REAL ESTATE
National Licensing
EXAM PREP

The SMART Guide to Passing

Marcia Darvin Spada

CENGAGE
Learning™

Australia • Brazil • Japan • Korea • Mexico • Singapore • Spain • United Kingdom • United States

333.33
SPA
2012

**Real Estate National Licensing Exam Prep:
The SMART Guide to Passing**
Marcia Darvin Spada

Vice President/Editor-in-Chief: Dave Shaut

Acquisitions Editor: Sara Glassmeyer

Developmental Editor: Arlin Kauffman,
LEAP Publishing Services

Senior Marketing and Sales Manager:
Mark Linton

Senior Manufacturing Buyer: Charlene Taylor

Senior Art Director: Pamela A. E. Galbreath

Rights Acquisitions Director: Audrey Pettengill

Permissions Acquisitions Manager: John Hill

Content Project Management: PreMediaGlobal

Production House/Compositor:
PreMediaGlobal

Internal Designer: PreMediaGlobal

Cover Designer: Cindy Dean Baldwin

Cover Image: © Flashon | Dreamstime.com

For product information and technology assistance, contact us at
Cengage Learning Customer & Sales Support, 1-800-354-9706

For permission to use material from this text or product,
submit all requests online at **www.cengage.com/permissions**
Further permissions questions can be emailed to
permissionrequest@cengage.com

Library of Congress Control Number: 2011923973

ISBN-13: 978-1-111-42713-9

ISBN-10: 1-111-42713-5

Cengage Learning
5191 Natorp Boulevard
Mason, OH 45040
USA

Cengage Learning products are represented in Canada by Nelson Education, Ltd.

For your course and learning solutions, visit **academic.cengage.com**

Purchase any of our products at your local college store or at our preferred online store **www.cengagebrain.com**

Printed in the United States of America
1 2 3 4 5 6 7 15 14 13 12 11

For my mother, Dorothy Darvin, who believed in me

Contents

Your Real Estate Exam and This Exam Guide   vi

About the Author   viii

How to Prepare for and Take Your Exam   x

1 PROPERTY OWNERSHIP 2

2 PROPERTY VALUATION, MARKET ANALYSIS, AND THE APPRAISAL PROCESS 18

3 LAND USE CONTROLS AND REGULATIONS 34

4 CONTRACTS AND RELATIONSHIPS WITH BUYERS AND SELLERS 50

5 FINANCING 68

6 LAW OF AGENCY 84

7 PROPERTY CONDITIONS, DISCLOSURES, AND TRANSFER OF TITLE 100

8 LEASES, RENTS, AND PROPERTY MANAGEMENT 116

9 BROKERAGE OPERATIONS AND THE PRACTICE OF REAL ESTATE 132

10 REAL ESTATE MATH 158

SALESPERSON 100-QUESTION PRACTICE EXAM 168

BROKER 100-QUESTION PRACTICE EXAM 188

ANSWER SECTION 209

Your Real Estate Exam and This Exam Guide

There are a number of different exams for real estate salesperson and broker licensure. The test you must take depends on the state where you will be receiving your real estate license. The three main testing service companies are AMP, PSI, and Pearson VUE. Alternatively, your exam may be generated by your state real estate commission or licensing agency. In some states, you will have to complete two exams: a national exam given by a testing service covering a number of real estate topics, and a more specific state exam covering state regulations.

This *Exam Guide* was prepared after a careful analysis of all of the testing formats that a real estate applicant may encounter. The questions address similar difficulty levels, question styles, and content that you are likely to find on your exam, no matter what testing entity offers the exam. (Note that the AMP broker exam consists of simulation questions that are a different format than the multiple choice questions found in this Guide.) The *Exam Guide* is composed of the 10 topics found on all of the testing service exams and many state exams. The topics chosen for this Guide are all topics you can expect to find on your exam, no matter which exam you take. When working with the questions, note that a few address concepts that may be unfamiliar. This is because the Guide covers content that may exist in one state but not in another. On your exam, you will only be responsible for concepts having to do with your state. In addition, you can choose to study only select topics or review them all. You will also find that similar concepts are grouped together within each question bank. The questions in a grouping may ask about the same concept but from a different point of view. This grouping will help you to think about the topic from different viewpoints and to become more familiar with its relevance.

The Guide also includes two 100-question practice exams: one salesperson practice exam and one broker practice exam. The salesperson and broker practice exams are weighted according to topic emphasis in a very similar fashion to the actual exams. The tests are captioned according to subject matter so you can gauge how you are doing with a specific topic. Most testing services offer the same topics for both the salesperson and broker exams. The difficulty level is generally higher for the broker exam. You will find this to be true of the practice exams in this Guide. Students can enhance their study by taking both practice exams for a more comprehensive study experience.

There are a total of 1,000 questions in this *Exam Guide*.

This Guide also offers you something that the actual exam does not. For each question, there is a complete explanation for both the correct and the incorrect answers. These explanations will help you better understand the subject that greatly aides in retention. Even if you have the correct answer, it is a good idea to read through the rationales to gain further insight into the correct answer as well as the incorrect answers (which may also appear on your actual exam).

The Guide also contains full explanations for all of the math questions including helpful and easy formulas that you can memorize and apply whenever you encounter a similar question on your actual exam.

Best of luck on your studies and forthcoming career as a real estate professional!

About the Author

Marcia Darvin Spada is the owner of the Albany Center for Real Estate Education, a New York licensed proprietary school. She is also the owner of Cram for Exam, a website that provides practice real estate exams and tutoring for the New York licensure exam.

A professional educator and nationally known real estate author, Marcia teaches real estate and has developed curricula for numerous real estate courses widely used in colleges, real estate–related organizations, and proprietary schools. In addition to the *National Real Estate Exam Prep: The SMART Guide to Passing*, her tenth real estate textbook, she is the author of

- *New York Real Estate for Salespersons*
- *Cram for Exam! Your Guide to Passing the New York Real Estate Salesperson Exam*
- *New York Real Estate for Brokers*
- *Cram for the Exam! Your Guide to Passing the New York Real Estate Broker Exam*
- *30-Hour Remedial Course for the New York Real Estate Licensure Qualifying Course*
- *New Jersey Real Estate for Salespersons and Brokers*
- *Cram for the Exam! Your Guide to Passing the New Jersey Real Estate Salespersons and Brokers Exam*
- *The Home Inspection Book: A Guide for Professionals*
- *Environmental Issues and the Real Estate Professional*

Marcia holds a B.A. and an M.A. in English from the University at Albany and a B.S. in Real Estate Studies from Empire State College.

She continues to update the material in the *Exam Prep* and welcomes all comments and questions. Also, visit her website www.cramforexam.net that contains downloadable practice real estate NYS licensing exams and licensure information. Also visit www.cengage.com/spada, the publishers' website where you can purchase Marcia's textbooks and support materials. Her email address is cramforexam@hotmail.com.

GENERAL STUDY HINTS

Additional exposure to the material and repetition will improve your confidence and help alleviate "exam anxiety." The more you know, the less stress you will have when taking the test.

Use questions in your book more than once.   Write your answers on a separate sheet of paper. This will make scoring easier as you compare your answers with the answer key and leave the questions unmarked for additional practice. This will also work with your regular textbook and any other practice exams you might decide to use.

Practice taking timed tests.   Duplicate the testing situation by practicing the questions under pressure. This is one of the best ways to overcome exam anxiety. Based on the time allowed on the state examination, your goal should be to complete 50 questions per hour. Missed items will quickly pinpoint your weak areas and help focus your attention on them for additional study.

Research wrong answers.   First, carefully read the explanation in the answer key. Determine why the correct answer is correct and the other distractors are not. Try not to memorize individual questions, as this may cause you to miss subtle wording differences on the exam, causing you to answer incorrectly. You need to concentrate on concepts, not memorization of all details.

Pace your studying.   Immediately test yourself after class discussion. Look up wrong answers. Remember that last-minute cramming before a final exam or the state licensing exam may cause you to panic when confronted with difficult material, or to become overly tired during the exam. Do not fall behind in your studying; it is difficult to catch up.

Limit your study time.   Most people more easily recall the first and last part of whatever they study, while the middle material may be less easily recalled. It is better to study with short breaks rather than a solid hour.

How to Prepare for and Take Your Exam

Get a good night's sleep before the test. A proper amount of sleep will help you think more clearly and avoid errors. Staying up all night will make you less able to concentrate during the exam.

Know where you are going. If you are going to a test site in another town, know the directions and give yourself extra time.

Know the testing rules. Review your examination guide to be sure you know how you will be tested and the general process. There are generally a few sample questions in the guide or even sample exams online through your testing service, as well as a list of content to be tested. There should also be a chart of how many questions will be asked in each general category.

If you are just beginning your class, try these additional tips:

Read the assigned material BEFORE class. If you are in a classroom setting, then the lecture should help reinforce what you have read. Highlight what you think are important points and jot down any questions. Do not highlight everything in your book! Hold your questions until the topic is completed as your question may be answered during the lecture.

Participate, do not just talk. Instructors appreciate relevant questions that offer them an opportunity to explain the content. However, no one enjoys a classroom where students are continuously speaking to one another or telling "war stories" that have little to do with the topic.

Organize your notes and handouts. Many students accumulate a number of handouts during a course, and they may become disorganized. Consider using a three-ring binder or a folder with pockets to store handouts and other paperwork.

If you are in a classroom, be on time, and listen for instructions. Lateness or lack of attention during class may ultimately mean missing a question or two on the exam. Information that you missed could make the difference between passing and failing.

TEST TAKING STRATEGIES

Read the question (RTQ). Some students go so far as putting a huge "RTQ" on scratch paper to remind them! It is imperative to know what is being asked. Look for words such as NOT, EXCEPT, or INCORRECT. For a math question, the numbers provided may be monthly, but the question asks for an annual number. Be sure you understand the question before you look at the answer choices!

Read the answers. Go through the four choices. Look for ones that can be easily eliminated. Some students write "A B C D" on a sheet of paper for tougher questions and check off incorrect answers as they are eliminated. If you eliminate two answers, you now have a 50-50 chance, even if you have to guess! You might want to approach a multiple choice question as four separate True/False questions—you are looking for the True answer. For questions with two Yes and two No answers, read what follows the Yes and No, as that is usually the key to answering correctly.

Review your answer. When done, review by reading the question and the answer you picked, asking yourself, "Does this completed sentence make sense?" If it is a "story problem," put yourself in the story. Does the correct answer make common sense to you? On math problems, put the answer back into the formula. Also, is the answer logical? It would not make sense for a $100,000 home to have annual real estate taxes of $50,000.

Make sure you immediately record your answer. Many students find that mistakes, such as recording "B" instead of "D" on their answer sheet, will cost them a point or two.

Manage your time during the exam. Go through the entire exam in order, answering the questions that come easily. If you are in doubt or do not know the answer, skip it, and move on. Many students use 45–60 minutes to answer about 70% of the questions. This leaves plenty of time to focus on the remaining 30%. On computerized exams, there should be an indicator of how many questions are answered and how much time is remaining.

Manage your panic. As you go through the exam for the first time, it is normal to leave some questions blank. When you come to a question that is difficult for you, remember that subsequent questions may jog your memory or provide answers to earlier questions; look for that help.

Stay comfortable and avoid stress. If necessary, get up, and stretch. Staying relaxed will help you to keep focused on the test.

Do not dwell on any one question. Rather than dwell on a single question, you could be answering several more questions to which you DO know the answer. Stay away from negative thinking and move on!

Answer all questions. Before handing your test in, or indicating on your computer that you are finished, be sure every question has an answer. If you are out of time, mark one answer for each randomly. It may help your score. If unsure about an answer, it is okay to change an original answer if you think that the new answer is better.

Additional information. There are three main testing agencies administering real estate exams to the majority of states. Their websites may also be a source for information and are:

AMP: http://www.goAMP.com
Pearson VUE: http://www.pearsonvue.com
PSI: http://www.psiexams.com

Congratulations—you've passed! If so, you may want to let your instructor know. If you fail, do not be discouraged. You will need further study. Now that you have some experience with the exam, you better know what to expect. Before leaving the test site, write down topic areas that need more study.

EXAM OUTLINES

The following are outlines from the three major testing providers. Check the websites for your state and its testing provider to ensure accurate and effective preparation.

AMP   http://www.goAMP.com
National Salesperson Licensing Examination Content Outline

1. **Agency Relationships and Contracts   28%**

   A. **Agency Relationships**
      1. Creating Agency
      2. Types of Agency (including implied agency)
      3. Rights, Duties, and Obligations of the Parties
      4. Termination and Remedies for Nonperformance
      5. Disclosure (related to representation)
   B. **General Legal Principles, Theory, and Concepts about Contracts**
      1. Unilateral/Bilateral
      2. Validity
      3. Void and Voidable
      4. Notice of Delivery/Acceptance
      5. Executory/Executed
      6. Enforceability
      7. Addenda to Contracts

C. **Purchase Contracts (contracts between seller and buyer)**
  1. General Principles and Legal Concepts
  2. Purchase Contract (contract of sale, purchase and sale agreement, etc.)
  3. Options (contractual right to buy)
  4. Basic Provisions Purpose/Elements
  5. Conditions for Termination/Breach of Contract
  6. Offer and Acceptance (counter offers, multiple offers, negotiation, and earnest money)
  7. Contingencies
  8. Duties and Obligations of the Parties

D. **Service/Listing Buyer Contracts (contracts between licensee and seller or buyer)**
  1. General Principles and Legal Concepts
  2. Basic Provisions/Purpose/Elements
  3. Duties and Obligations of the Parties
  4. Conditions for Termination/Breach of Contract
  5. Remuneration/Consideration/Fees
  6. Types of Service/Listing Contracts

E. **Employment Agreements between Broker and other Licensees (including supervision)**

2. **Real Property Ownership/Interest   14%**

  A. **Freehold Estates (rights of ownership)**

  B. **Types of Ownership (estates in land)**
    1. Joint Tenancy
    2. Tenancy in Common
    3. Condominiums

  C. **Leasehold Interest**
    1. Basic Concepts and Terminology
    2. Types of Leases
    3. Basic Elements and Provisions of Leases
    4. Rights and Duties of the Parties
    5. Remedies for Default/Nonperformance

  D. **Forms of Business Ownership**
    1. Sole Proprietorship
    2. General or Limited Partnership
    3. LLC

  E. **Private Restrictions on Real Property/Land Use and Matters Affecting Ownership**
    1. Liens
        a. Voluntary
        b. Involuntary
        c. Priority
    2. Easements/Rights of Way/Licenses
    3. Preexisting Leases or Other Agreements
    4. Encroachment

   5. Deed Conditions, Covenants, and Restrictions
   6. Property Owner Association Agreements
 F. Government Powers and Control of Land Use
   1. Americans with Disabilities Act (ADA)
   2. Land Use Restrictions and Regulations (i.e., zoning)
   3. Police Powers
   4. Eminent Domain
   5. Property Taxation
   6. Subdivision Regulations (e.g., condominiums, cooperatives, and planned unit developments)

3. **Finance   15%**
 A. Basic Concepts and Terminology
   1. Equity
   2. Loan-to-Value Ratio
   3. Term and Payment
   4. Principal and Interest
   5. Direct and Indirect Costs (points, discounts, etc.)
   6. Return on Investment/Rate of Return
 B. Types of Financing
   1. Amortized
   2. Interest Only
   3. ARM
   4. Construction Loan
   5. Home Equity
 C. Methods of Financing
   1. Government Programs (e.g., FHA and VA)
   2. Conventional
   3. Owner-financed
   4. Land Contract
 D. Financing Instruments (mortgages, trust deeds, promissory notes)
   1. Basic Elements and Provisions of Financing Instruments
   2. Legal Principles
   3. Nonperformance
 E. Government Oversight
   1. RESPA
   2. Regulation Z
   3. Truth in Lending Act
   4. Antitrust
   5. Mortgage Fraud
   6. Equal Credit Opportunity Act
 F. Lending Process
   1. Preapproval and Prequalification (e.g., debt ratios, credit scoring, and history)
   2. Parties to the Lending Process (e.g., loan originator, underwriter, and mortgage broker)

4. **Real Property   14%**

   A. **Methods of Legal Description of Land**
      1. Metes and Bounds
      2. Rectangular Survey
      3. Lot and Block

   B. **Methods of Measurement**
      1. Structures (space and volume)
      2. Livable Area
      3. Land Measurement

   C. **Property Valuation**
      1. Basic Concepts and Terminology
      2. Influences and Characteristics Affecting Value
      3. Comparative Market Analysis (performed by a real estate licensee)
      4. Broker Price Opinion
      5. Real Property—fixtures *vs.* personal property (e.g., chattel)

   D. **Methods of Valuation (performed by an appraiser)**
      1. Sales Comparison (Market Data) Approach
      2. Cost Approach
      3. Income Analysis Approach
      4. Appraisal Process/Procedure

   E. **Conveyance of Real Property**
      1. Definition of Clear (Marketable) Title
      2. Matters Affecting Title
      3. Recordation
      4. Title Insurance
      5. Deeds
      6. Will
      7. Court-Ordered Sale (e.g., foreclosure)
      8. Adverse Possession
      9. Settlement Procedures (closing the transaction)

5. **Marketing Regulations (purchase and rental)   8%**

   A. **Property Advertising (including Fair Housing) Disclosures**
      1. Environmental Concern (e.g., lead-based paint and radon)
      2. Property Condition

   B. **Licensee Advertising**
      1. Antitrust
      2. Do-not-Call List
      3. CAN-SPAM Act
      4. Fair Housing (e.g., blockbusting and steering)

6. **Property Management   8%**

   A. General Principles of Property Management Agreements
   B. Basic Provisions/Purpose/Elements of Property Management Agreements

  C. Types of Contracts

  D. Duties and Obligations of the Parties

  E. Market Analysis and Tenant Acquisition

  F. Accounts and Disbursement

  G. Property Maintenance and Improvements

  H. Evictions

7. Real Estate Calculations   13%

  A. Compensation, Commission, and Fees

  B. Valuation/Market Sale Price and Yields

  C. Net to Seller, Cost to Buyer (credits and debits)

  D. Tax and Other Prorations

  E. Amortization

  F. Points

  G. Prepayment Penalties

  H. Loan-to-Value Ratios

  I. Measurement (e.g., square footage, acreage, and volume)

  J. Property Management/Investment (e.g., rate of return)

National Broker Simulation Licensing Examination Content Outline

	Broker Simulation Specifications	
# of Problems	Primary Issues	Section Topics
3	Agency Relationships and Property Representations	A. Agency
2	Fair Housing and Other Governmental Regulations	B. Contracts
2	Handling Money	C. Freehold & Leasehold
1	Training and Supervision of Licensees	D. Property management
Plus one primary issue varying by examination form.		E. Finance
		F. Government Regulations & Private Restrictions
	Property Types	G. Description & Measurement
4	Residential	H. Valuation
2	Commercial	I. Conveyance
1	Property Management	J. Calculations
Plus two property types varying by examination form.		K. Ethical behavior

Other Topics on the Broker Simulation Exam may include but are not limited to:

✎ Mortgage Fraud

✎ Pre-Approval and Pre-Qualification (e.g., debt ratios, credit scoring, and history)

✎ Court-Ordered Sale (e.g., foreclosure)

✎ Do-Not-Call List

✎ CAN-SPAM Act (Federal law regulating the sending of commercial e-mails)

Pearson VUE   http://www.pearsonvue.com

National Exam Content Outlines For Real Estate Salespersons and Brokers

I. **Real property characteristics, definitions, ownership, restrictions, and transfer (Salesperson 16, Broker 12)**
- A. Definitions, descriptions, and ways to hold title
  1. Elements of real and personal property
  2. Property description and area calculations
  3. Estates in real property
  4. Forms of ownership, rights, interests, and obligations
- B. Land use controls and restrictions
  1. Government controls
  2. Private controls—non-monetary
  3. Private controls—mortgage (deed of trust) and liens
- C. Transfer/alienation of title to real property
  1. Voluntary
  2. Involuntary
  3. Protections
  4. Partition/severance (voluntary or involuntary)
  5. Deeds and warranties: validity, types, covenants
  6. Title and title insurance

II. **Property valuation and appraisal (Salesperson 6, Broker 6)**
- A. Principles, types, and estimates of property value
  1. Valuation definition, purpose, and process
  2. Characteristics
  3. Valuation principles
  4. Approaches to value
  5. Depreciation/obsolescence
  6. Value
  7. Appraisals and list price
  8. Math
  9. Influences on property value
- B. Investment analysis
  1. Application of principles
  2. Math calculations

III. **Contracts and relationships with buyers and sellers (Salesperson 18, Broker 20)**
- A. Contract elements
  1. Validity
  2. Void/voidable
  3. Enforceable/unenforceable (Statute of Frauds)
  4. Unilateral/bilateral
  5. Executory/executed
- B. Listing contracts
  1. General purpose/definition of listing
  2. Types

        3. Required elements
        4. Establishing listing price
        5. Responsibilities
   C. Commission agreements
        1. Negotiation of commission
        2. Who may collect
        3. Other compensation arrangements
        4. Math: licensee compensation/commission
   D. Sales contracts
        1. Terminology
        2. Procedures
        3. Standard parts
        4. Contingencies and misc. provisions
        5. Contractual rights and obligation
        6. Disputes and dispute resolution terms
   E. Option contracts
   F. Licensee–client relationships and responsibilities
        1. Types of relationships—terminology
        2. Relationship powers and obligations

IV. **Property conditions and disclosures (Salesperson 7, Broker 7)**
   A. Federal environmental regulations
        1. Lead-based paint
        2. CERCLA
        3. Asbestos
        4. Wetlands and flood plains
   B. Environmental issues
        1. Mold
        2. Radon
        3. Protected species
        4. Other
   C. Material and other property disclosures
   D. Liability considerations

V. **Federal laws governing real estate activities (Salesperson 8, Broker 9)**
   A. Civil Rights Acts/Fair Housing Acts
        1. Provisions
        2. Violations
        3. Enforcement/penalties
        4. Exceptions
        5. Advertising
        6. Required poster
   B. Americans with Disabilities Act (ADA)
   C. Antitrust—(Sherman Act, etc.)

D. Marketing and financial controls
   1. Truth in Lending Act (TILA—Regulation Z)
   2. Real Estate Settlement Procedures Act (RESPA)
   3. Equal Credit Opportunity Act (ECOA)
   4. Equal Employment Opportunity Commission (EEOC)
   5. UCC/Interstate/Securities (Broker only)
   6. Do Not Call/Privacy Act

VI. **Financing the transaction and settlement (Salesperson 17, Broker 13)**
   A. Financing components
      1. Financing instruments
      2. Financing sources (primary and secondary mortgage markets, seller financing)
      3. Types of loans
      4. Financing clauses, terminology, and cost of money (calculation)
      5. Lending issues
   B. Lender requirements and obligations
      1. Private mortgage insurance (PMI)
      2. FHA requirements
      3. VA requirements
      4. Escrow/impound account
      5. Credit report
      6. Assumption requirements
      7. Appraisal requirements
      8. Hazard and flood insurance
      9. Federal financing and credit regulation
   C. Settlement/Closing
      1. Procedures and forms
      2. Closing costs and calculations
      3. Documents, title, and recording

VII. **Leases, rents, and property management (Salesperson 5, Broker 6)**
   A. Types and elements of leases
      1. Leasehold estates
      2. Types of leases
      3. Lease clauses and provisions
   B. Lessor and lessee rights, responsibilities, liabilities, and recourse
      1. Owned and leased inclusions
      2. Reversionary rights of owners
      3. Rental related discriminatory laws
      4. Unit-related disclosures
      5. Effect of sale/transfer/foreclosure
      6. Evictions
      7. Tenant improvements
      8. Termination of a lease
      9. Breach

    C. Property management contracts and obligations of parties

        1. Contracts and contractual relationships

        2. Manager's obligations, duties, liabilities

        3. Owner's obligations, duties, liabilities

        4. Management/owner math calculations

VIII. **Brokerage operations (Salesperson 3, Broker 7)**

    A. Broker management of funds

        1. Earnest money

        2. Commingling

        3. Conversion of funds

    B. Broker–salesperson relationship

    C. Advertising

    D. Ethical and legal business practices

        1. Misrepresentation

        2. Implied duty of good faith

        3. Due diligence

        4. Unauthorized practice of law

        5. Marketing practices

    E. Forms of business ownership

        1. Corporation

        2. Partnership (general and limited)

        3. Limited liability company

        4. Sole proprietorship

    F. Independent contractors vs. employee

PSI   http://www.psiexams.com

National Portion Content Outline

Property Ownership (Salesperson 6 Items, Broker 5 Items)

1. Classes of Property

    a. Real versus Personal Property

    b. Defining Fixtures

2. Land Characteristics and Legal Descriptions

    a. Physical Characteristics of Land

    b. Economic Characteristics of Land

    c. Types of Legal Property Descriptions

    d. Usage of Legal Property Descriptions

3. Encumbrances

    a. Liens (Types and Priority)

    b. Easements and Licenses

    c. Encroachments

4. Types of Ownership

    a. Types of Estates

    b. Forms of Ownership

    c. Leaseholds

    d. Common Interest Properties

    e. Bundle of Rights

5. Physical Descriptions of Property

    a. Land and Building Area

    b. Basic Construction Types and Materials

Land Use Controls and Regulations (Salesperson 5 Items, Broker 5 Items)

1. Government Rights in Land

    a. Property Taxes and Special Assessments

    b. Eminent Domain, Condemnation, Escheat

    c. Police Power

2. Public Controls Based in Police Power

    a. Zoning and Master Plans

    b. Building Codes

    c. Environmental Impact Reports

    d. Regulation of special land types (floodplain, coastal, etc.)

3. Regulation of Environmental Hazards

    a. Abatement, mitigation and cleanup requirements

    b. Contamination levels and restrictions on sale or development of contaminated property

    c. Types of hazards and potential for agent or seller liability

4. Private Controls

    a. Deed Conditions or Restrictions

    b. Covenants (CC&Rs)

    c. HOA Regulations

Valuation and Market Analysis (Salesperson 8 Items, Broker 7 Items)

1. Value

    a. Market Value and Market Price

    b. Characteristics of Value

    c. Principles of Value

    d. Market Cycles and other Factors Affecting Property Value

2. Methods of Estimating Value/Appraisal Process

    a. Market or Sales Comparison Approach

    b. Replacement Cost or Summation Approach

    c. Income Approach

    d. Basic Appraisal Terminology (Replacement versus Reproduction Cost, Reconciliation, Depreciation, Kinds of Obsolescence)

3. Competitive/Comparative Market Analysis (CMA)

    a. Selecting and Adjusting Comparables

    b. Factors to Consider in a CMA

    c. Contrast CMA, Broker Opinion of Value (BOV), Appraisal

    d. Price/Square Foot

    e. Gross Rent and Gross Income Multipliers

4. When Appraisal by Certified Appraiser is Required

Financing (Salesperson 7 Items, Broker 7 Items)
1. General Concepts
   a. LTV Ratios, Points, Origination Fees, Discounts, Broker Commissions
   b. Mortgage Insurance (PMI)
   c. Lender Requirements, Equity, Qualifying Buyers, Loan Application Procedures
2. Types of Loans
   a. Term or Straight Loans
   b. Amortized and Partially Amortized (Balloon) Loans
   c. Adjustable Rate Loans (ARMS)
   d. Conventional versus Insured
   e. Reverse mortgages; equity loans; subprime and other nonconforming loans
3. Sources of Loan Money
   a. Seller/Owner Financing
   b. Primary Market
   c. Secondary Market
   d. Down Payment Assistance Programs
4. Government Programs
   a. FHA
   b. VA
5. Mortgages/Deeds of Trust
   a. Mortgage Clauses (Assumption, Due-On-Sale, Alienation, Acceleration, Prepayment, Release)
   b. Lien Theory versus Title Theory
   c. Mortgage/Deed of Trust and Note as Separate Documents
6. Financing/Credit Laws
   a. Truth in Lending, RESPA, Equal Credit Opportunity
   b. Mortgage Loan Disclosure and Seller Financing Disclosure
7. Mortgage Fraud, Predatory Lending Practices (Risks to Clients)
   a. Usury and Predatory Lending Laws
   b. Appropriate Cautions to Clients Seeking Financing

Laws of Agency (Salesperson 10 Items, Broker 11 Items)
1. Laws, Definitions, and Nature of Agency Relationships
   a. Types of Agents/Agencies (Special, General, Designated, Subagent, etc.)
   b. Possible Agency Relationships in a Single Transaction
   c. Fiduciary Responsibilities
2. Creation and Disclosure of Agency and Agency Agreements (General; Regulatory Details in State Portions)
   a. Creation of Agency and Agency Agreements
   b. Express and Implied
   c. Disclosure of Representation
   d. Disclosure of Acting as Principal or other Conflict of Interest
3. Responsibilities of Agent to Seller, Buyer, Landlord or Tenant as Principal
   a. Traditional Common Law Agency Duties ("COALD")
   b. Duties to Client/Principal (Buyer, Seller, Tenant or Landlord)
   c. Effect of Dual Agency on Agent's Duties

4. Responsibilities of Agent to Customers and Third Parties
5. Termination of Agency
   a. Expiration
   b. Completion/Performance
   c. Termination by Operation of Law
   d. Destruction of Property/Death of Principal
   e. Termination by Acts of Parties

Mandated Disclosures (Salesperson 7 Items, Broker 8 Items)
1. Property Condition Disclosure Forms
   a. Agent's Role in Preparation
   b. When Seller's Disclosure Misrepresents Property Condition
2. Warranties
   a. Types of available warranties
   b. Coverages provided
3. Need for Inspection and Obtaining/Verifying Information
   a. Agent Responsibility to Verify Statements included in Marketing Information
   b. Agent Responsibility to Inquire about "Red Flag" Issues
   c. Responding to Non-Client Inquiries
4. Material Facts Related to Property Condition or Location
   a. Land/Soil Conditions
   b. Accuracy of Representation of Lot or Improvement Size, Encroachments or Easements affecting Use
   c. Pest Infestation, Toxic Mold and other Interior Environmental Hazards
   d. Structural Issues, including Roof, Gutters, Downspouts, Doors, Windows, Foundation
   e. Condition of Electrical and Plumbing Systems, and of Equipment or Appliances that are Fixtures
   f. Location within Natural Hazard or Specially Regulated Area, Potentially Uninsurable Property
   g. Known Alterations or Additions
5. Material Facts Related to Public Controls, Statutes, or Public Utilities
   a. Local Zoning and Planning Information
   b. Boundaries of School/Utility/Taxation Districts, Flight Paths
   c. Local Taxes and Special Assessments, other Liens
   d. External Environmental Hazards (lead, radon, asbestos, formaldehyde foam insulation, high-voltage power lines, waste disposal sites, underground storage tanks, soil or groundwater contamination, hazardous waste)
   e. Stigmatized/Psychologically Impacted Property, Megan's Law Issues

Contracts (Salesperson 10 Items, Broker 10 Items)
1. General Knowledge of Contract Law
   a. Requirements for Validity
   b. Types of Invalid Contracts
   c. When Contract is Considered Performed/Discharged

    d. Assignment and Novation

    e. Breach of Contract and Remedies for Breach

    f. Contract Clauses (Acceleration, etc.)

2. Listing Agreements

    a. General Requirements for Valid Listing

    b. Exclusive Listings

    c. Non-Exclusive Listings

3. Management Agreements [Broker Only]

4. Buyer Broker Agreements/Tenant Representation Agreements

5. Offers/Purchase Agreements

    a. General Requirements

    b. When Offer becomes Binding (Notification)

    c. Contingencies

    d. Time is of the Essence

6. Counteroffers/Multiple Counteroffers

    a. Counteroffer Cancels Original Offer

    b. Priority of Multiple Counteroffers

7. Lease and Lease-Purchase Agreements

8. Options and Right of First Refusal

9. Rescission and Cancellation Agreements

Transfer of Title (Salesperson 4 Items, Broker 6 Items)

1. Title Insurance

    a. What is Insured Against

    b. Title Searches/Title Abstracts/Chain of Title

    c. Cloud on Title/Suit to Quiet Title

2. Conveyances After Death

    a. Types of Wills

    b. Testate vs. Intestate Succession

3. Deeds

    a. Purpose of Deed, when Title Passes

    b. Types of Deeds and when used (General Warranty, Special Warranty, Quitclaim)

    c. Essential Elements of Deeds

    d. Importance of Recording

4. Escrow or Closing

    a. Responsibilities of Escrow Agent

    b. Prorated Items

    c. Closing Statements/HUD-1

    d. Estimating Closing Costs

5. Foreclosure, Short Sales

6. Tax Aspects of Transferring Title to Real Property

7. Special Processes [Broker Only]

Practice of Real Estate (Salesperson 12 Items, Broker 11 Items)

1. Trust Accounts (General; Regulatory Details in State Portions)
   a. Purpose and Definition of Trust Accounts
   b. Responsibility for Trust Monies
   c. Commingling/Conversion
   d. Monies held in Trust Accounts
2. Fair Housing Laws
   a. Protected Classes
   b. Covered Transactions
   c. Specific Laws and their Effects
   d. Exceptions
   e. Compliance
   f. Types of Violations and Enforcement
   g. Fair Housing Issues in Advertising
3. Advertising
   a. Incorrect "Factual" Statements versus "Puffing"
   b. Uninformed Misrepresentation versus Deliberate Misrepresentation (Fraud)
   c. Truth in Advertising
4. Agent Supervision
   a. Liability/Responsibility for Acts of Associated Agents
   b. Responsibility to Train and Supervise
   c. Independent Contractors
   d. Employees
5. Commissions and Fees
   a. Procuring Cause/Protection Clauses
   b. Referrals and Finder Fees
6. General Ethics
   a. Practicing within Area of Competence
   b. Avoiding Unauthorized Practice of Law
7. Issues in Use of Technology (electronic signatures, document delivery, Internet advertising)
8. Antitrust Laws
   a. Antitrust Laws and Purpose
   b. Antitrust Violations in Real Estate

Real Estate Calculations (Salesperson 7 Items, Broker 5 Items)

1. General Math Concepts
   a. Addition, Subtraction, Multiplication, and Division
   b. Percentages/Decimals/ Fractions
   c. Areas, including Acreage
2. Property Tax Calculations (not Prorations)
3. Lending Calculations
   a. Loan-to-Value Ratios
   b. Discount Points
   c. Equity
   d. Qualifying Buyers

4. Calculations for Transactions
   a. Prorations (Utilities, Rent, Property Taxes, Insurance, etc.)
   b. Commissions and Commission Splits
   c. Seller's Proceeds of Sale
   d. Total Money Needed by Buyer at Closing
   e. Transfer Tax/Conveyance Tax/Revenue Stamps
5. Calculations for Valuation
   a. Comparative Market Analyses (CMA)
   b. Net Operating Income
   c. Depreciation
   d. Capitalization Rate
   e. Gross Rent and Gross Income Multipliers (GIM, GRM)
6. Mortgage Calculations
   a. Down Payment/Amount to be Financed
   b. Amortization
   c. Interest Rates
   d. Interest Amounts
   e. Monthly Installment Payments

Specialty Areas (Salesperson 4 Items, Broker 5 Items)
1. Property Management and Landlord/Tenant
2. Common Interest Ownership Properties
3. Subdivisions
4. Commercial, Industrial, and Income Property

REAL ESTATE
National Licensing
EXAM PREP

THE SMART GUIDE
TO PASSING

Topic

1

MULTIPLE CHOICE

Identify the choice that best completes the statement or answers the question.

1. The main difference between the terms real estate and real property is that only real property includes

   A. ownership rights
   B. landscaping
   C. improvements
   D. fences

2. The bundle of rights refers to

   A. real property rights
   B. condemnation
   C. water rights only
   D. chattel

3. Which of the following is evidence of a definite ownership right in real property?

   A. Possess
   B. Lease
   C. Occupy
   D. Sell

Property Ownership

4. Sima's property borders a gorgeous lake. She owns

   A. littoral rights
   B. legal rights
   C. riparian rights
   D. squatter's rights

5. The land and improvements, and all legal rights, powers, and privileges of real estate ownership are called

   A. personal property
   B. real property
   C. license
   D. subsurface rights

6. All property that is readily movable is known as

   A. real property
   B. personal property
   C. realty
   D. real estate

7. H plans to sell his tired, worn-out household furnishings when he sells his house. H will most likely use a document called a

   A. sales contract
   B. bill of sale
   C. transfer affidavit
   D. purchase offer

8. The process of the gradual addition to one's land by the deposit of soil from a flowing river or stream is

   A. alluvion
   B. avulsion
   C. accretion
   D. accrual

9. Isaac bought a property that borders a river that also has a quarry on the land. What are the rights that Isaac has in the property?

   A. Riparian rights
   B. Mineral rights
   C. Subsurface rights
   D. All of the answers shown

10. The legal notice that a lawsuit is pending affecting title or possession of a specific property is called a(n)

    A. transcript of judgment
    B. involuntary lien
    C. *lis pendens*
    D. general lien

11. Chattel is another name for

    A. real property
    B. personal property
    C. air rights
    D. cattle

12. Ownership rights that belong to the owner of property bordering a flowing body of water are

    A. percolating water
    B. littoral rights
    C. riparian rights
    D. river rights

13. An accurate legal description on a deed must include

    A. street address of the property only
    B. assessor's tax number only
    C. a legal description of the land
    D. a picture of the property

14. A description by reference

    A. may be in addition to another description
    B. may be the only description in the deed
    C. may refer to a plat as part of a subdivision that has been recorded
    D. refers to all of the answers shown

15. A reference to a lot and block number can generally be found on a

    A. mortgage
    B. closing statement
    C. deed
    D. contract of sale

16. One of the most important recognizable factors of the metes and bounds description is the

    A. number of degrees north
    B. point of beginning
    C. size of the property being described
    D. placement of the monuments

17. The metes and bounds description is generally

    A. made up by an attorney
    B. written by the real estate agent
    C. used only if a survey is not available
    D. written from a survey of the property

18. Tayisha had attached built-in bookshelves to the walls of her retail store and removed them when her lease was up. These items are called

    A. estates in land
    B. trade fixtures
    C. a stick in the bundle of rights
    D. common elements

19. Items become fixtures and part of real property in a number of ways. Which of the following is NOT a method by which an item becomes a fixture?

    A. Attachment
    B. Application
    C. Adaptation
    D. Agreement

20. Personal property that attaches permanently to the land or improvements and becomes part of the real property is called

    A. chattel
    B. common elements
    C. attachment
    D. a fixture

21. Habib deeds his land to his friend, Selena, with the condition that she only uses it for residential purposes. This deed is an example of a

    A. fee simple defeasible estate
    B. life estate
    C. tenancy in common
    D. partnership

22. Ownership, possession, and control of a property that is contingent upon living and lost at death define a

    A. fee simple absolute
    B. joint tenancy
    C. life estate
    D. cooperative

23. Telly and Michael hold title to a parcel of land. Neither will inherit the other's portion should one of them die. This is probably a

    A. joint tenancy
    B. life estate
    C. corporation
    D. tenancy in common

24. Ownership for an undetermined length of time is called a

    A. freehold estate
    B. nonfreehold estate
    C. leasehold estate
    D. life estate

25. When the possession of the property reverts back to the owner at the end of the life estate, it is called a(n)

    A. dower
    B. reversionary interest
    C. remainder interest
    D. act of waste

26. When a property is in the name of only one person or entity, it is a(n)

    A. estate (ownership) in severalty
    B. joint tenancy
    C. partnership
    D. sole proprietorship

27. For joint tenancy, which of the following is NOT a unity required between the co-owners? Unity of

    A. occupation
    B. time
    C. interest
    D. possession

28. Stacy has fee simple absolute ownership in a property that she has recently purchased. Which of the following rights in the property does she have? To

    A. sell by deed or will
    B. control use within legal limits
    C. dispose by gift
    D. do all of the answers shown

29. A type of estate that exists for a fixed time period is called a(n)

    A. estate at sufferance
    B. estate at will
    C. freehold estate
    D. estate for years

30. Neal, Oscar, and Dwayne were friends since high school. Over time they have bought a property together with the only unity being that of possession. This arrangement is called

    A. ownership in severalty
    B. joint tenancy
    C. tenancy in common
    D. leasehold

31. E and E hold title to a property together with no right of survivorship. They most likely hold the property

    A. as joint tenants
    B. as tenants in common
    C. in severalty
    D. at sufferance

32. An estate in land that implies possession but not ownership is called a

    A. freehold
    B. life estate
    C. leasehold
    D. fee simple absolute

33. Z's mother deeds Z her beach house for Z's lifetime. Then the property goes to the A.S.P.C.A. in memory of mother's favorite cat upon daughter Z's death. This is an example of a

    A. fee simple absolute
    B. leasehold
    C. joint tenancy
    D. life estate in remainder

34. F and H recently purchase a property and are advised by their attorney that title to the property offers them the most complete form of ownership. Their ownership right is

    A. fee simple on condition
    B. fee simple absolute
    C. fee simple defeasible
    D. a life estate

35. A deed that reads "to Xavier Pilar as long as the premises are not used for the sale of alcohol" is an example of

    A. fee simple absolute
    B. qualified fee simple
    C. life estate
    D. nonfreehold estate

36. Fee simple estates and life estates are two examples of

    A. freehold estates
    B. leasehold estates
    C. periodic tenancies
    D. nonfreehold estates

37. Which of the following regarding a fee simple absolute estate is FALSE? It

    A. includes the right to dispose of the property
    B. is the most comprehensive form of title
    C. is a type of freehold estate
    D. must be conveyed as an estate in severalty

38. Carmine conveys 20 acres to Vito for Vito's life. This type of ownership is called a(n)

    A. defeasible estate
    B. life estate
    C. estate for years
    D. estate in severalty

39. Beverly and Jeff own their home free and clear. Beverly believes that if they take out a home equity loan, the loan will jeopardize their fee simple absolute ownership. Which of the following is TRUE?

    A. Homeowners cannot obtain home equity loans with fee simple ownership
    B. The loan will not jeopardize their ownership if they pay it back in a timely manner
    C. Home equity loans are only for homeowners in target areas
    D. Homeownership of any kind, including fee simple, is not required for a home equity loan

40. Tony owns property with four others. In his will, he leaves his share of the property to his brother who is not a co-owner. Tony probably owns the property as a

    A. joint tenant
    B. remainderman
    C. tenant in common
    D. life tenant

41. A life tenant

    A. can possess and enjoy the property
    B. must preserve and protect the property
    C. may have the right to lease the property depending on the wording of
       the life estate
    D. all of the answers shown

42. Winona and Aaron own a property together as tenants in common. Each of them
    wants to divide their interest in the property and destroy the tenancy in common
    relationship. This may be accomplished through

    A. a court proceeding (partition action)
    B. a divorce only
    C. disclosure and informed consent
    D. a real estate closing

43. Both dower and curtesy refer to the automatic life estate owned by a surviving spouse
    in inheritable property previously owned by the deceased spouse in his or her name
    alone during the marriage. If the landowner was the husband, the wife has a life estate
    called _____. If the owner of the land was the wife, the husband has a life estate that
    in most states is called _____.

    A. dowager, courtesy
    B. curtesy, dower
    C. dower, curtesy
    D. life tenant, remainder

44. An act of waste on the part of a life tenant violates which of the following rights?

    A. Estovers
    B. Alienation
    C. Reversion
    D. Encumbrance

45. Periodic estates and estates for years are what types of estates?

    A. Life
    B. Dower
    C. Freehold
    D. Leasehold

46. Jeremy and Melissa own their townhouse together but are not married. Melissa purchased her share six months after Jeremy purchased the property. They are

    A. joint tenants
    B. owners of a leasehold estate
    C. tenants in common
    D. tenants *pur autre vie*

47. Debbie conveys a condominium to Raul until the death of Jack. This type of ownership is called

    A. *caveat emptor*
    B. unencumbered
    C. *pur autre vie*
    D. estate in severalty

48. The grounds, roof, hallways, elevators, and pools in a cooperative and condominium development are called

    A. chattel
    B. personal property
    C. common elements
    D. life estates

49. The right of occupancy to a cooperative is evidenced by a(n)

    A. proprietary lease
    B. deed
    C. articles of incorporation
    D. bill of sale

50. Gerald conveys a condominium to Felicia for life. Upon Felicia's death, the property goes to Jennifer. What is the type of estate that Jennifer has?

    A. Reversion
    B. Recession
    C. Rescission
    D. Remainder

51. A cooperative apartment purchase is different from other types of property transactions because

    A. cooperatives are generally more expensive than other property purchases
    B. a cooperative purchase involves purchasing an interest in a corporation and receiving shares of stock
    C. a cooperative purchase cannot be handled by real estate licensees
    D. a cooperative purchaser must always commit to a minimum five-year lease on the apartment

52. Clarissa and James are disappointed to find out that they will not be able to extend the balcony on their new condo. They might have known about this regulation if they had read which of the following documents?

    A. Covenants, conditions, and restrictions
    B. Chattel
    C. Bill of sale
    D. Shares of stock

53. Evidence of a condominium purchase is through

    A. a deed
    B. shares of stock
    C. a proprietary lease
    D. a mortgage

54. Purchasers of a cooperative receive

    A. a deed
    B. shares of stock
    C. a rental agreement
    D. a bill of sale

55. Which of the following about condominium ownership is FALSE?

    A. Ownership applies to both residential and commercial property
    B. Financing is not readily available
    C. The owner owns the individual unit exclusively
    D. Tenants use the common areas together

56. The term appurtenance refers to all rights of a property owner EXCEPT the

    A. reversion of an intestate decedent's property to the state
    B. right to give a license to use one's land
    C. right to allow someone to profit from the land
    D. right to allow someone to access water features

57. A satellite dish that reaches over a property's boundaries to a neighboring property is an example of a(n)

    A. nuisance
    B. encroachment
    C. appurtenance
    D. license

58. All of the following are encumbrances. Which one is also NOT a lien?

    A. mortgage
    B. deed restriction
    C. judgment
    D. property taxes

59. The "trespass on the land of another" describes a(n)

    A. encroachment
    B. encumbrance
    C. easement
    D. profit

60. Ramon cashed in on a silver mine he found on his land. We can assume that Ramon owned

    A. air rights
    B. mineral rights
    C. littoral rights
    D. water rights

61. To determine whether physical encroachments exist, the buyer or the buyer's lender will order a

    A. survey
    B. vendor's affidavit
    C. title insurance
    D. perc test

62. Which of the following is NOT an appurtenant right?

    A. Profit
    B. License
    C. Water rights
    D. Title to the property

63. Which of the following is FALSE concerning encroachments?

    A. An encroachment is necessary when there is no access to roads from the property
    B. The encroaching owner is responsible for removing the encroachment
    C. One way to determine if an encroachment exists is to survey the boundary lines
    D. An encroachment may lead to legal action

64. Cyrus has an easement right. He

    A. owns the land where the easement lies
    B. can never terminate the easement
    C. owns the right to use or have access to the land
    D. cannot use the easement for commercial purposes

65. Which of the following is an example of an easement? The

    A. intrusion of a driveway into the land of another
    B. right a landlocked property owner has to cross his or her neighbor's property to the road
    C. right of an owner to the crops his or her land produces
    D. permission to do a particular act on another's land without possession

66. An easement by prescription

    A. exists when land has no access to roads and is landlocked
    B. is obtained by the use of land without the owner's permission for a legally prescribed length of time
    C. is created with the written express agreement of the landowners
    D. arises by implication from the conduct of the parties

67. An easement created by the government's right of eminent domain is called easement by

    A. necessity
    B. prescription
    C. grant
    D. condemnation

68. An example of an easement in gross is a

    A. utility pole
    B. party wall
    C. shared driveway
    D. recorded right-of-way agreement

69. Which of the following is FALSE regarding an easement?

    A. It can be created by need
    B. It may be owned by the government
    C. It may be affirmative or negative
    D. The easement in gross is the least used form of easement

70. Property owner A and property owner B have adjoining residential properties. Property owner B has permission from property owner A to use property owner A's driveway. Property B would be described as the_____ tenement.

    A. servient
    B. dominant
    C. easement
    D. appurtenant

71. If property owner Cartwright sells his property, including an easement appurtenant, to property owner Purcell, the easement is said to_____

    A. run with the land
    B. create an additional easement by prescription
    C. create an additional easement in gross
    D. create an additional easement by implication

72. When an owner is landlocked and has no access to roads, the landowner may go to court and ask for an

    A. easement by condemnation
    B. easement by necessity
    C. encroachment
    D. easement by grant

73. Property owner, John, gives his neighbor, Odetta, the right to use his driveway to reach her garage. Odetta's interest or right is called a(n)

    A. encroachment
    B. sublease
    C. implied easement
    D. easement

74. Most road widening, sidewalk, alley, and utility easements are created by easements by

    A. prescription
    B. necessity
    C. condemnation
    D. grant

75. In a lawsuit, Nadia wins a judgment against Casey and all of Casey's property. This type of lien is known as a

    A. general lien
    B. specific lien
    C. mechanics' or construction lien
    D. mortgage lien

76. Mechanics' or construction liens may receive priority for payment because of

    A. the type of documentation required to record
    B. time and date of the filing
    C. the amount of the lien
    D. the penalties assessed if they are not paid

77. Adam filed a lien against his contractor for not completing work on a roof on his property. This type of lien (in many states) is called a(n)

    A. laborer's
    B. mechanic's or construction
    C. *lis pendens*
    D. *in rem*

78. A party wall is a type of

    A. easement
    B. lien
    C. appurtenance
    D. *lis pendens*

79. Which of the following would NOT constitute a lien?

    A. State income tax
    B. Mechanic's or construction
    C. Real property tax
    D. Egress

80. Which of the following is FALSE regarding liens?

    A. A lien creates an encumbrance on the property
    B. All liens should be paid in full before a transfer of title take place
    C. An unpaid lien cannot trigger foreclosure proceedings for a new owner
    D. All of the answers shown

MULTIPLE CHOICE

Identify the choice that best completes the statement or answers the question.

1. The highest and best use of a property is defined as

   A. its present use
   B. its market value
   C. the use that best suits the neighborhood
   D. the use that will produce the highest present value

2. The major difference between market price and market value is

   A. market price is what the property sells for while market value is what the sales price should be to a typical buyer
   B. market price is the same as replacement cost while market value is the same as value in use
   C. market price is what the seller is asking and market value is what the buyer pays
   D. none of the answers shown

3. A property valued at $325,000 appreciates by 3% each succeeding year. What is its value after three years?

   A. $340,719.30
   B. $344,792.50
   C. $350,175.45
   D. $355,136.27

Property Valuation, Market Analysis, and the Appraisal Process

4. In an analysis of highest and best use, the appraiser would NOT consider which of the following?

   A. Possible use
   B. Permissible use
   C. Feasible use
   D. Value in use

5. A difference between valuation and evaluation is

   A. valuation is the actual determination of a probable price; evaluation does not result in an estimate of value
   B. evaluation requires a license; valuation does not
   C. evaluation provides a legal value
   D. valuation is the same as a CMA; evaluation is a formal appraisal

6. In the construction of a property, if time schedules are not met or other construction problems occur, which the following would most likely apply? The

   A. market value will equal the cost
   B. cost may exceed the market value
   C. cost will be less than the market value
   D. price will have to equal the cost

7. A value analysis that does not necessarily produce an estimate of value can be best defined as a(n)

   A. evaluation
   B. appraisal
   C. comparative market analysis
   D. competitive market analysis

8. A property will probably NOT sell for market value under which of the following conditions?

   A. Buyer and seller are equally motivated
   B. A reasonable time is allowed for exposure in the market place
   C. The buyer and seller are related to each other
   D. It is an arm's-length transaction

9. Depreciation of real property may be defined as loss of value

   A. due to poor upkeep
   B. due to external influences only
   C. from any cause
   D. from economic obsolescence only

10. A measurement meaning one-foot wide along a property frontage is called a(n)

    A. front foot
    B. fixture
    C. acre
    D. depth frontage ratio

11. The area of a lot with front footage of 100 ft. and depth of 150 ft. is

    A. 15,000 sq. ft.
    B. 7,500 sq. ft.
    C. 1.5 sq. ft
    D. one acre

12. Highest and best use

    A. is often not the best use for the property
    B. is the use that will bring the highest rate of return
    C. does not necessarily take community development goals into consideration
    D. is the same as value in use

13. Surveyors' and appraisers' fees in relation to the development of a property are called

    A. hard costs
    B. indirect costs
    C. direct costs
    D. impact fees

14. A physical force that affects real estate value is

    A. plottage
    B. geographic distribution of social groups
    C. climate
    D. zoning regulations

15. An arm's-length transaction means that

    A. no salesperson or broker is involved in the transaction
    B. the transaction is a cash transaction and no financing is required
    C. the transaction takes place within six months of the property being placed on the market
    D. the parties are not related as relatives, friends, or business associates

16. An economic factor that will decrease when excess competition occurs is

    A. supply
    B. capital
    C. contribution
    D. profit

17. The plottage value of land refers to the

    A. value associated with the plot of land indicating an improvement
    B. value of a plot of land according to tax rolls
    C. increase in value created by combining two or more sites to produce a larger lot with greater utility
    D. total value of a parcel of land that has been subdivided

18. The expression for the value of a particular property to a given investor is

    A. insured value
    B. investment value
    C. value in exchange
    D. production value

19. A study of the supply-and-demand conditions in a specific area for a specific product or service is referred to as

   A. anticipation
   B. economic base
   C. projection analysis
   D. market analysis

20. The economic principle that underlies the income approach to value is

   A. conformity
   B. anticipation
   C. substitution
   D. contribution

21. Topography is defined as the

   A. process of mapping an area by metes and bounds
   B. square footage of boundary lines
   C. configuration of the surface of the land
   D. soil condition of a site

22. The principle of anticipation states that

   A. property depends on its production value
   B. value is the present worth of all prospective future benefits
   C. change is constantly occurring
   D. excess profit is not good for competition

23. A social characteristic to analyze value for an appraisal report is

   A. race
   B. religion
   C. national origin
   D. population growth

24. Which type of value would be most relevant to a city or a county budget official?

   A. Assessed value
   B. Insurance value
   C. Value in use
   D. Mortgage value

25. A site is most profitably used if it

    A. provides the most aesthetic value to the land
    B. is unique to the area
    C. has the same use when improved
    D. provides the highest monetary returns

26. Which effect would be created from a seller's market?

    A. New construction offering more choices to the buyer
    B. Reduced absorption of units
    C. Decrease in prices
    D. Change in population distribution

27. An appraisal is best defined as

    A. an exact determination of value
    B. the sales price agreed upon by a buyer and a seller
    C. an unbiased estimate of value
    D. an approximate cost to replace subject plus site value

28. In the sales comparison approach, if the comparable property has two bathrooms and the subject property has only one, the appraiser must

    A. subtract a certain amount from the comparable
    B. add a certain amount to the comparable
    C. not use the comparable for the appraisal
    D. add a certain amount to the subject

29. The appraisal approach most closely related to a comparative market analysis is the

    A. income approach
    B. cost approach
    C. capitalization approach
    D. sales comparison approach

30. The appraisal approach to value that considers the price to reproduce a property when it was new is the

    A. cost approach
    B. sales comparison approach
    C. income approach
    D. capitalization approach

31. Which appraisal approach to value is the MOST applicable approach for appraising single-family residential properties?

    A. Cost
    B. Income
    C. Sales comparison
    D. Cost and income together

32. The Board of Directors of Wingate Academy, a preparatory school, decided to replace the aging structure with a similar but modern facility. What approach to value would be used to estimate the cost of the new academy?

    A. Cost approach-replacement cost
    B. Income approach
    C. Sales comparison approach
    D. Cost approach-reproduction cost

33. Why is the economic principle of substitution important to performing an appraisal? It is the basis for

    A. reconciliation
    B. conformity
    C. demand
    D. the sales comparison approach

34. All of the following are elements of the income approach to value EXCEPT that it

    A. is based on the principle of anticipation
    B. estimates the potential gross income
    C. requires an estimate of net operating income of property
    D. is a type of sales comparison approach

35. Properties such as schools, hospitals, and government office buildings are generally appraised using the

    A. gross rent multiplier
    B. cost approach
    C. sales comparison approach
    D. income approach

36. Reproduction cost as compared to replacement cost is

    A. the cost to produce an exact duplicate of a building while replacement cost does not produce an exact duplicate
    B. normally far less accurate than the replacement cost
    C. exactly the same
    D. the cost to produce a similar structure while replacement cost is the cost to produce an exact duplicate of the structure

37. A value estimate of real property is a(n)

    A. appraisal of a single-family home
    B. feasibility study
    C. highest and best use study
    D. land utilization study

38. When writing an appraisal report, the appraiser must consider

    A. federal and state fair housing laws
    B. Uniform Standards of Professional Appraisal Practice
    C. Appraisal Board Advisory Opinions
    D. all of the answers shown

39. In order to arrive at the gross rent multiplier, two essential components must be extracted from the market. They are

    A. comparable sales price and its economic rent
    B. comparable net operating income and economic rent
    C. market value of the comparable and depreciation
    D. comparable replacement value and site value

40. If a seller has one bathroom instead of the market standard of two bathrooms in a two-story residential property, the loss in value is considered as

    A. physical deterioration
    B. lack of conformity
    C. external obsolescence
    D. functional obsolescence

41. Which appraisal approach to value depends most heavily upon replacement value?

    A. Gross rent multiplier
    B. Income
    C. Sales comparison
    D. Cost

42. In trying to decide whether or not to add an additional room to an existing home, the owners, Jan and Tom, weigh the future resale value of the home compared to what they must spend to build the addition. Their analysis represents the economic value principle of

    A. conformity
    B. substitution
    C. contribution
    D. supply and demand

43. In a residential appraisal report, adjustments may be made to the

    A. comparables to make them like the subject
    B. subject to make it like the comparables
    C. subject to make it like the market
    D. comparables to make them like the market

44. A valid adjustment for an appraisal report

    A. must be statistically valid
    B. must be supported with data from the market
    C. must be from properties that are sold for the same price
    D. may be based on nothing more than an educated guess

45. The first step in the appraisal process is to

    A. define the purpose of the appraisal
    B. prepare the written appraisal report
    C. arrive at a value estimate
    D. reconcile the data

46. Zev and Tiffany recently had an appraisal performed on their property, which they will put up for sale shortly. They wish to have an exact sales price for the property. What will they receive from the appraiser?

   A. An estimate
   B. The legal value
   C. The lowest amount a seller will accept
   D. The book value

47. While preparing the comparative market analysis, the sales agent, Emily, should NOT consider

   A. similar properties that were sold recently
   B. similar properties being built
   C. properties currently listed for sale
   D. recent expired listings

48. One of the most important aspects of marketing a property is

   A. pricing the property at the lowest possible price for a quick and timely sale
   B. ignoring the competition and allowing the property to sell, based on its own merits
   C. knowing the competition and adjusting pricing and marketing accordingly
   D. effecting a sale within 18 months of the listing date

49. When analyzing data for a comparative market analysis, Tammy, a real estate agent, should not use

   A. sales of similar property
   B. pending offers on similar properties
   C. expired listings over six months old
   D. listings on similar properties

50. Seller Suzanne and real estate broker Jamison agree upon a price to market Suzanne's property. This price is called the

   A. listing price
   B. mortgage value
   C. market position
   D. highest possible use

51. A valuation of the subject property for sales purposes is best described by the term

    A. credit
    B. sales contract
    C. title search
    D. appraisal

52. What is the difference between the sales comparison approach and the comparative market analysis in valuing property?

    A. The sales comparison approach is used for income-producing property and comparative market analysis is used for residential property
    B. The sales comparison approach is a direct approach and the comparative market analysis approach is an indirect approach
    C. Adjustments are generally made only when using the sales comparison approach
    D. There is no difference

53. Expired listings

    A. are never used for a comparative market analysis
    B. are often indicative of properties that were priced below market value
    C. are properties that were not sold during the term of their listing
    D. have little or no information that is useful to marketing a subject property

54. Which of the following is TRUE of housing demand in a single-family residential market analysis?

    A. When market prices fall below the cost of construction, building will accelerate
    B. Incomes have a minimal effect on housing demand
    C. Government regulation does little to impact housing demand
    D. If financing terms are not favorable, housing demand will decrease even though incomes increase

55. Typically, when pricing a property, a real estate agent should NOT use comparables that date back more than

    A. two years
    B. one year
    C. six months
    D. six weeks

56. The name of the listing system available to real estate agents or subagents is the

    A. sales comparison approach
    B. URAR
    C. MLS
    D. CMA

57. Which of the following regarding the price of a property is TRUE? Price

    A. always equals cost
    B. is always more than the cost
    C. is always equivalent to the market value of the property
    D. is not always equivalent to the market value of the property

58. In any real estate investment, the expenses and mortgage costs may well exceed the returns if the investor

    A. uses too much leverage
    B. uses too little leverage
    C. does not make use of available financing
    D. pays cash

59. Jerome's office building produces a net annual operating income of $140,000. If Jerome paid $1,166,666 for the property, what rate of return is he receiving on the investment?

    A. 8.3%
    B. 14%
    C. 12%
    D. 16.3%

60. Which of the following is FALSE regarding investment in vacant land?

    A. Land investment is seldom profitable
    B. Unimproved land cannot be depreciated for tax purposes
    C. Money must be invested in the approval process
    D. Generally, the investor must wait longer for profits than with other types of investments

61. Rent roll refers to which of the following? The

    A. names and addresses of the residents in the building
    B. number of rental units that are currently occupied multiplied by the rental amount per unit
    C. estimated rent for the year
    D. total amount needed monthly to pay the mortgage

62. Property taxes may be deducted from which types of property?

    A. Investment property only
    B. Personal property only
    C. Vacant land only
    D. All types of property

63. In the sale of a real estate investment, the taxpayer is taxed on the

    A. full sales price
    B. full sales price less commission
    C. gain or profit
    D. time value of money

64. Carlotta and Sam buy a second home for vacation purposes only. Their purchase exemplifies which type of value?

    A. Investment value
    B. Depreciated value
    C. Value in use
    D. Insured value

65. The percentage of income per dollar amount earned that an investor receives back on an investment is called the

    A. loan-to-value ratio
    B. time value of money
    C. rate of return
    D. interest

66. Income received without deducting expenses is known as

    A. net operating income
    B. gross income
    C. debt service
    D. mortgage principal

67. G was able to use a minimal amount of personal funds and a substantial amount of borrowed funds to purchase a four-family apartment building. G had a great deal of

    A. leverage
    B. good fortune
    C. negative cash flow
    D. depreciation

68. Unfortunately, Gary's investment property is not yielding income equal to the investment. The economic principle behind Gary's misfortune could be

    A. anticipation
    B. excess profit
    C. decreasing returns
    D. supply and demand

69. Latisha and Toby sell their home for $122,000. They purchased it for $68,500 in 2008, and added central air-conditioning costing $12,000 in 2010 and a small bathroom costing $7,500 in 2011. What is their adjusted basis in the home?

    A. $68,500
    B. $80,500
    C. $88,000
    D. $122,000

70. Which of the following is NOT a method by which equity builds up in an investment property?

    A. Increased value of the property
    B. Principal reduction on the amortized loan
    C. Obtaining a second mortgage on the property
    D. Reduction of interest rates

71. A benefit of tax depreciation is

    A. tax credit
    B. tax deduction
    C. tax evasion
    D. adjusted basis

72. Accrued depreciation

    A. is the total loss in the value of a property over a period of time
    B. is the total cost to replace a building
    C. is the breakdown method of analysis
    D. never goes above 10% of a building's value

73. Tax depreciation

    A. means depreciation due to physical deterioration
    B. means capital loss
    C. means a deductible allowance from net income of property when arriving at taxable income
    D. is also known as the adjusted basis

74. For income tax purposes for a business, which of the following is NOT a deductible expense for a business property?

    A. Advertising
    B. Utilities
    C. Mortgage principal
    D. Insurance

75. Anthony, a Certified General Real Property Appraiser, receives an assignment to conduct a mass appraisal on a housing development in a low-income community that has a significant minority population. The lender tells Anthony that the valuation should be on the low side as compared with other similar developments. Anthony should

    A. accept the assignment and do what he is told by the lender
    B. refuse the assignment
    C. accept the assignment and include a disclaimer stating that the conclusions are partially based on neighborhood statistics
    D. accept the assignment but refuse any future assignments from this particular lender

76. An appraisal performed by a licensed or certified appraiser is required for all real estate–related financial transactions except for those in which the transaction value is

    A. $250,000 or less
    B. less than $300,000
    C. less than $500,000
    D. less than $1 million

77. A Certified General Real Property Appraiser, with regard to federally regulated or insured properties, can appraise

    A. industrial property only
    B. multipurpose property only
    C. agricultural property only
    D. all types of real property

78. Which of the following is NOT a federal category of appraisal licensure?

    A. Licensed Real Property Appraiser
    B. FDIC-Certified Real Property Appraiser
    C. Certified Real Property Appraiser
    D. Certified General Real Property Appraiser

79. Helen has received her appraiser trainee license. Which laws, codes, and regulations apply to her as she performs appraisals under the supervision of a Certified General Real Property Appraiser?

    A. Fair housing laws
    B. Fair lending laws
    C. Uniform Standards of Professional Appraisal Practice (USPAP)
    D. All of the answers shown

80. Miranda, a Certified General Real Property Appraiser, is asked to appraise a property that has ramps, widened doorways, lowered counters, and other accommodations for the disabled. How should she state this information in the appraisal report?

    A. State that these features enhance the value of the property
    B. State that these features detract the value of the property
    C. Not draw an unsupported conclusion that the features either enhance or detract from the property's value
    D. State that the property is stigmatized

Topic 3

Identify the choice that best completes the statement or answers the question.

1. The study of the social and economic statistics of a community is known as

    A. infrastructure
    B. demography
    C. geography
    D. topography

2. Which of the following statements is FALSE?

    A. Private land use control is enforced by public law
    B. Enforcement of covenants is limited to the original purchasers
    C. An injunction prevents a use contrary to the restrictions of record
    D. Failing to enforce restrictions in a timely manner may result in the loss of the right to enforce them at all

3. Which of the following is an example of private land use control?

    A. Eminent domain
    B. Escheat
    C. Police power
    D. Deed restrictions

Land Use Controls and Regulations

4. Cameron was astonished when a group of homeowners in her subdivision informed her that she could not have a toolshed in her yard. Cameron felt that this was not fair especially since most of the other subdivision owners had toolsheds in their yards. What might best explain this?

    A. Cameron was not a good neighbor
    B. Cameron's house did not look good with a toolshed behind it
    C. Many zoning ordinances require that a homeowner live in the house for at least one year before building any outside structures
    D. Cameron has a restriction in her deed preventing her from having the toolshed

5. The best example of direct public ownership is

    A. a subdivision of residential homes
    B. condominiums
    C. a shopping mall
    D. streets, highways, parks

6. Which of the following is NOT a privately imposed land use control?

    A. Covenant
    B. Variance
    C. Condition
    D. Restriction

7. If a municipality does not have the services to support a new development, it may impose a

    A. variance
    B. spot zoning ordinance
    C. nonconforming use
    D. moratorium

8. Zane is building a strip mall in a small community. The community now has to re-build some roadways for increased traffic. Which of the following is FALSE? Zane

    A. must apply for a nonconforming use permit
    B. may be subject to a moratorium
    C. most likely will submit the building plan to the local planning board
    D. may pay impact fees

9. The government's right to tax real property is derived from

    A. the power of escheat
    B. police power
    C. the right of eminent domain
    D. IRS regulations

10. The power of escheat allows the state to

    A. take a private property for public use
    B. take the property of a deceased owner who leaves no heirs or will
    C. levy taxes according to property value
    D. seize property without compensation

11. The Interstate Land Sales Full Disclosure Act regulates developers of subdivisions of

    A. 25 or more lots offered across state lines
    B. 25 or fewer lots offered across state lines
    C. 25 or more lots offered within state lines
    D. 25 or fewer lots offered within state lines

12. If a state takes property under its power of escheat, it is because the property owner died

    A. testate
    B. intestate
    C. *pur autre vie*
    D. bankrupt

13. Which of the following is NOT a government restriction on real property?

    A. Taxation
    B. Eminent domain
    C. Police power
    D. Restrictive covenant

14. Compensation by a government agency in a property matter often follows a court action related to which of the following?

    A. *Caveat emptor*
    B. Police power
    C. Condemnation
    D. Restrictive covenants

15. The purpose of cluster development is to

    A. preserve the land
    B. preserve the aesthetic quality of the subdivision
    C. preserve open space
    D. increase the developer's profits

16. Specific regulations governing materials used in construction, fire and safety standards, and sanitary equipment facilities are referred to as

    A. zoning ordinances
    B. restrictive covenants
    C. deed restrictions
    D. building codes

17. The document that permits occupation of a structure by tenants or owners is called a(n)

    A. property report
    B. certificate of occupancy
    C. declaration of restrictions
    D. enabling act

18. Developers offering 25 or more lots across state lines must provide a property report to the prospective buyer and a statement of record to HUD according to

    A. the Interstate Land Sales Full Disclosure Act
    B. local building codes
    C. the Superfund Amendment
    D. the Truth in Lending Act

19. Although the block where Z's travel agency was located was rezoned to residential use, Z was allowed to keep his agency in the same location. This is an example of

   A. a variance
   B. cluster zoning
   C. spot zoning
   D. a nonconforming use

20. The first step in community planning is to

   A. develop a master plan for the community
   B. make changes to the zoning ordinance
   C. develop a strong police force
   D. issue building permits to developers

21. Zoning ordinances are established by the

   A. planning board
   B. legislature
   C. federal government
   D. HUD

22. A permitted deviation from specific requirements of the zoning ordinance defines

   A. variance
   B. nonconforming use
   C. planned unit development
   D. subdivision regulations

23. After a public hearing, the planning board allows Dwayne to open a computer warehouse in a residential neighborhood. The planning board most likely granted him a

   A. nonconforming use
   B. special use permit
   C. variance
   D. spot zoning permit

24. Homeowners in Lakeside Manor subdivision did nothing for three years to enforce a covenant stating that residents may not park an RV on their front driveways. The homeowners may lose their rights to enforce this covenant under

   A. the Statute of Frauds
   B. articles of incorporation
   C. zoning regulations
   D. the Doctrine of Laches

25. Ramone wishes to construct a house that is larger than allowed by local zoning regulations for that neighborhood. Which of the following would NOT be a necessary step in the building process?

   A. Lead-based paint disclosure
   B. Variance
   C. Building permit
   D. Certificate of occupancy

26. Teri wishes to add another story to her home, but the new height would not comply with local zoning regulations. She would have to apply for a

   A. nonconforming use
   B. variance
   C. spot zone
   D. special permission

27. Which of the following does NOT describe typical planning and zoning?

   A. Provides for the orderly growth of the community
   B. Based on the police power of government
   C. Requires the unanimous consent of all property owners within a community
   D. Results in social and economic benefits to the community

28. A zoning issue raised by the conversion of apartments into condominiums might include

   A. changes to the green space
   B. lot size and setback requirements
   C. infrastructure requirements such as increased road frontage and accessibility
   D. all of the answers shown

29. In general, changes to a community's master plan are

    A. voted in by the state legislature
    B. decided by the mayor's office
    C. voted in by a majority referendum of the community
    D. only changed by judicial review in court

30. Zoning ordinances consist of which two parts?

    A. Nonconforming use and spot zoning
    B. Planned unit developments and the zoning map
    C. Cluster development and planned unit developments
    D. The zoning map and the text of the zoning ordinance

31. The zoning board of appeals does NOT

    A. grant or deny exceptions and special permits
    B. review rulings made by the zoning board
    C. establish zoning policy
    D. deal with applications for variances

32. If zoning of a property is solely for the benefit of the property owner and has the effect of increasing the land value, the rezoning is

    A. legal
    B. illegal spot zoning in most states
    C. referred to as a nonconforming use
    D. referred to as a variance

33. A warehouse is left standing and in use after the entire street is rezoned as residential. The warehouse then converts to a retail store. Which of the following applies?

    A. It is an example of nonconforming use
    B. It is an example of spot zoning
    C. The nonconforming use is violated
    D. It is an example of a special use permit

34. An outlot can be defined as a(n)

    A. parcel of land that is outside the main area of development
    B. extra lot
    C. lot developed from a wetland
    D. lot that is undesirable for development

35. An element that is friable and can cause lung cancer when released into the air is

    A. formaldehyde
    B. radon
    C. asbestos
    D. PCBs

36. An innocent landowner would not be liable for the presence of hazardous waste under the Superfund Amendment to the Comprehensive Environmental Response, Compensation, and Liability Act (CERCLA). These parties may include

    A. landowners who did not know the property was contaminated when it was purchased
    B. landowners who reacted responsibly to the contamination when found
    C. property owners who made inquiries into past usage to see if the property was contaminated at the time of purchase
    D. all of the answers shown

37. An element that is radioactive and measured in picocuries

    A. are electromagnetic waves
    B. is formaldehyde
    C. are PCBs
    D. is radon

38. Due-diligence reviews of a property before title transfer protect which of the following from liability for environmental problems after title transfer?

    A. Seller
    B. EPA
    C. Local planning boards
    D. Purchaser

39. Which of the following laws seek reimbursement from responsible parties who have caused hazardous waste?

    A. Real Estate Settlement Procedures Act
    B. Comprehensive Environmental Response, Compensation, and Liability Act
    C. Interstate Land Sales Full Disclosure Act
    D. Residential Lead-Based Paint Hazard Reduction Act

40. Which of the following is TRUE?

    A. Construction on or near a wetland requires an application and permit
    B. Construction on or near a wetland does not require an application or permit
    C. Construction is not permitted under any circumstances on or near a wetland
    D. Wetlands are not protected areas in most places

41. The federal government organization that oversees navigation, flood control, and dredging projects is the

    A. Army Corps of Engineers
    B. Environmental Protection Agency (EPA)
    C. Department of Housing and Urban Development (HUD)
    D. State and local departments of health

42. If a property is termite infested,

    A. it must be completely rebuilt
    B. the property cannot close within 120 days of treatment
    C. it cannot be placed for sale
    D. a real estate licensee must disclose information regarding termite infestation, if known, to prospective buyers

43. A member of the fungi kingdom that is caused by excess moisture and high humidity in and about a property is called

    A. PCBs
    B. mold
    C. asbestos
    D. formaldehyde

44. The federal agency that oversees the regulation of underground storage tanks is

    A. FHA
    B. HUD
    C. EPA
    D. Fannie Mae

45. Which of the following is NOT generally a consideration in the development of a site or subdivision plan?

    A. Environmental considerations
    B. Easements running through the property
    C. The power of escheat
    D. Zoning surrounding the site

46. An environmental impact statement

    A. is always necessary for the transfer and/or development of real property
    B. becomes necessary if a government agency finds that further evaluation of the property is needed before a project can be developed
    C. is a voluntary environmental assessment
    D. is needed only for hazardous waste sites

47. When an environmental impact statement for a development is completed, which of the following will occur next?

    A. A public comment period and public hearing
    B. A judicial ruling on the development
    C. A zoning ordinance
    D. A state agency's permission to go forward or not go forward with the development

48. Which of the following is FALSE regarding owners of underground storage tanks?

    A. Owners must test the tanks periodically for leakage
    B. Owners must repair or replace the tank if compromised by leakage
    C. If there is contamination, the owner may need to restore the environment
    D. If there is leakage from the tank, the owner should not remove the product from the tank

49. Wayne is purchasing an industrial plant to manufacture chemicals for swimming pools. The plant owns five underground storage tanks, and Wayne plans to add five more and expand the building to cover another acre of land to use for storage of more chemicals. What might be the process(es) that Wayne faces in the transfer of this property?

    A. Environmental impact statement
    B. Due-diligence review
    C. Underground storage tank inspection
    D. All of the answers shown

50. Broker L showed prospective buyers a property that was in close proximity to a toxic waste site. Although the broker knew about the site, he did not inform the buyers. Later, the buyers bought the property and sued the broker and the sellers. Who may be liable?

    A. No one
    B. The seller only
    C. Both the sellers and the broker
    D. The agent only

51. Tanisha is a buyer broker. Her clients request that the property they are purchasing be tested for radon. Neither Tanisha nor the buyers' attorney adds a radon contingency to the contract. After purchase, the property tests high for radon levels. Who may be liable?

    A. No one because radon testing is not mandatory in Tanisha's state
    B. The attorney only
    C. Tanisha, the buyers' broker, only
    D. Tanisha, the buyer broker, and the buyers' attorney

52. Which of the choices below is FALSE under the Comprehensive Environmental Response, Compensation, and Liability Act (CERCLA)? A program exists to

    A. identify sites containing hazardous substances
    B. seek reimbursement from the responsible party
    C. blame innocent landowners who unknowingly purchase contaminated property
    D. ensure cleanup by the parties responsible or by the government

53. An agent lists a property, built after 1978, in a rural area that uses oil heat and a well and septic system. From this information, which of the following contingencies would not appear in the contract for purchase?

    A. Radon contingency
    B. Well condition and water flow contingency
    C. Septic system contingency
    D. Lead-based paint contingency

54. The danger of radon lies in its

    A. fumes
    B. friability
    C. magnetic strength
    D. radioactivity

55. An issue that developers must consider in building near tidal waters or wetlands includes

    A. extra cost of construction
    B. government regulations restricting the project
    C. approval of private drinking water and wastewater systems
    D. all of the answers shown

56. The only true and impartial standard for setting assessments is

    A. the market value
    B. the cost approach
    C. the income approach
    D. a uniform percentage

57. When an action is brought against the real property and not against the individual and his personal property, this is known as

    A. an *in rem* legal proceeding
    B. an *ad valorem* legal proceeding
    C. *caveat emptor*
    D. the Doctrine of Laches

58. The tax rate is determined by the amount of the

    A. tax levy
    B. assessment
    C. tax lien
    D. tax exemption

59. Which of the following is NOT classified as a homestead property?

    A. Two-family home
    B. Residential condominium
    C. Warehouse
    D. Farmhouse and land used for agricultural production

60. If the tax value is 50% of the assessed value, and the assessed value is $89,990, what are the annual taxes if the rate is $4.10 per $100 (rounded)?

    A. $1,844.80
    B. $10,822.22
    C. $1,484.44
    D. $5,444.44

61. A tax bill is determined by

    A. the property's taxable assessment and the tax rates of the taxing jurisdiction in which the property is located
    B. the number of properties on the assessment roll divided by the tax levy
    C. the total cost of the municipality's operations
    D. an estimate by the local assessor

62. Which of the following properties are ALWAYS fully exempt from property taxes?

    A. Properties owned by senior citizens
    B. Properties owned by veterans
    C. Gas stations
    D. Churches

63. Serena is purchasing a property for $325,000. She finds out that the sellers purchased the property for $200,000 eight years ago. She asks her real estate agent, Eva, if she has to pay increased property taxes once title transfers to her. How should Eva respond?

    A. Serena's property taxes will increase immediately upon transfer
    B. Serena's property taxes will probably not immediately increase upon transfer
    C. Serena's assessment will not increase upon transfer, only her property taxes
    D. None of the answers shown

64. Tom is 66 years old and has owned and lived in his house for 25 years. He is a U.S. Army veteran. Tom is disabled because of his service in the military. For which of the following reasons may Tom be eligible for a school or property tax exemption?

    A. Senior citizen
    B. Veteran
    C. Disability
    D. All of the answers shown

65. Decisions regarding the assessments to real property are made by the

    A. local assessor
    B. state taxing agency
    C. county government body
    D. mayor's office

66. The tax rate is usually expressed by number of tax dollars per $1,000 of assessed value. If a town levy is $5 million and the entire town has an assessed value of $100 million, what would be the tax rate for the town?

    A. $500
    B. $200
    C. $50
    D. $20

67. Appropriation

    A. occurs when a government agency sets aside funds for a certain purpose
    B. is the amount that the municipality must raise by taxing real property
    C. is the cumulative assessment figures on all properties in a municipality
    D. is used to calculate the property tax bill

68. When a taxpayer is delinquent in paying property taxes, which of the following attaches to the property?

    A. Judgment
    B. Tax lien
    C. Foreclosure
    D. Equity of redemption

69. Which of the following is FALSE concerning back taxes?

    A. Back taxes are unpaid property taxes
    B. If title is to be transferred, back taxes are paid at closing
    C. Generally, owing of back taxes will affect the reassessment of a property
    D. If a property owner takes title to a new property not fully assessed upon moving in, the town is not entitled to back taxes when the property is fully assessed

70. A type of map, drawn to scale, showing all of the real property parcels in a city, town, or other assessing unit is a(n)

    A. tax map
    B. plat
    C. homestead diagram
    D. assessment roll

71. A property whose market value is $100,000 in a community where the uniform percentage for assessment is 70% will have an assessed value of

    A. $7,000
    B. $10,000
    C. $70,000
    D. $100,000

72. There would be no need for equalization if all municipalities assessed all property at what percentage of market value each year?

    A. 100%
    B. 80%
    C. 75%
    D. 60%

73. If a property is assessed at 90% of market value, the market value is $200,000, and the tax rate is 6%, what is the amount of the property tax?

    A. $10,000
    B. $10,800
    C. $16,600
    D. $29,600

74. A property owner's tax rate is 0.045, and the annual tax bill is $9,500. What is the assessed value of the property (rounded)?

    A. $211,111
    B. $200,111
    C. $200,000
    D. $231,426

75. Which of the terms below refers to the division of property and school tax monies so that school districts, counties, towns, and cities in the different municipalities all pay their fair share of the tax levy?

    A. Apportionment
    B. Appropriation
    C. Assessment
    D. Equalization

76. A house has an assessed value of $150,000. The property is taxed at 75% of assessed value at a rate of $4.50 per $100. If the assessed valuation is increased by 15%, what is the amount of taxes to be paid on the property (rounded)?

    A. $1,293.75
    B. $5,882.10
    C. $5,821.88
    D. $12,938

77. The difference between proposed expenditures and revenues from various sources such as state and federal aid determines the

    A. apportionment
    B. tax levy
    C. special assessment
    D. tax rate

78. Makeda has applied for a tax exemption because of her age and income. She will be allowed a 25% reduction in her assessment. Her current assessment (before the exemption) is $80,000. The current tax rate for all properties in the town is $32 per $1,000. What will Makeda owe in property taxes for the year?

    A. $2,560
    B. $1,920
    C. $60,000
    D. $2,150

79. A home is valued at $94,000 and is assessed at 40% of value. The tax rate is 17 mills. One mill = $1/10$ of one cent. What is the amount of the tax bill?

    A. $159.80
    B. $639.20
    C. $958.80
    D. $1,598

80. If a town levy is $1.5 million and the entire town has an assessed value of $75 million, what would the tax rate be for the town expressed by number of tax dollars per $1,000 of assessed value?

    A. $10
    B. $20
    C. $25
    D. $50

Topic 4

MULTIPLE CHOICE

Identify the choice that best completes the statement or answers the question.

1. Consideration is

   A. a promise of quiet enjoyment
   B. the giving of something, which need not be monetary value, as an inducement to contract
   C. always expressed as a dollar value
   D. a power of attorney

2. What is the main benefit of the mortgage contingency clause? If the

   A. buyer does not like the mortgage rate, the contract may be canceled
   B. buyer does not receive a mortgage commitment, the contract may be canceled
   C. seller does not receive a mortgage for his or her next house before the closing, the contract may be canceled
   D. buyer does not receive a mortgage commitment, the contract is not canceled but his or her deposit is refunded to the seller

3. Which of the following is NOT a contract?

   A. deed
   B. lease
   C. mortgage
   D. option

Contracts and Relationships with Buyers and Sellers

4. When two parties have made sincere promises to each other, the contract that exists is known as a(n)

   A. unilateral contract
   B. void contract
   C. bilateral contract
   D. option contract

5. Vince, a salesperson, wants to avoid the unlawful practice of law in filling out a contract of sale. What should he include in his contract?

   A. A rider
   B. A copy of his salesperson's license
   C. An attorney review clause
   D. The right of first refusal

6. An example of liquidated damages is

   A. a penalty for extremely bad behavior by a party
   B. forfeiture of earnest money
   C. money actually lost
   D. a penalty for a party taking fraudulent advantage over another party

7. A contract that is always binding and enforceable on all parties to it is known as

   A. valid
   B. void
   C. voidable
   D. executed

8. Carolanne is 15 years old and has entered into a written real estate contract with a person who is 25. From the point of view of Carolanne, this contract is

   A. void
   B. voidable
   C. unilateral
   D. implied

9. Why is it important that an earnest money deposit accompany an offer to purchase? It

   A. shows the sincerity of buyer
   B. demonstrates financial capability to raise the money called for in the purchase offer
   C. may serve as possible liquidated damages to the seller if the buyer defaults
   D. includes all of the answers shown

10. A contract is drawn to convey Lot #3 from Green Hill Developers, Inc. to Matthew Morton. Upon further investigation, it is discovered that the lot selected by Matthew was Lot #4. Both parties recognize an error was made and agree to correct the contract. The error is an example of

   A. fraud
   B. mutual mistake
   C. misrepresentation
   D. legality of object

11. Which of the following is NOT a purpose of the earnest money deposit?

   A. Shows the sincerity of the buyer
   B. Helps demonstrate the buyer's capability to raise sufficient funds to purchase the property
   C. To buy down the interest rate of the mortgage loan
   D. Serves as liquidated damages to the seller should the buyer default

12. An executed contract means that

   A. only one party to the contract has made a promise
   B. at least one party to the contract may still sue for specific performance
   C. all of the parties have fully performed their duties
   D. one of the conditions of the contract has been completed

13. B entered into a contract to buy land from C. It was soon discovered that C was not the owner of the land. The contract between the two of them is

    A. valid
    B. void
    C. enforceable
    D. executed

14. Which of the following is NOT an essential element of a contract?

    A. Capacity of the parties
    B. Legality of object
    C. Consideration
    D. Value of comparable sales

15. Which of the following is NOT a form of real estate contract?

    A. Condominium contract of sale
    B. Option to buy
    C. Installment sales contract
    D. Mortgage contingency

16. If a contract is signed and pending and another contract comes in, this is known as a(n)

    A. assignment
    B. novation
    C. counteroffer
    D. back-up offer

17. A valid contract

    A. is always bilateral
    B. must be filed with the county clerk
    C. is never broken
    D. is binding and enforceable on all parties

18. When the parties to a contract have definitely agreed to all terms and conditions in the contract, the type of contract that exists is known as

   A. promissory
   B. executed
   C. express
   D. implied

19. Seller R received an order from the court stating that he must pay the commission to the broker exactly as stated in the agreement. The court has ordered

   A. specific performance
   B. rescission
   C. compensatory damages
   D. liquidated damages

20. The portion of the money paid to purchase a property that is paid in cash and is not part of the mortgage loan is called the

   A. upfront deposit
   B. boot
   C. down payment
   D. contingency

21. Frank and Debbie sign a contract to purchase a house for their daughter. The daughter decides that she does not like the house. Luckily, Frank's son decides that he wants it. The contract is amended with Frank's son as the purchaser. This is a(n)

   A. counteroffer
   B. installment contract
   C. assignment
   D. contingency

22. The rights, duties, and responsibilities of the parties to a contract are wholly expressed through the

   A. offer
   B. contract
   C. acceptance
   D. application

23. Legal capacity to contract includes which of the following considerations?

    A. Emotional ability
    B. Mental ability
    C. Competency
    D. All of the answers shown

24. Essential elements of a valid contract do NOT include

    A. consideration
    B. lawful objective
    C. mutual agreement
    D. assignment

25. Deposits for real estate transactions negotiated by brokers may be held by all of the following EXCEPT

    A. real estate brokers
    B. attorneys
    C. lenders
    D. sellers

26. In a brokerage firm, the listing contracts are typically owned by the

    A. salesperson who listed the property
    B. multiple listing service together with the brokerage firm
    C. principals who engaged the firm to market their properties
    D. brokerage firm

27. A brokerage firm received an order from the court to immediately stop soliciting listings in a certain geographic area. This order is called a(n)

    A. rescission
    B. reformation
    C. injunction
    D. assignment

28. Scott lists his farm with A.J., a local broker, who specializes in farm and land transactions. Scott retains the right to sell the property himself, but assures A.J. that he is the only broker Scott wants to work with. A.J. advises Scott to sign a contract for a(n)

    A. open listing
    B. exclusive-right-to-sell
    C. exclusive agency
    D. nonexclusive agency

29. The two tests that entitle a broker to compensation is a buyer who is

    A. ready and willing; seller acceptance
    B. ready; seller acceptance
    C. ready, willing, and able; seller acceptance
    D. financially capable; seller acceptance

30. At closing, the sellers refuse to pay Jacob the full commission agreed upon in the listing agreement because they think it is too high. What recourse does Jacob have to obtain the full commission?

    A. Sue for the commission
    B. File a *lis pendens*
    C. Petition for a hearing to the real estate commission
    D. None of the answers shown

31. In general, a valid written listing agreement between a seller and a real estate agent where a buyer has not been found is a(n)

    A. implied contract
    B. void contract
    C. executory contract
    D. unenforceable contract

32. "The seller lists the property with several brokers" describes a(n)

    A. exclusive-right-to-sell listing
    B. contract for deed
    C. open listing
    D. option

33. A contract of sale includes a "time is of the essence" clause. However, the parties to the contract do not close by the date specified in the contract. This contract may be

    A. executed
    B. fully performed
    C. unenforceable
    D. implied

34. The law that requires that all contracts that create an interest in real estate be in writing to be enforceable in court is the

    A. Statute of Limitations
    B. Regulation Z
    C. Statute of Frauds
    D. Real Estate Settlement Procedures Act

35. Which of the following statement is TRUE?

    A. A buyer's agent represents the seller
    B. The buyer broker generally holds the deposit
    C. A buyer begins the contractual process as the offeror
    D. A lead-based paint disclosure and contingency need only be added to contracts of sale for properties built after 1978

36. At what point is a real estate contract of sale binding?

    A. When it is signed by buyer and seller
    B. When it is signed by buyer and seller and agents for each
    C. When it is reviewed and approved by the attorneys for buyer and seller
    D. At closing

37. Typically, a deposit that accompanies an offer to purchase or contract of sale is which of the following?

    A. A percentage of the purchase price
    B. Always 10% of the purchase price
    C. At least 50% of the purchase price
    D. None of the answers shown

38. A real estate salesperson sells a property for $90,000. The commission on this sale to the real estate firm with whom the salesperson is associated is 6%. The salesperson receives 60% of the total commission paid to the real estate firm. What is the amount of the salesperson's commission?

    A. $2,240
    B. $3,240
    C. $4,500
    D. $4,750

39. In certain places, which of the following is used in place of an offer to purchase when a buyer makes an offer on a property?

    A. Proprietary lease
    B. Binder
    C. Deed of trust
    D. Mortgage

40. Which statement is FALSE about an accepted offer to purchase? The

    A. purchase contract is a bilateral express contract
    B. parties are assumed to be in equal bargaining positions
    C. principals have formed an agency relationship with each other
    D. parties have equal ability from opposing viewpoints

41. If a contract for purchase and sale states that "time is of the essence," this means that the contract must be performed

    A. within a reasonable time period
    B. within one year
    C. on or before the date stipulated on the contract
    D. within three months

42. Goldie and Sam, college graduates, are ready to buy their first home, and receive a lender promise of $275,000 on a property with a purchase price of $325,000. The seller agrees to pay all closing costs. They are unable to purchase the property because they do not have the

    A. legal capacity
    B. down payment
    C. right of first refusal
    D. mortgage commitment

43. A broker earns a commission of $12,000 in the sale of a residential property. His rate of commission is 6%. What is the selling price?

    A. $100,000
    B. $150,000
    C. $200,000
    D. $250,000

44. Which of the following is NOT a part of a real estate contract of sale?

    A. Contingency
    B. Addenda
    C. Rider
    D. Codicil

45. Who signs the offer to purchase first?

    A. The seller
    B. The purchaser
    C. Seller and purchaser must sign at the same time
    D. The purchaser's attorney

46. Seller Belle signs a purchase agreement with buyer Leroy, contingent upon a pest inspection. In this contract, seller Louise agrees that she will pay up to 2% of the purchase price for any repairs that a licensed pest inspector indicates must be completed. Upon inspection, it is discovered that the repairs will exceed 4% of the purchase price. The purchase agreement is now

    A. void
    B. voidable
    C. executed
    D. unenforceable

47. Justine enters into a written contract of sale with Pietro. The closing is scheduled for the following month. This contract is

    A. express
    B. implied
    C. unilateral
    D. executed

48. Pet restrictions, repair obligations, and use of the common elements are disclosed in a condominium's

    A. bylaws
    B. letter of intent
    C. contract of sale
    D. deed

49. Which of the following is NOT included in a condominium offering plan?

    A. Initial declaration
    B. Prospectus
    C. Initial price of the units
    D. Proprietary lease

50. In the sale of a cooperative, a board package, submitted to the cooperative board of directors, consists mainly of

    A. societal status information
    B. family history
    C. financial data
    D. reasons for purchase

51. The type of contract used for the transfer of cooperative properties is a(n)

    A. cooperative contract of sale
    B. proprietary lease
    C. installment sales contract
    D. letter of intent

52. Which of the following is FALSE regarding an installment land contract? It

    A. provides equitable title to the buyer
    B. must be in writing to be enforceable
    C. cannot be used on land purchases
    D. is binding on the heirs and estates of the parties

53. Evan has an option to lease a movie theatre when the current lease runs out. In the meantime, another buyer expresses an interest in leasing the same movie theatre. The property owner contacts Evan and asks him if he wants to exercise his option, or else the property owner will lease it to the other interested party. What must Evan have in his option contract? A(n)

    A. binder

    B. right of first refusal

    C. "time is of the essence" clause

    D. injunction

54. A written option agreement is a contract that

    A. specifies a time limit within which the optionee may choose to purchase or lease a piece of real property

    B. not enforceable in court

    C. does not define a specific sales price

    D. conveys title when the optionee signs the option contract

55. Aunt May promises to hold 10 acres of her land to sell to her nephew 10 months from today for $100,000. Her nephew promises nothing in return. The legal agreement they both sign is

    A. bilateral

    B. an option

    C. unenforceable

    D. executed

56. Often, a seller agrees to finance a portion, or all of the selling price of the property. A seller financing contract is which of the following?

    A. Assumable mortgage

    B. Home equity loan

    C. FHA loan

    D. Purchase money mortgage

57. The Havenots make an offer for a property that was rejected by the sellers. The sellers then make a higher offer to the Havenots. In this situation, the sellers have

    A. voided the contract

    B. counteroffered

    C. violated their fiduciary duty to their agent

    D. breached the contract

58. Brad, age 21, and Donna, age 19, enter into a contract to construct a gambling casino on some land in New York State where gambling casinos are illegal except on Native American lands. This contract is void because

    A. there is no consideration
    B. gambling casinos are illegal in New York
    C. Brad and Donna are too young to enter into a contract
    D. it is implied

59. A legal remedy for breach of contract would NOT be

    A. novation
    B. specific performance
    C. compensatory damages
    D. liquidated damages

60. The substitution of a new contract for a prior contract is known as

    A. novation
    B. injunction
    C. full performance
    D. release

61. When brokers improperly pay any part of their compensation to anyone who is not licensed or who is not exempt from the license law, they violate the license law. This payment is called

    A. a kickback
    B. fee splitting
    C. commingling
    D. an illegal net listing

62. A real estate broker who convinces a party to a contract of sale to break the contract in order to substitute a new contract with another party is guilty of

    A. violating federal and state fair housing statutes
    B. inducing a breach of contract
    C. failing to disclose his or her interest in the real estate
    D. commingling funds

63. Agent Uri was about to accept a deposit from purchaser Palani, when Agent Uri discovered that the seller had decided to withdraw his property from the market. Agent Uri

   A. should accept the deposit anyway
   B. should accept the deposit for a limited time only
   C. should not accept the deposit
   D. should accept the deposit and place it in his personal checking account until further notice

64. A false statement regarding an important matter in a real estate transaction to induce someone to contract is called

   A. the unauthorized practice of law
   B. reciprocity
   C. "buyer beware"
   D. misrepresentation

65. In the sale of his single-family home, homeowner D refused an offer from a qualified buyer who was Asian. Which of the following is CORRECT?

   A. He has violated federal fair housing laws
   B. He has violated no laws
   C. He has only violated the law if he has used the services of a real estate agent
   D. The sale of single-family homes is exempt from all fair housing laws

66. Sales agent A works for broker B who is selling his vacation home to buyer P. Agent A does not mention to buyer P that the owner of the property he is selling is his broker. Which of the following is TRUE?

   A. The theory of "buyer beware" applies
   B. Broker B is engaging in illegal self-dealing
   C. Agent A need not disclose this information because it is the broker's property, not his
   D. The buyer must wait for his attorney to divulge this information at closing

67. Agent Gamal tells prospective purchasers at a listing presentation that he would guarantee them $200,000 for their property, and keep whatever he procured over that amount for his commission. In many states, this type of arrangement is

   A. perfectly fine
   B. illegal
   C. legal only with disclosure and informed consent
   D. only legal if there is a signed listing agreement

68. Broker Yardley, the listing broker, did not inform broker Wynn, who was showing the property, that he had just found out about a recent zoning change that affected the ingress and egress to the street. Broker Yardley

   A. has not violated license laws
   B. has committed an act of misrepresentation
   C. has no duty to know about zoning laws or pass them on to other brokers
   D. is not showing the property so he does not have a duty to disclose this information

69. Raphael, a real estate salesperson, advises his buyer clients not to sign a contract of sale prepared by their attorney because he believes that the "as is" clause in the contract will cause them trouble later. Which of the following is TRUE? Raphael

   A. can advise his clients as to legal matters as long as they don't have an attorney
   B. can advise his clients about any matters as long as they have signed the agency disclosure form
   C. can advise his clients on all contractual matters
   D. may be engaging in the illegal practice of law

70. Broker Carlton initially placed a client's deposit money in his escrow account as required by law. Later, he transferred the sum to the office operating account and paid the rent with it. Broker Carlton is guilty of

   A. conversion
   B. self-dealing
   C. specific performance
   D. failure to disclose

71. Sales agent S, the listing agent, informed sales agent P that there were no other offers on a property even though there were. Relying on this information, sales agent P told his prospective buyers to take some time to think about an offer. This activity is

    A. an act of misrepresentation on the part of sales agent S
    B. acceptable because agents are in competition with each other
    C. acceptable in the sale of residential property
    D. an attempt by sales agent S to protect the seller

72. Salesperson Omar placed an ad in the newspaper for a four-bedroom property but did not indicate that he was a real estate salesperson or that the property was offered by a real estate firm. This ad

    A. violates license law
    B. is allowable under the license law
    C. is allowable if it mentions the geographical location of the property
    D. is only allowable for residential properties

73. If a real estate salesperson should receive a deposit, which of the following is TRUE? He or she

    A. must keep it in his checking account
    B. must lock it in a safe place until the closing
    C. must turn it over to his broker
    D. can keep it as his commission

74. A broker persuades his or her customers to purchase an overpriced property immediately to obtain a higher commission even though he or she knows of less expensive properties that would fulfill their needs and wants. This action could be interpreted as

    A. undue influence
    B. duress
    C. misrepresentation
    D. fraud

75. K lists her condominium with broker B for $150,000. Broker B then tells a prospective buyer to submit a low offer because seller K is going through a divorce and needs the money. The buyer offers $120,000 and K accepts this offer. In this circumstance, broker B

    A. violated her fiduciary relationship to the seller
    B. did nothing wrong since an offer came through that K was happy with
    C. acted properly as long as K does not complain
    D. was correct to tell the buyers this information under his duty to disclose

76. R, a broker, negotiated the sale of a single-family house. Both the buyer and seller signed the contract of sale, the contract was reviewed and approved by attorneys for both parties, and financing was approved. A day before closing, the buyers want to back out of the deal. R

    A. must now forfeit his commission because it is unearned
    B. must take a lesser commission than arranged because of the new circumstances
    C. is entitled to the full commission as originally agreed upon
    D. must forfeit his commission because the deal involves residential real estate, and if it does not close, the broker cannot be compensated

77. Broker Tiffany received two purchase offers at the same time. Although the offers were for the same amount, one offer had better terms than the other. Broker Tiffany decided to submit only the better offer to the sellers. This activity is

    A. perfectly acceptable
    B. a violation of license law
    C. dependent on the in-house policy in the brokerage firm
    D. allowable only if submitted by the broker and not the salesperson

78. With respect to real estate commissions and compensation, which of the following is FALSE?

    A. A broker is not entitled to a commission if the seller refuses to or cannot complete the transaction with a ready, willing, and able buyer
    B. Antitrust laws prohibit competing brokers from collaborating on a commission percentage to charge collectively
    C. A brokerage firm, not the salesperson, owns the listings
    D. A broker may elect to charge different commission percentages for different types of properties based on price, location, or other considerations

79. Vito, a real estate broker, advises his clients that they should not sign their contract of sale because he does not agree with the wording of the contract. Which of the following applies?

    A. Vito should advise his clients because he is their broker
    B. Vito's advice could constitute the illegal practice of law
    C. A broker can give legal advice to his clients if they do not have an attorney
    D. Advice on contracts of sale by real estate brokers is exempt from the prohibition against giving legal advice

80. After numerous negotiations, Kendra and Dan contract to buy a two-story income property. When the closing takes place, their broker tells them they have fulfilled the terms of the contract. Which of the following has occurred?

    A. Full performance
    B. An executory contract
    C. Meeting of the minds
    D. Novation

Topic 5

MULTIPLE CHOICE

Identify the choice that best completes the statement or answers the question.

1. Which of the following describes a mortgage?

   A. A cash sale
   B. A two-party instrument between the lender and the borrower
   C. Only available through a bank
   D. All of the answers shown

2. The lowest point in the economic cycle is which of the following?

   A. Recession
   B. Stagflation
   C. Inflation
   D. Depression

3. What does the mortgagee require of the borrower?

   A. Pay all real property taxes and assessments on a timely basis
   B. Keep the buildings in proper repair
   C. Protect against loss by insuring the building for at least 80% of its value
   D. All of the answers shown

Financing

4. Which of the following describes the term interest?

   A. The money paid for using someone else's money
   B. The amount of money borrowed
   C. The amount of money the lender has lent
   D. It provides evidence that a valid debt exists

5. Barry has borrowed $40,000 against his home with a second mortgage note from EZ Pay Mortgage Company. In this transaction, EZ Pay Mortgage Company is the

   A. mortgagee
   B. mortgagor
   C. trustor
   D. beneficiary

6. Which of the following is NOT a tax deductible expense for a business property?

   A. Advertising
   B. Utilities
   C. Mortgage principal
   D. Insurance

7. A consideration for a lender in making a mortgage loan would NOT be the

   A. borrower's income
   B. borrower's ability to repay the loan
   C. borrower's credit history
   D. whether the property is redlined or not

8. A mortgage is a

   A. loan
   B. security instrument
   C. note
   D. defeasance

9. Jacob's mortgage broker has informed him that interest on his loan will be calculated in arrears. This concept of arrears means

   A. if Jacob is behind in his payments, the lender will foreclose
   B. the payment of monthly interest will be for use of the money during the previous month and not for the upcoming month
   C. Jacob will be allowed a short grace period before a late charge will be assessed
   D. Jacob may obtain additional funds advanced at a later time

10. The lender of mortgage money is known as the

   A. trustee
   B. mortgagor
   C. mortgagee
   D. trustor

11. With regard to a mortgage, another name for a promissory note is

   A. acceleration clause
   B. defeasance clause
   C. power of attorney
   D. bond

12. A property has three subordinate mortgage liens encumbering it: a first mortgage, a second mortgage, and a third mortgage. These numbers refer to

   A. the priority of the liens
   B. the size of the liens
   C. the dates of the liens
   D. whether the liens are from a seller, a mortgage company, or a third-party lender

13. What does the right of assignment provide to the lender?

   A. Repayment of the debt
   B. Liquidity
   C. Shorter lending period
   D. Insurance on its investment

14. The amount of money that is advanced by the lender and ultimately repaid by the borrower is referred to as

   A. interest
   B. principal
   C. note
   D. mortgage

15. The monthly mortgage payment generally consists of

   A. principal and interest
   B. taxes
   C. insurance
   D. all of the answers shown

16. The loan-to-value ratio is the relationship between the amount of the

   A. loan and the property value
   B. property's income-producing value and the mortgage value
   C. property's sales value and its listing value
   D. interest value and the remaining loan balance

17. If a property value is $500,000 and the loan amount is $475,000, what is the loan-to-value ratio (rounded)?

   A. 80%
   B. 90%
   C. 95%
   D. 100%

18. Personal liability for the mortgage is evidenced by the

   A. alienation clause
   B. note
   C. lien itself
   D. borrower's ability to pay

19. The primary importance of a loan-to-value ratio is in determining the

    A. interest rate
    B. down payment
    C. financial capability of the borrower
    D. appraised value of the property

20. A request by a purchaser to reserve a certain loan interest rate for a specified time is called a(n)

    A. rate lock
    B. commitment
    C. rate cap
    D. interest lock

21. Some mortgage loans allow a specified time for payment to be made before the loan is in default. This is called

    A. in arrears
    B. in advance
    C. in escrow
    D. a grace period

22. Because current interest rates on mortgage loans are very low, Kathy would most likely choose which of the following for her mortgage?

    A. Fixed
    B. Adjustable
    C. Graduated
    D. Growing equity

23. Creditor A, whose lien is secured by Y's property, obtained a judgment against Y on July 10; banker B lent money to Y and took back a mortgage on August 1; Y's wife obtained a judgment for failure to pay child support on August 20. Which of these listed liens will be paid first at foreclosure?

    A. Creditor A
    B. Banker B
    C. J's wife
    D. The liens will be paid on a pro rata basis

24. Timothy is several months behind in his payments. The lender is starting foreclosure proceedings with the full balance due immediately. The lender may legally demand the balance under the terms of the

    A. granting clause
    B. alienation clause
    C. acceleration clause
    D. defeasance clause

25. Sandy is paying off his loan 18 years early to refinance to a lower interest rate. His current lender is asking for a one point fee additionally on the balance because of early payoff. This event describes a(n)

    A. acceleration penalty
    B. discount point
    C. defeasance clause
    D. prepayment penalty

26. The lender on Janicqua's mortgage has elected to force Janicqua to pay off her mortgage rather than let a new buyer assume that loan. This is the lender's right under the

    A. acceleration clause
    B. reconveyance clause
    C. alienation clause
    D. assumption clause

27. If an assumption of an existing loan takes place and the original borrower is relieved of liability, this is referred to as a(n)

    A. alienation
    B. novation
    C. defeasance
    D. equity of redemption

28. Which of the following mortgages contain a "release clause" that allows certain parcels of property to be removed from the mortgage lien if the loan balance is reduced by a specific amount?

    A. Installment land contract
    B. Shared appreciation mortgage
    C. Commercial mortgage
    D. Blanket mortgage

29. A mortgage loan, payable in monthly installments of principal and interest that will fully retire the debt, is known as a(n)

    A. balloon mortgage
    B. subordinate mortgage
    C. amortized mortgage
    D. gap financing

30. A bridge loan is a(n)

    A. home equity loan
    B. short-term loan
    C. long-term loan
    D. illegal type of financing instrument

31. Any mortgage that is subordinate to another mortgage is called

    A. term
    B. junior
    C. amortized
    D. adjustable rate

32. A deed of trust contains which of the following parties?

    A. Trustor
    B. Trustee
    C. Beneficiary
    D. All of the answers shown

33. When borrower Ramsey actually conveys title to his home to a disinterested third party pending full payoff of the debt to the lender, this demonstrates

    A. title theory
    B. lien or mortgage theory
    C. contract for deed
    D. nonrecourse note

34. When the adjustable rate mortgage (ARM) index rises and the payment is fixed, the shortfall is added to the principal. This is called

    A. amortized payment
    B. negative amortization
    C. growing equity payment
    D. balloon payment

35. An example of seller financing is

    A. blanket mortgage
    B. wraparound mortgage
    C. straight term mortgage
    D. bridge loan

36. A type of mortgage in which two or more parcels of real estate are pledged as security for repayment of a mortgage debt is called a(n)

    A. shared appreciation mortgage
    B. bridge loan
    C. installment land contract
    D. blanket mortgage

37. A type of gap financing, sometimes not secured by a mortgage, in which the borrower uses the equity that he has in one property to obtain the funds to buy another property, is called a

    A. purchase money mortgage
    B. wraparound mortgage
    C. swing loan
    D. package mortgage

38. When a payment is made on an amortized loan, which of the following items is paid last?

    A. Principal
    B. Interest
    C. Taxes
    D. Insurance

39. A loan that does NOT meet the Federal Reserve Bank loan criteria for funding is known as

    A. illegal
    B. secondary
    C. nonconforming
    D. straight term

40. A type of loan in which the mortgage rate floats based on the fluctuations of a standard index is called a(n)

    A. fixed rate
    B. fluctuating mortgage
    C. straight term mortgage
    D. adjustable rate mortgage

41. A house sells for $165,000. If the seller agrees to pay 5.5% discount points on a $155,000 mortgage loan, and the broker's fee is 6% of the sales price, how much is the seller's net?

    A. $146,575
    B. $148,275
    C. $156,575
    D. $158,375

42. A construction loan made to a developer is generally a(n)

    A. long-term loan
    B. based on the appraised value of the property
    C. home equity loan
    D. a structured loan

43. Merilee obtains a mortgage in which she pledges her personal property in addition to her condominium to secure payment of the loan. This type of mortgage is known as a(n)

    A. purchase money mortgage
    B. home equity loan
    C. wraparound mortgage
    D. package mortgage

44. Marta has pledged her home and a neighboring parcel as blanket security for a note but retains possession of both. This pledging is an example of

    A. hypothecation
    B. a mortgage
    C. a deed of trust
    D. liquidity

45. Royale is an investor with many properties. To facilitate his many investments and streamline the lending of funds, Royale has a(n)

    A. open-end mortgage
    B. blanket mortgage
    C. bridge loan
    D. purchase money mortgage

46. What term describes a priority rather than a type of mortgage?

    A. Junior mortgage
    B. Secondary mortgage
    C. Subordinate mortgage
    D. All of the answers shown

47. In what type of mortgage does the borrower pay interest only for a specified term, and at the end of the term, pay the principal?

    A. Straight term
    B. Amortized
    C. Open-end
    D. Graduated payment

48. A second mortgage for an amount equal to or larger than the existing mortgage against the same property is called

    A. participation mortgage
    B. growing equity mortgage
    C. wraparound mortgage
    D. blanket mortgage

49. A type of mortgage in which the lender makes payments to the borrower for a contracted period of time and then recaptures the equity upon the death of the homeowner or sale of the property is known as a

    A. balloon mortgage
    B. reverse annuity mortgage
    C. straight term mortgage
    D. deed of trust

50. In a sale-leaseback arrangement, which of the following applies to the new owner-lessor of the property? He or she

    A. must pay rent
    B. must maintain possession and control of the property
    C. does not fully own the property
    D. obtains income tax benefits of ownership

51. Odetta amortized a 15-year mortgage loan that was not enough to pay off the principal and interest. Instead, she would owe a large final payment. This type of mortgage is called a(n)

    A. straight term
    B. growing equity
    C. blanket
    D. balloon

52. Which of the following is a secondary mortgage institution?

    A. VA
    B. FHA
    C. HUD
    D. Fannie Mae

53. A conventional loan

    A. involves participation by the federal government
    B. is always an amortized loan
    C. involves no participation by any agency of the federal government
    D. is an FHA loan

54. Which of the following offer conventional loans?

    A. Department of Veterans Affairs
    B. Rural Housing Service
    C. Federal Housing Authority
    D. None of the answers shown

55. The main purpose of the secondary mortgage market is to provide

    A. an alternate form of primary lending
    B. liquidity to the lending process
    C. loans to first-time buyers
    D. higher credit ratings to lenders

56. A government agency that may loan 100% of the mortgage up to a certain amount without down payment is called

    A. VA
    B. FHA
    C. Fannie Mae
    D. RHS

57. Which mortgage "warehouse" is an agency of the federal government that purchases FHA, VA, and RHS loans?

    A. FHA
    B. Ginnie Mae
    C. VA
    D. RHS

58. Which of the following is FALSE regarding the FHA?

    A. FHA's mission is to make home ownership available to more people
    B. FHA makes mortgage loans
    C. FHA loan programs allow lenders to make high loan-to-value loans
    D. FHA is an agency of HUD

59. The main function of the FHA is to

    A. make mortgage loans
    B. buy mortgages on the secondary market
    C. insure loans to protect lenders against financial loss
    D. make loans for targeted low-income housing

60. The secondary mortgage market is

    A. where one might obtain a second mortgage
    B. where a borrower who has poor credit may seek a loan
    C. regulated by state organizations
    D. where mortgages are bought and processed after they have been originated

61. Ronnie borrows $350,000 at a 6% interest rate for 30 years. The lender requires two months interest to be placed in escrow. What is the amount to be escrowed?

    A. $3,500
    B. $4,000
    C. $6,000
    D. $7,000

62. If the sales proceeds are insufficient to pay all of the costs of the foreclosure and the secured liens, the borrower may still be held responsible for any remaining debts through which of the following?

    A. Nonrecourse debt
    B. Redemptive right
    C. Buy down
    D. Deficiency judgment

63. A mortgage broker who represents a purchaser in negotiating a mortgage loan is which of the following?

    A. Agent
    B. Intermediary
    C. Facilitator
    D. None of the answers shown

64. One of the main differences between a residential and commercial loan is that with a commercial loan the

    A. lender evaluates the financial strength of the borrower
    B. loan process demands a cash flow projection
    C. loan process evaluates the condition of the property
    D. loan process demands an appraisal of the property

65. A mortgage broker who represents the purchasers in negotiating a mortgage while also representing the sellers as a real estate broker in the same transaction is acting as a

    A. general agent
    B. facilitator
    C. dual agent
    D. single agent

66. Carlos has obtained a new loan on his home. Two months later, the lender notifies Carlos that future payments should be made to Central States Mortgage Co. The original mortgagee has executed its right of

    A. assignment
    B. foreclosure
    C. acceleration
    D. novation

67. A certain bank's guidelines state that the maximum housing debt a borrower may have is 29% of his or her gross income. If the borrower's gross income is $4,200 per month, what is the maximum housing expense?

    A. $499
    B. $1,218
    C. $1,722
    D. $2,940

68. Sanjay receives a statement from his lender indicating that it will loan him a certain sum of money to purchase a property. This statement is called a(n)

    A. contract
    B. mortgage commitment
    C. rate lock
    D. bond

69. At what point in the loan application does the loan underwriting take place?

    A. At the time the loan application is made
    B. After the loan documentation has been assembled and verified
    C. At the time of closing
    D. At any point in the transaction depending on lender policies

70. What considerations must the lender take in the evaluation process before granting a loan?

    A. Neighborhood location
    B. Condition of the property
    C. Comparable value to similar properties
    D. All of the answers shown

71. If a fully amortized 30-year mortgage loan of $128,000 at 8.5% has monthly payments of $984.21, how much interest will be paid over the life of the loan?

    A. $10,880
    B. $226,316
    C. $326,400
    D. $354,316

72. If Jerome pays five points at closing on a mortgage of $325,000, how much did he pay in points?

    A. $3,250
    B. $13,250
    C. $16,250
    D. $32,500

73. To ensure disclosure in the loan process, Congress enacted legislation that contains four disclosures included in Regulation Z. This Act is known as

    A. RESPA
    B. TILA
    C. MIP
    D. APR

74. Which of the following real estate loans is NOT covered by Regulation Z, which is a section of the Truth in Lending Act (TILA)?

    A. Personal
    B. Household
    C. Commercial
    D. Agricultural

75. The federal law that makes it unlawful for any creditor to discriminate against an applicant, with regard to a credit transaction, based on race, color, religion, national origin, sex, marital status, or age (provided the applicant has the capacity to contract) is called the

    A. Truth in Lending Act
    B. Equal Credit Opportunity Act
    C. Real Estate Settlement Procedures Act
    D. Community Reinvestment Act

76. Which of the following is FALSE regarding the Community Reinvestment Act?

    A. It is also called the Fair Lending Law
    B. Its purpose is to encourage lenders to meet the credit needs of the community where they are located
    C. The law only applies to commercial mortgages
    D. The lender's records in helping to meet the needs of the community are periodically evaluated

77. The financing of the purchase of a cooperative is governed by the rules set forth

    A. in the Uniform Commercial Code
    B. by the Real Estate Settlement Procedures Act
    C. by HUD
    D. by local zoning ordinances

78. Justy bought her home one year ago at a prevailing and relatively low-fixed interest rate. The lender contacts her to refinance her loan to obtain additional cash. This illegal practice is called

    A. acceleration
    B. redlining
    C. loan flipping
    D. point adjustment

79. Which of the following is NOT a predatory lending practice?

    A. Making loans to unqualified buyers
    B. Increasing the interest rate because of borrower default
    C. Taking kickbacks
    D. Lending based on the borrower's ability to pay

80. Subprime lenders provide loans

    A. that are secondary mortgages
    B. that are always junior mortgages
    C. to borrowers who are risky candidates for repayment
    D. to heirs of an estate to pay off inherited debt

Topic 6

MULTIPLE CHOICE

Identify the choice that best completes the statement or answers the question.

1. The seller who selects another to act on his behalf is called a(n)

   A. agent
   B. fiduciary
   C. principal
   D. customer

2. The client is the

   A. customer
   B. principal
   C. supervising broker
   D. sales agent

3. In a buyer agency relationship, the buyer is the

   A. customer
   B. principal
   C. subagent
   D. third party

Law of Agency

4. A buyer employing a broker ONLY to assist in finding a certain type of property to purchase has authorized a(n)

   A. power of attorney
   B. general agency
   C. special agency
   D. attorney in fact

5. In a real estate transaction, a principal who selects an agent to represent him or her may be a

   A. seller
   B. buyer
   C. lessor
   D. all of the answers shown

6. A broker engaged to act on behalf of a principal as a listing agent for a property is what type of agent?

   A. General
   B. Personal
   C. Special
   D. Unilateral

7. The business of bringing buyers and sellers together and assisting in negotiations for the sale of real estate is called a(n)

   A. corporation
   B. brokerage
   C. agency
   D. listing

8. An agent, such as a property manager, who has the authority to represent the principal in all matters concerning a certain property is a(n)

   A. dual agent
   B. general agent
   C. unlimited agent
   D. special agent

9. Greta, a real estate agent, brings Dominique to view Perry's property. Greta represents seller Perry. This makes Dominique the

   A. client
   B. principal
   C. customer
   D. fiduciary

10. A principal who lists a property

   A. automatically permits subagency
   B. has the option of accepting or rejecting subagency when signing the listing agreement
   C. automatically allows subagency if his agent belongs to the multiple listing service
   D. is not liable, under any circumstances, for the acts of subagents

11. Which of the following is NOT a subagent? An agent

   A. from a listing firm who markets a property through MLS
   B. who markets a listing under his primary broker
   C. from a firm that does not have the listing but who markets the property through MLS
   D. for a buyer client

12. Seller Clare allows broker Gregory to take a prospect through her property but has not signed a listing agreement. Gregory is operating with what kind of authority?

    A. Express
    B. Implied
    C. Special
    D. None

13. Which of the following persons would best be described as a subagent?

    A. Listing broker
    B. Salesperson
    C. Buyer
    D. Seller

14. Under buyer agency, the

    A. seller must pay the buyer broker's commission
    B. buyer broker may not be compensated by the seller
    C. buyer broker's commission may be paid by either party as determined through negotiations
    D. buyer always pays for his broker's commission

15. Although a buyer agent represents a buyer and a subagent represents a seller, they are both

    A. dual agents
    B. subagents
    C. seller agents
    D. cooperating agents

16. A salesperson may receive compensation from

    A. his client
    B. his customer
    C. his sponsoring broker
    D. any licensed broker

17. Salesperson Joyce brings three offers to a seller, although none have been accepted. No written agency contract exists between Joyce and the seller, nor have any disclosures or disclaimers been put forth. Joyce probably has a(n)

    A. general agency
    B. dual agency
    C. express agency
    D. implied agency

18. Subagents of the seller

    A. have no duty to the buyer
    B. only have the duty to disclose whom they represent to the buyer and no other obligation
    C. must deal fairly and ethically with the buyer
    D. owe the same loyalties to the seller as to the buyer

19. Broker Wong has listed seller Peterson's home. Which of these people would NOT be a possible subagent of the seller?

    A. Wong's sales staff
    B. Other agents who are members of the local multiple listing service
    C. An out-of-state broker who refers Wong a buyer with the expectations of a referral
    D. Broker Clarice, who has disclosed a buyer agency relationship

20. Melissa is working with some buyers who want to view a property that is NOT listed with a real estate firm. Melissa, as an agent,

    A. cannot show a property not listed with a real estate firm
    B. cannot show a property that is not listed with multiple listing
    C. can show the property with the permission of the sellers and her broker and attempt to negotiate a commission
    D. has a fiduciary relationship with all sellers

21. The real estate broker usually is hired by a seller as an agent through a document known as a(n)

    A. listing agreement
    B. finder's agreement
    C. binder
    D. option to buy

22. An agency relationship is created

    A. when a property is placed on the market
    B. by the conduct of the agent
    C. by the fact that the agent has a real estate license
    D. through a contract with a principal or the conduct and actions of the parties

23. If broker White has a customer for a property listed by broker Green, then

    A. broker White represents the buyer
    B. broker White represents broker Green
    C. broker Green is a subagent of broker White
    D. broker Green represents the seller

24. In a listing arrangement with a real estate agent, the principal has an agency relationship with

    A. the multiple listing service
    B. the agent and broker
    C. any prospective customers
    D. the agent only

25. Under the usual commission split agreement between the broker and the sales agents in a firm,

    A. the broker initially receives the entire commission
    B. the broker pays a portion to the listing agent
    C. the broker pays a portion to the agent who sold the property
    D. all of the answers shown

26. Agency does NOT exist without the

    A. mutual consent between the principal and the agent
    B. consent of the principal only
    C. consent of the agent only
    D. consent of the customer

27. A written listing agreement is an example of a(n)

    A. single agency
    B. implied agency
    C. express agency
    D. cooperative agency

28. A system that pools the listings of all member firms is known as a(n)

    A. corporation
    B. brokerage
    C. franchise
    D. multiple listing service

29. What is NOT a possible advantage of a multiple listing service (MLS) for a seller?

    A. MLS offers a greater exposure for a listed property
    B. MLS gives agents a greater inventory of properties to offer buyers
    C. The seller may be liable for the actions of subagent members of MLS
    D. MLS may help to sell a property faster than if it were not listed since more agents are marketing it

30. A listing contract creates a(n)

    A. sales contract
    B. agency relationship
    C. transfer of title
    D. license

31. The overall purpose of agency disclosure laws is to

    A. protect the commissions earned by real estate agents
    B. ensure that buyers do not communicate with sellers
    C. make consumers aware of the agency relationship of a real estate agent and the choices available to them
    D. protect the broker from being liable for the acts of principals who have listed with them

32. A broker, in accepting commissions from both buyer and seller without disclosing the fact to both parties, is

    A. committing an illegal act
    B. following standards of real estate practice
    C. guilty of commingling
    D. guilty of conversion

33. A broker, who represents the seller, must disclose to the buyer

    A. the amount of the commission
    B. the seller's financial status
    C. the seller's reason for selling
    D. structural defects

34. Real estate agent C was told by her sellers that the basement of their house flooded every spring. The sellers said that since it was winter and the basement was dry, they did not wish to inform any prospective purchasers. Agent C should

    A. agree with her sellers
    B. inform her sellers that this information must be disclosed to all interested parties
    C. obtain a signed release from her sellers so that C is not liable should a purchaser eventually sue
    D. refuse to take a listing under any circumstances since the property has a material defect

35. Agent Regina tells a customer that her client's home is 5,000 square feet when in fact she has no idea about the measurements of the property. Regina has

    A. committed an act of misrepresentation
    B. done nothing wrong
    C. no duty to be truthful to customers
    D. engaged in self-dealing

36. When a listing agent discloses a material defect that he or she has knowledge of to a prospective buyer, the agent

    A. has breached the fiduciary duty to the seller
    B. has done the right thing under the duty to disclose
    C. may only disclose this defect with permission of the sellers
    D. should report the information to multiple listing for publication so that prospective buyers will see it and let the agent off the hook

37. Owner Fannie agrees to list a property with broker Olie. Broker Olie, however, will receive a commission if owner Fannie sells the property. This type of listing agreement is a(n)

    A. exclusive-right-to-sell
    B. open listing
    C. net listing
    D. exclusive agency

38. In a brokerage firm, the listing contracts are typically owned by the

    A. salesperson who listed the property
    B. multiple listing service together with the brokerage firm
    C. principals who engage the firm to market their properties
    D. brokerage firm

39. Sabrina has signed several listing agreements with different brokers. The broker who sells the property will receive a commission. She has probably signed a(n)

    A. exclusive agency agreement
    B. exclusive-right-to-sell agreement
    C. open listing agreement
    D. option to purchase

40. A broker must always

    A. present all offers to purchase to the property owner
    B. discuss a first offer with a later offer
    C. tell the owner not to take an offer below the desired price
    D. advise the seller on legal matters

41. Sales agents, associated with a supervising broker, can legitimately receive a fee directly from

    A. their supervising broker
    B. the seller
    C. the buyer
    D. a cooperating broker

42. The most common type of commission is calculated

    A. as a flat fee
    B. by whatever the principal decides
    C. as a percentage of the sales price
    D. by the commission rates established by the local real estate board

43. Broker Jack's seller-client wants to give agent Kerry a bonus for bringing a buyer to the client who paid full price for the property. Broker Jack is a cooperating broker from another firm. Kerry must receive the bonus from

    A. her sponsoring broker
    B. the principal
    C. any cooperating broker
    D. the attorney for the seller at closing

44. A net listing is one

    A. that requires the broker to have a fixed price for the property
    B. that is generally legal
    C. that most agents would prefer
    D. in which the seller specifies a certain amount of money to be received upon sale of the property and all monies above that amount are the agent's commission

45. Naomi lists her property with ABC Brokerage. She agrees that she will take $200,000 for the property and any money above that amount will be the broker's commission. This arrangement is a(n)

    A. net listing
    B. open listing
    C. exclusive-right-to-sell
    D. exclusive agency

46. Salesperson Vincenzo sells a property for $100,000. The commission on this sale to the real estate firm with whom Vincenzo is associated is 6%. Vincenzo receives 70% of the total commission paid to the real estate firm. What is the firm's share of the commission in dollars?

    A. $618
    B. $6,000
    C. $180
    D. $1,800

47. The commission rate that a broker charges is decided by the

    A. agent and principal
    B. multiple listing service
    C. real estate board
    D. broker and agent

48. Which of the following is NOT a broker's obligation?

    A. Disclosure of a seller's personal circumstances
    B. Disclosure of property defects to the buyer
    C. Accounting of funds through a trust account
    D. Loyalty to the principal

49. Which one of the following does NOT constitute an agent's responsibility to the principal?

    A. Loyalty
    B. Reasonable care
    C. Confidentiality
    D. Legal advice

50. From the choices below, which one is a part of the fiduciary relationship between a broker and a principal? The broker

    A. need not disclose any material defects to prospective buyers
    B. must follow the seller's instructions as to what classes of protected groups under the fair housing laws should be shown the property
    C. may refuse any low offers that he feels will not interest the sellers
    D. must obey reasonable and lawful instructions from the principal

51. A fiduciary duty of the agent to the principal does NOT include

    A. full disclosure
    B. loyalty
    C. protection
    D. obedience

52. When real estate brokers fail to train and supervise their new salespeople, they violate the fiduciary duty of

    A. accountability
    B. reasonable care
    C. confidentiality
    D. obedience

53. Which of the following is FALSE regarding buyer agents? They

    A. can help in negotiating an offer
    B. owe complete loyalty to the buyer client
    C. can perform a market analysis of the property for the buyer client
    D. can negotiate for the sellers without giving up their role as fiduciary

54. A real estate agent's obligation to a seller principal does NOT include

    A. accounting of funds through a trust account
    B. disclosure of property defects to the buyer
    C. reducing the broker's commission to make the deal
    D. loyalty

55. In addition to the broker, what other party in the agency relationship has the duty to disclose all information bearing on the agency agreement?

    A. Principal
    B. Customer
    C. Buyer
    D. None of the answers shown

56. A seller's broker, in a fiduciary role, may NOT do which of the following?

    A. Advise a seller that a listing price is too high
    B. Negotiate, on behalf of the seller, a price below that at which the property is listed
    C. Advise a buyer that the seller is anxious to sell because of a job transfer
    D. Represent both the buyer and seller with disclosure and informed consent from both parties

57. Real estate broker Bert may

    A. never sell a property that he owns
    B. only sell a property he owns if he gives the listing to another firm
    C. sell a property he owns through proper disclosure
    D. only sell a property he owns if he does not place it on multiple listing

58. If a broker accepts deposit money, it may be kept in which of the following? In

    A. the office operating account
    B. a separate escrow account in an insured bank
    C. a safety deposit box
    D. an interest-bearing stock portfolio account

59. Bob Buyer asked Tom, a salesperson, if a home was well insulated. Tom thought that it was since it was in such a nice neighborhood. After Bob bought the house, he found that his heating bills were outrageous due to poor insulation. Which of the following is TRUE?

    A. Since salesperson Tom did not really know, he is not responsible
    B. Since buyer Bob completed the transaction, he has no basis for further action against anyone
    C. Salesperson Tom may be held liable for misrepresentation
    D. Only Tom's broker may be held liable for misrepresentation

60. When brokers commingle funds of clients and customers with their operating account, they have violated the fiduciary duty of

    A. disclosure
    B. loyalty
    C. accountability
    D. care

61. The sellers tell Dewey, their real estate listing agent, that they do not want Dewey to show their property to anyone who has children. Which of the following is TRUE?

    A. If Dewey does not comply, he is violating his fiduciary duty of obedience
    B. The sellers are within their legal rights to make this request
    C. Dewey cannot violate fair housing law so must withdraw from the agency relationship
    D. Dewey can comply with the seller's request with his broker's permission

62. An agent does not inform the buyer of the fact that the property is not on the city sewer system but instead has a septic system. The agent knows this information and forgets to tell the buyer. Which of these statements is TRUE?

    A. The buyer cannot sue the agent
    B. The agent has done nothing wrong since the agent did not actually say anything one way or the other and no one asked
    C. The agent has misrepresented to the buyer through this act of omission
    D. The agent is guilty of fraud

63. To avoid a misrepresentation concerning a property being marketed, brokers are responsible for

    A. what they should know from disclosure by the principal
    B. what they should know because of their skill and training
    C. what they should know through an inspection of the property
    D. all of the answer shown

64. Lainie, an agent, exaggerates her experience in order to obtain a listing. Lainie

    A. is guilty of misrepresentation
    B. is guilty of constructive notice
    C. is guilty of negligent misrepresentation
    D. has done nothing improper if she effectuates a sale on the seller's terms

65. Stella, a salesperson, represents the sellers. She has, however, suggested to the buyers that she is trying to obtain the full amount of the listing price as there are several other lower offers on the property. In this scenario,

    A. Stella is acting appropriately as agent of the seller
    B. a possible dual agency situation has arisen
    C. price fixing has occurred
    D. Stella has now switched her representation to the buyers only

66. Generally, dual agency is legal

   A. all of the time
   B. with disclosure and informed consent
   C. in residential transactions only
   D. in commercial transactions only

67. If the parties to a residential real estate transaction agree to dual agency representation,

   A. all confidential information given to the agent by the seller or buyer must be disclosed to both parties
   B. both seller and buyer must pay a full commission to the agent
   C. both seller and purchaser forfeit the right to undivided loyalty by the agent
   D. the real estate commission must be informed of the agreement

68. Salesperson Hersh owns a 25% share in a three-family property that he is listing and selling through the brokerage firm where he is employed. This is an example of a(n)

   A. arm's-length transaction
   B. agency coupled with an interest
   C. exclusive agency
   D. all of the answers shown

69. When both parties to a transaction (buyer and seller) are expressly represented by one brokerage firm (even though by two separate sales agents at the brokerage), there exists a(n)

   A. dual agency
   B. illegal agency
   C. double agency
   D. ostensible agency

70. A broker has a listing with a seller and one of the broker's sales agents wants to submit a purchase offer for himself. In this case, which of the following is TRUE?

   A. The broker must give up the listing
   B. The sales agent is prohibited by law from purchasing the property
   C. A dual agency relationship exists
   D. None of the answers shown

71. In a designated agency relationship within the brokerage firm, the client gives up the fiduciary duty of

    A. reasonable care
    B. obedience
    C. accountability
    D. undivided loyalty

72. If the parties to a residential real estate transaction agree to dual agency representation,

    A. all confidential information given to the agent by the seller or buyer must be disclosed to both parties
    B. both seller and buyer must pay a full commission to the agent
    C. both seller and purchaser forfeit the right to undivided loyalty by the agent
    D. the real estate commissioner must be informed of the agreement

73. When an agent attempts to represent the buyer and seller in the same transaction, this is an example of a(n)

    A. subagency
    B. dual agency
    C. buyer agency
    D. undivided loyalty

74. If sales agent A from one real estate branch office represents the seller and sales agent B from another branch office represents the buyer,

    A. all agents represent the seller only
    B. salesperson B must renounce the buyer's representation
    C. all agents are acting in a dual agency capacity
    D. none of the answers shown

75. Tihera and Constance work for broker Sumner. After disclosure and informed consent, Tihera is appointed by the broker to represent the seller client, Felicity. Constance is appointed by the broker to represent to buyer client, Rachel, in the sale of Felicity's property. Tihera and Constance are

    A. buyer agents
    B. designated agents
    C. general agents
    D. none of the answers shown

76. Which of the following is TRUE of a transaction agent or broker?

    A. Represents either party
    B. Protects the interest of the seller or the buyer
    C. Facilitates the transaction
    D. Is a dual agent

77. Hannah, a real estate agent, represents Sean, the seller. She does not represent anyone but Sean throughout the transaction. She has placed Sean's listing on the MLS. Which of the following agency relationships does NOT apply to Hannah?

    A. Dual agent
    B. Single agent
    C. Seller agent
    D. Subagent

78. Olivia is a sales agent in a brokerage firm. She is working with both a buyer and seller but has no agency relationship with either one. She does not advise or counsel either party as to how to gain an advantage at the expense of the other. Yet, she will work with both to arrive at an agreement to close a property. Olivia is best described as a

    A. designated agent
    B. seller agent
    C. dual agent
    D. transaction agent

79. Martin signs an exclusive-right-to-sell listing agreement for six months with broker Gerald. Within one month, Martin sells his house himself and refuses to pay a commission to broker Gerald. Martin's behavior is a possible

    A. reformation
    B. breach of contract
    C. injunction
    D. assignment

80. A listing contract terminates if

    A. the principal moves out of the property
    B. the agent does not hold open houses
    C. a brokerage license is revoked
    D. the principal gives the agent 24 hours notice

Topic 7

MULTIPLE CHOICE

Identify the choice that best completes the statement or answers the question.

1. A type of toxic mineral that is found in soil, paint, and water is

   A. asbestos
   B. radon
   C. lead
   D. formaldehyde

2. A device that may become hazardous because chemicals can seep into the ground is a(n)

   A. underground storage tank
   B. well
   C. shingle
   D. underground cable

3. A dangerous gas that can seep into a property, through cracks in the foundation, concrete slab, or chimney is

   A. Electromagnetic waves
   B. Formaldehyde
   C. PCBs
   D. Radon

Property Conditions, Disclosures, and Transfer of Title

4. One of the biggest concerns about water safety is that highly corrosive water may contain dangerous amounts of

   A. bacteria
   B. radon
   C. lead
   D. polychlorinated biphenyls

5. The land mass added to land over time by deposits of silt and sand is called

   A. alluvion
   B. avulsion
   C. accretion
   D. accession

6. Theresa lives in a flood hazard area and is applying for a mortgage from a federally regulated lender. Which of the following is TRUE?

   A. She should be required to purchase flood insurance
   B. She should be given a choice to purchase or not
   C. The bank appraiser will determine if flood insurance is required
   D. None of the answers shown

7. Which of the following is FALSE regarding underground storage tanks? They

   A. are out of sight
   B. are protected against vandalism
   C. need not be disclosed when a property is transferred
   D. are generally protected against fire

8. Jaqueena owns a vacation home on a lakefront. Land that accumulates on the property by avulsion and reliction fall under which category?

   A. Escheat
   B. Eminent domain
   C. Accession rights
   D. Adverse possession

9. A real estate agent, Jeffrey, notices a small patch of oily soil near the location of a home's underground fuel storage tank. Jeffrey

   A. does not have to disclose anything about the small patch of oily soil or existence of the UST as the buyers will probably see it for themselves
   B. must mention this information
   C. must obtain the property owner's approval to disclose
   D. must obtain the lender's approval to disclose

10. Broker G showed prospective buyers a property that was in close proximity to a toxic waste site. Although the broker knew about the site, he did not inform the buyers. Later, the buyers bought the property and sued the broker and the sellers. Who may be liable?

    A. No one
    B. The seller only
    C. Both the seller and the broker
    D. The broker only

11. B, a broker, told the buyers that the home she had listed had a solid roof with no leakage, although she knew that the roof was badly in need of repair or replacement. B

    A. need not disclose this information to the buyers
    B. must disclose this information to the buyers
    C. must receive permission from the sellers before disclosing this information to the buyers
    D. must only disclose this information if the house is an income property

12. Before closing on the sale of a residential property, an inspection is generally performed. The completion date of the inspection is important for all of the following reasons EXCEPT

    A. a real estate closing may be pending
    B. a real estate contract may be subject to a property inspection
    C. zoning changes may be imminent and the homeowner is anxious to sell before the change in zoning
    D. a decision to purchase may depend on the results of the inspection

13. Certain problems regarding a property may not be observed by prospective buyers, real estate agents, and home inspectors because they are hidden from sight. These problems are called

    A. liabilities
    B. errors
    C. omissions
    D. latent defects

14. During a home inspection of the property, besides the home inspector, which party should definitely accompany the home inspector? The

    A. agent for the seller
    B. attorney for the seller
    C. attorney for the buyer
    D. buyers

15. Property condition disclosure forms are completed by which of the following?

    A. Seller
    B. Buyer
    C. Listing broker
    D. Cooperating broker

16. In many states, a document called a property condition disclosure form is completed by the sellers. Which of the following is not a benefit of this form?

    A. Complements seller's duty to disclose
    B. Complements an agent's duty to disclose
    C. Immediately gets the seller "off the hook" in remediating any negative conditions
    D. Informs the buyer of issues affecting the property

17. Which of the following facts is FALSE under the Residential Lead-Based Paint Hazard Reduction Act?

    A. Seller disclosure of lead paint
    B. Law applicable to commercial properties
    C. Distribution of lead hazard pamphlet
    D. Lead paint assessment

18. So that liability for hazardous substances and other problems are not passed to new owners, lenders and purchasers may conduct certain reviews of the property called

   A. remedial evaluations
   B. due diligence
   C. feasibility studies
   D. highest and best use studies

19. Violators of the Residential Lead-Based Paint Hazard Reduction Act may have to pay a fine of up to

   A. $1,000
   B. $5,000
   C. $10,000
   D. $25,000

20. The Residential Lead-Based Paint Hazard Reduction Act does NOT mandate

   A. a 10-day period for lead paint assessment
   B. disclosure of lead-based paint information
   C. removal of all lead-based paint before a property is leased or sold
   D. distribution of a lead hazard pamphlet

21. The Residential Lead-Based Paint Hazard Reduction Act applies to

   A. all residential properties
   B. residential properties built before 1978
   C. residential and commercial properties
   D. senior citizen housing only

22. Which of the following is NOT a component of the Comprehensive Environmental Response, Compensation, and Liability Act (CERCLA)?

   A. Identify sites containing hazardous substances
   B. Seek reimbursement from the responsible party
   C. Ensure cleanup by the parties responsible or by the government
   D. Prohibition against transferring property that has hazardous waste

23. Which of the following is NOT a type of voluntary alienation of title?

   A. Sale of a property
   B. Gift of a property
   C. Dedication of a property
   D. Bankruptcy

24. The recipient of title through a deed is a

    A. grantor
    B. grantee
    C. vendor
    D. vendee

25. Oscar deeded his property to Yoko. Oscar is the

    A. grantee
    B. mortgagee
    C. mortgagor
    D. grantor

26. A type of deed that contains no warranties of title is called a

    A. full covenant and warranty deed (general warranty deed)
    B. dedication by deed
    C. bargain and sale deed with covenants
    D. quitclaim deed

27. A transfer of personal property during one's lifetime is evidenced by a bill of sale. The equivalent document to transfer real property is a(n)

    A. affidavit
    B. will
    C. deed
    D. abstract of title

28. The term for the transfer of property is

    A. delivery and acceptance
    B. dedication
    C. execution
    D. alienation

29. Dooley's deed contains a covenant against encumbrances, a covenant of quiet enjoyment, and a covenant of further assurance, among others. Dooley's deed is a(n)

    A. full covenant and warranty deed
    B. quitclaim deed
    C. executor's deed
    D. None of the answers shown

30. Caroline is the grantee on the prior deed. She becomes which of the following on the new deed?

    A. Vendor
    B. Grantor
    C. Party of the second part
    D. Purchaser

31. A type of deed that contains the strongest and broadest form of guarantee of title is a

    A. full covenant and warranty deed
    B. quitclaim deed
    C. bargain and sale deed
    D. judicial deed

32. When the grantor, or his or her representative, gives the deed to the grantee or his or her representative, transfer of title has occurred. This act is known as

    A. dedication
    B. probate
    C. delivery and acceptance
    D. adverse possession

33. To provide constructive notice, evidence of a document must be

    A. seen and read by all interested parties
    B. recorded
    C. validated by a court of competent jurisdiction
    D. a real estate–related document only

34. Which of the following is NOT necessary for Dorothy to claim ownership of Jared's land under adverse possession?

    A. Continuous possession
    B. Open and notorious use
    C. Jared's permission
    D. Exclusive use apart from Jared

35. Which of the following title transfers is voluntary during one's lifetime?

    A. Conveyance by deed
    B. Eminent domain
    C. Involuntary alienation
    D. Adverse possession

36. To claim ownership under adverse possession, the possession must be continuous and uninterrupted

    A. for at least one month
    B. as agreed to by the claimant and the property owner
    C. for a number of years
    D. for as long as a court dictates

37. The essential elements of a valid deed include

    A. that it be in writing
    B. the signature of the grantee
    C. recording
    D. all of the answers shown

38. In a deed, the clause that begins with the words "to have and to hold" and describes the estate granted is the

    A. consideration
    B. acknowledgement
    C. limitation and subject to clauses
    D. *habendum* clause

39. Calvin is the devisee of his aunt's estate. This means that he is

    A. appointed by the court to distribute the property of a person dying intestate
    B. conveying the title
    C. the recipient of a gift of personal property by will
    D. the recipient of a gift of real property by will

40. Baron has died leaving a sizable estate and a complicated will. A court action has been filed to test the validity of the will. This process is called

    A. execution of the will
    B. distribution
    C. descent
    D. probate

41. Personal property given to someone by a will is called a

    A. devise
    B. inheritance
    C. gift
    D. legacy

42. Miguel Fernandez has died and named his sister, Lupe, to handle the affairs of his estate until all real and personal property are distributed to Lupe and their other brother, Manuel. Which term would NOT properly describe Lupe's role?

   A. Executrix
   B. Probate
   C. Devisee
   D. Beneficiary

43. The term "intestate" means that a

   A. person has died and all of his or her property is located in the state in which the decedent resided
   B. person has died without a valid will
   C. deceased person has insufficient assets to cover his or her debts
   D. deceased person's assets will pass to the state

44. Who has the right to name the executor (executrix) of an estate?

   A. Devisee
   B. Trustee
   C. Administrator
   D. Testator

45. The seller accepts a purchase money mortgage from the buyer. On the closing statement, this amount appears as a

   A. seller debit
   B. seller credit
   C. buyer debit
   D. balancing disbursement

46. One of the main purposes of a survey before closing is to

   A. ensure that no encroachments exist
   B. ensure that a deed exists
   C. verify the chain of title
   D. prepare an abstract of title

47. A document that is NOT usually required at a closing is the

    A. contract of sale
    B. broker's commission statement
    C. title insurance policy
    D. comparative market analysis

48. Which of the following documents are NOT required for a closing to take place?

    A. Survey
    B. Certificate of occupancy
    C. Prior deed
    D. Census statement

49. At closing, the specific name for the division of expense and income between a buyer and a seller is called a(n)

    A. appraisal fee
    B. proration
    C. survey
    D. computation

50. Rachel and Evan and are purchasing an income property in which the rental income is $2,581 per month. For a closing taking place on August 18, if the seller has collected the rent for the month, how much of the rent should the buyer be credited (to be rounded)?

    A. $1,082
    B. $1,097
    C. $2,101
    D. $2,581

51. At closing, if the purchaser is given a proprietary lease, he or she has purchased a(n)

    A. condominium
    B. industrial property
    C. cooperative
    D. income property

52. The annual real property taxes of $3,600 have not been paid in conjunction with a closing to be held September 15. What amount will the seller pay in property taxes?

    A. $150
    B. $2,400
    C. $2,550
    D. $3,600

53. Which of the following regarding closings is FALSE?

    A. A salesperson's role before closing involves inspection of the property with the purchaser
    B. The buyer arranges for a final walk-through on the day of closing
    C. The seller generally pays for the structural inspection
    D. Perc tests are generally performed for new construction

54. When a property transfers, liens are generally paid

    A. before closing
    B. after closing
    C. not necessarily paid at all
    D. when the seller is ready either before or after the closing

55. The closing on the sale of a rental property is to be held Sept 15. The seller has received the rent for September in the amount of $600. What entry will appear on the seller's and the buyer's closing statements?

    A. $300 credit to buyer
    B. $300 credit to seller
    C. $400 credit to buyer
    D. $400 credit to seller

56. Should an escrow closing take place, which of the following may serve as a neutral escrow agent?

    A. Escrow department of a bank or savings and loan
    B. An independent escrow company
    C. Escrow department of a title insurance company
    D. All of the answers shown

57. Homeowners' policies have different numbers such as: HO-1, HO-4, and HO-5. These policy numbers refer to

    A. the length of time the policy has been in force and the premium discount earned
    B. policies covering differing needs of various insureds such as tenants, homeowners, or condominium owners
    C. the number of units in the dwelling
    D. the number of people in the household

58. In reference to condominiums and cooperatives, which of the following defines an assessment?

    A. An attorney's written opinion as to which person owns a property or title
    B. Sets forth the distribution of monies involved in a closing transaction
    C. Payable to the homeowners' association for the maintenance of common elements
    D. A condensed history of the title

59. A type of real estate closing involving a neutral third party is called a(n)

    A. escrow closing
    B. deed in lieu of foreclosure
    C. good faith estimate
    D. trust

60. A sale closes on February 12. The buyer is assuming the seller's mortgage that has an outstanding balance of $28,000 as of the closing date. The last mortgage payment was made on February 1. The annual interest rate is 7.75%, and interest is paid in arrears. What interest proration appears in the buyer's closing statement?

    A. $72.36 credit
    B. $77.52 credit
    C. $180.83 debit
    D. $253.19 credit

61. A complete examination of a property's title typically involves

    A. researching the public record from the present to back in time
    B. a survey
    C. examination of the property
    D. verifying only the last transfer of property

62. Corcos is buying a home. He is concerned about the quality of the property's title. Which of these is NOT a method of inspecting and assuring that Corcos will have marketable title?

    A. Abstract and opinion
    B. Title insurance
    C. Recording his deed
    D. All of the answers shown

63. The seller must provide evidence of marketable title for transfer. This proof can be provided by a(n)

    A. abstract of title
    B. sales contract
    C. survey
    D. settlement statement

64. A title to real property that is reasonably free and clear of encumbrances is said to be

    A. profitable
    B. enforceable
    C. "judgment proof"
    D. marketable

65. Peggy and Sue are buying a condominium and paying cash. They do not require a mortgage loan. Before closing, which of the following documents will they receive?

    A. HUD Form No. 1
    B. A good faith estimate
    C. HUD booklet
    D. None of the answers shown

66. Although the coverage period for warranties on new home construction vary from state to state, which of the following categories are generally not warranted by a builder?

    A. Siding, stucco, doors and trim, and drywall and paint
    B. HVAC, plumbing, and electrical systems
    C. Major structural defects
    D. Household appliances

67. Which of the following is NOT included in a builder's new home warranty?

    A. Limited coverage on workmanship and materials related to components of the home
    B. Definition on how repairs will be made
    C. Components covered under a manufacturer's warranty
    D. Duration of the coverage

68. Consuela owed $25,000 on her home mortgage that she did not pay due to a foreclosure on her property. She also did not pay income tax on the debt. She can lawfully do this according to the

    A. Real Estate Settlement Procedures Act
    B. Community Reinvestment Act
    C. Mortgage Forgiveness Debt Relief Act
    D. IRS Form 1040

69. Which of the following is TRUE under the Mortgage Forgiveness Debt Relief Act?

    A. Owners of a principal residence may not have to pay income tax on a mortgage debt due to a foreclosure of their property
    B. The Act applies to owners of commercial property
    C. Provisions of the Act apply until 2030
    D. Provisions of the Act apply to an unlimited amount of debt on the principal residence

70. Which of the following regarding a short sale is FALSE?

    A. Both the lender and the borrower must agree to the sale
    B. The lender may take a deficiency judgment against the borrower after the sale
    C. The borrower sells the property for less than the outstanding balance on the mortgage loan
    D. A foreclosure proceeding is quicker and less costly than a short sale

71. Heath could not pay his mortgage debt and was in default. He decided to convey the title to his property to the lender, to avoid a record of foreclosure. This arrangement is known as a

    A. deficiency judgment
    B. equity of redemption
    C. deed in lieu of foreclosure
    D. short sale

72. Cynthia lost her property because of a foreclosure on a property tax lien. This is an example of

    A. involuntary alienation
    B. voluntary alienation
    C. caveat emptor
    D. escheat

73. If a taxpayer's tax rate is above the 15% income bracket and he or she has held a property for longer than 12 months, when the taxpayer sells the property, the capital gains tax will be at a rate of

    A. 5%
    B. 10%
    C. 15%
    D. 20%

74. The profit realized from the sale of any capital investment including real estate is called

    A. capital loss
    B. capital gain
    C. the capitalization rate
    D. the adjusted basis

75. Which of the following is TRUE regarding tax-deferred exchanges?

    A. Do not always have to be "like-kind" properties
    B. Can include an exchange of residences between two homeowners
    C. Can include foreign property
    D. Are allowable only for investment or business property

76. Which of the following items are allowed federal tax deductions on home ownership?

    A. Maintenance and repairs
    B. Mortgage principal
    C. Property taxes
    D. Fuel and water bills

77. Annie and Xavier, a married couple, bought their house five years ago for $350,000. They are in the 35% tax bracket. They recently sold it for $400,000. What is the amount of capital gains tax they must pay when they file their tax return?

    A. $2,500
    B. $7,500
    C. $50,000
    D. No capital gains tax

78. Which IRS rule allows first-time homebuyers to use IRA distributions to fund up to $10,000 of their new home cost without paying an early distribution penalty?

    A. Rule of four
    B. Age 59½ rule
    C. Safe harbor law
    D. IRA exemption clause

79. In a tax-deferred exchange, any cash in the exchange is called the

    A. equity
    B. collateral
    C. cache
    D. boot

80. The major drawback of boot is that it

    A. is tax deductible
    B. may be taxed in an otherwise tax-deferred exchange
    C. must be paid to balance the exchanged equities
    D. causes the whole exchange to become taxable

Topic

8

MULTIPLE CHOICE

Identify the choice that best completes the statement or answers the question.

1. Which of the following does NOT describe a temporary right of possession by a non-owner of the property?

   A. Freehold
   B. Estate
   C. Tenancy
   D. None of the answers shown

2. Sam was in lawful possession of Larry's property but now refuses to leave after his right to possession has been terminated. Sam is known as a tenant _____ during eviction proceedings.

   A. for years
   B. at will
   C. at sufferance
   D. trespasser

3. Jenkins has a lease that requires NO notice to terminate upon the original expiration date. Jenkins has a(n)

   A. estate for years
   B. periodic estate
   C. estate at will
   D. estate at sufferance

Leases, Rents, and Property Management

4. Tamara's lease is described as open-ended. This must be a(n)

   A. estate for years
   B. periodic estate
   C. estate at will
   D. estate at sufferance

5. Tenants who do NOT have leases and pay rent on a monthly basis are called

   A. month-to-month tenants
   B. tenants at sufferance
   C. trespassers
   D. rightful heirs

6. The only type of leasehold that would NOT be negotiated in advance with an owner would be a(n)

   A. estate for years
   B. periodic estate
   C. estate at will
   D. estate at sufferance

7. A contract that temporarily transfers the right to possession of a property is a(n)

   A. deed
   B. tenancy
   C. lease
   D. option

8. The consideration in a lease is

   A. the apartment
   B. the rent
   C. the tenant's possessions
   D. none of the answers shown

9. A lease requires

   A. a formal legal description
   B. recordation of the document
   C. identification of the term and method to terminate
   D. an option to renew

10. The term of a lease

   A. must be for a minimum period of one year
   B. will always require notice to terminate
   C. may be reduced by breach of contract
   D. none of the answers shown

11. Commercial lessees may view the difference between the rentable and usable area in a commercial space as which of the following?

   A. Vacancy factor
   B. Loss factor
   C. Unused perimeter
   D. Common areas

12. The party transferring the right to possession under a lease is the

   A. lessee
   B. lessor
   C. tenant
   D. vendor

13. The warranty of habitability clause in a lease provides

   A. for a security deposit for all leases for more than one year
   B. that oral leases are not enforceable in court
   C. that the tenant must keep the apartment in good repair
   D. that the landlord must provide services such as heat and water

14. A lease clause that states that the landlord's lender and future owners of the building CANNOT terminate the lease as long as the tenant fulfills lease obligations is called a(n)

    A. escalation clause
    B. estoppel
    C. subordination clause
    D. nondisturbance clause

15. A lease can be between how many parties?

    A. One
    B. Two
    C. Three
    D. All of the answers shown

16. Which of the following is a type of lease escalation clause in a commercial lease?

    A. Porter's wage formula
    B. Estoppel
    C. Use clause
    D. Subordination

17. The main purpose of a security deposit is to

    A. prove the tenant's creditworthiness
    B. collect the last month's rent before the tenant vacates
    C. provide for routine maintenance
    D. ensure the return of the property in good repair

18. Barring any wording in the lease to the contrary, the tenant may

    A. not assign the leasehold rights
    B. sublease the property
    C. share the apartment with as many individuals as he wishes
    D. not sublease the property

19. Generally, property owners lease commercial space according to the

    A. rentable square footage
    B. usable square footage
    C. effective square footage
    D. carpetable area

20. A lease agreement for commercial property is generally

    A. standard throughout a state
    B. customized to the particular space and tenant
    C. for 10 years or more
    D. an estate for years

21. An investor purchases a five-family property whose tenants hold leases at the time of the closing. The new owner assumes the responsibilities of the seller. This is an example of

    A. novation
    B. specific performance
    C. assignment
    D. accord and satisfaction

22. In a commercial lease, if property taxes go up, the tenant is charged a proportionate share of the increase if there is which type of clause in the lease?

    A. Tax pass through escalation clause
    B. Expense stop clause
    C. Porter's wage escalation clause
    D. Index clause

23. Which of the following terms does NOT describe a type of commercial lease?

    A. Ground
    B. Package
    C. Percentage
    D. Net

24. A lease that has a base rent plus a percentage of the gross sales of a business is known as a(n)

    A. triple net lease
    B. percentage lease
    C. index lease
    D. ground lease

25. A long-term lease of unimproved land usually for construction purposes is known as a(n)

    A. percentage lease
    B. index lease
    C. graduated lease
    D. ground lease

26. Shanelle rented an office space and is paying for all of the expenses associated with the property including the rent. Shanelle has a(n)

    A. gross lease
    B. percentage lease
    C. ground lease
    D. triple net lease

27. Goldie is letting her friend, Mattie, use her apartment while she travels for a year in Europe. Mattie will make payments to her each month and then Goldie will pay the landlord. This arrangement is called a(n)

    A. sublease
    B. assignment
    C. constructive eviction
    D. net lease

28. The obligations of the owner and tenant to each other are mostly dictated by

    A. statutory law
    B. common law
    C. the terms of the lease contract
    D. the laws addressing rentals

29. Katy sold her building containing six rental units. The new owner can raise the rent

    A. immediately
    B. upon lease renewal
    C. never
    D. only when the current tenants move out

30. Which of the following acts by the owner would be an act of negligence? Failure to

    A. install window screens
    B. replace air filters
    C. repair a leaking gas heater
    D. replace a broken window

31. Marisol has inherited a home for which she has placed an ad in the newspaper for tenants. One of the applicants is African American. She refuses to rent to this woman because she prefers renters of her own national origin with whom she shares a common cultural background. What is the first law prohibiting discrimination that Marisol has violated?

    A. Civil Rights Law of 1866
    B. Fair Housing Law of 1968
    C. Fair Housing Law of Amendments of 1988
    D. All of the answers shown

32. Trudy needed to move in the middle of her lease term. She transferred all of her lease obligations to her friend, Sue. This transfer is called a(n)

    A. assignment
    B. sublet
    C. option to renew
    D. breach of lease

33. Which of the following is NOT a method of lease termination?

    A. Expiration
    B. Mutual cancellation
    C. Eviction
    D. Negligence

34. The simplest method for a lease to terminate is

    A. for it to expire
    B. through constructive eviction
    C. a breach of the lease terms
    D. sublet

35. A tenant who vacates the premises due to unlivable circumstances has been deprived of

    A. a written lease agreement
    B. quiet enjoyment
    C. owner eviction proceedings
    D. self-help

36. Legal actions for evictions and rental collections can be minimized if

    A. the building is 100% occupied
    B. property managers carefully select tenants
    C. owners manage property for themselves
    D. property managers change the locks of tenants who are in arrears with rents

37. Bruce, a property owner, changed the locks on his tenant's door and moved the tenant's belongings to a storage facility. This behavior is an example of

    A. illegal use of self-help
    B. legal eviction
    C. constructive eviction
    D. owner's rights

38. Another name for actual eviction is

    A. self-help
    B. constructive eviction
    C. reversion
    D. mitigation of damages

39. If tenants must leave a leased premise because of lack of heat, they may be able to forfeit their lease obligations and claim that which of the following has occurred?

    A. Constructive eviction
    B. Actual eviction
    C. Forfeiture
    D. *Lis pendens*

40. When a tenant is removed from the premises without the aid of the court system, this is known as

    A. legal eviction
    B. actual eviction
    C. constructive eviction
    D. none of the answers shown

41. If a real estate broker enters into a property management agreement with an owner, this broker becomes a

    A. trustee
    B. fiduciary
    C. facilitator
    D. lessor

42. The relationship between the property manager and the owner is most similar to what other relationship?

    A. Seller and listing agent
    B. Buyer and listing agent
    C. Buyer and seller
    D. Buyer and selling agent

43. Which of the following statements about property management is FALSE?

    A. Property management is a specialized field within the real estate industry
    B. A property manager acts as an agent of the property owner
    C. The terms property manager and resident manager always have the same meaning
    D. A property manager is a fiduciary

44. A management agreement should NOT include a

    A. complete description of the property
    B. the duration of the agreement
    C. document citing the management fee
    D. building code for the municipality

45. Jamison, a real estate broker, is also a property manager for an eight-unit residential property. In his role as property manager, Jamison is a

    A. facilitator
    B. special agent
    C. general agent
    D. licensee

46. A document submitted to the property owner outlining the commitment of the property owner once the manager is employed is called the

    A. management proposal
    B. management agreement
    C. property projection
    D. operating budget

47. Which of the following is NOT a function of the property manager? To

    A. advertise to solicit tenants
    B. hire, train, and supervise employees
    C. maintain adequate insurance to protect the owner
    D. maintain records on the racial composition of the neighborhood

48. The property manager's authority to represent the principal is established by

    A. property management laws
    B. the state and local board of REALTORS® committee on property management
    C. local custom and tradition
    D. the express terms of the property management agreement

49. The designation Certified Property Manager (CPM) is

    A. available through state real estate commissions
    B. a special designation affiliated with the Institute of Real Estate Management
    C. a special national license in property management
    D. a required designation to be a property manager

50. Advisors to property managers who focus on long-term financial planning rather than day-to-day operations of the property are

    A. real estate agents
    B. property managers
    C. asset managers
    D. insurance brokers

51. How is the manager's fee determined?

    A. State law sets the fee for property managers
    B. It is always a flat fee with no consideration of the rents collected
    C. It is typically 10% of rents collected for all structures regardless of size
    D. None of the answers shown

52. A property manager's fee

    A. is always a percentage of the gross rental income
    B. always requires a down payment together with a percentage of the rents actually collected
    C. is always a flat fee agreed to between the owner and manager
    D. is negotiable between the property owner and the manager

53. A function that would most likely be outside of a residential property manager's authority is

    A. dispatching repairmen
    B. decision-making regarding eviction of delinquent tenants
    C. representing the owner in court proceedings such as evictions
    D. checking credit histories, references, and employment status of potential tenants

54. A document prepared by a property manager that relates expense items to the operating budget for the period is the

    A. property management agreement
    B. property management report
    C. current rent roll
    D. stabilized budget

55. Cory was recently hired to manage a property. Which of the following is not part of his job?

    A. Preparing the deed to the property
    B. Renting the property
    C. Leasing the property
    D. Selling the property

56. Which statement is FALSE?

    A. The current rent roll is the number of occupied units multiplied by the amount of rent per unit
    B. A planned unit development is a neighborhood of cluster housing with supporting business
    C. The agency relationship between the manager and owner is formalized with a clause in the management proposal
    D. Net operating income is the gross income minus the operating expense

57. What does the term risk management refer to?

    A. The concern for controlling and limiting risk in property ownership
    B. The importance of obtaining public liability insurance
    C. The careful selection process of tenants
    D. Maintaining an accurate property management report

58. In her position as managing agent for a small apartment complex, Alexa, a real estate broker, accepts a small bonus from the landscapers since she hired them to maintain the complex. Alexa does not tell the owners about the bonus. Which of the following is TRUE?

    A. Alexa is violating her fiduciary duty to the owners
    B. Alexa may not accept the bonus without disclosing the bonus to the owners
    C. Alexa is breaching her fiduciary duty of accountability to the owner
    D. all of the answers shown

59. The type of insurance that covers a building owner in case of an injury is

    A. homeowner's
    B. liability
    C. boiler and machinery
    D. equipment riders

60. To be eligible for insurance coverage of any type, the insured must have a legitimate financial interest, known in the insurance policy as the

    A. loss payee clause
    B. insurable interest clause
    C. risk management
    D. coinsurance clause

61. One of the main problems in dealing with the management of office space is

    A. business tenants are more difficult than residential tenants
    B. keeping vacancies at a minimum
    C. excessive maintenance
    D. difficult owners

62. A well-known establishment in a shopping mall that draws customers is called a(n)

    A. magnet store
    B. anchor tenant
    C. discount center
    D. PUD

63. Which of the following is NOT considered in the management of industrial property?

    A. Transportation systems
    B. Utility services
    C. Components of the surrounding infrastructure
    D. Retail customers

64. Several anchor tenants would most likely be found in a(n)

    A. regional shopping mall
    B. strip shopping center
    C. neighborhood shopping center
    D. area without any other adjacent stores

65. A type of residential housing that requires a property manager is

    A. apartments
    B. condominiums
    C. mobile home parks
    D. all of the answers shown

66. Which of the following is NOT a fixed expense of a property?

    A. Insurance
    B. Corrective maintenance
    C. Taxes
    D. Permits

67. If a building is 98% occupied, the property manager may feel justified in

    A. believing that the laws of supply and demand are not in favor of the property
    B. rewriting the leases during the lease term
    C. lowering the rents
    D. raising the rents

68. The expense required to improve or maintain a building is called

    A. operating budget
    B. capital reserve budget
    C. capital expense
    D. variable expense

69. When a property manager calculates the income received on a property without deducting expenses, he or she is calculating the

    A. net income
    B. gross income
    C. projected budget
    D. debt service

70. An economic principal considered in setting rental prices is

    A. anticipation
    B. conformity
    C. substitution
    D. supply and demand

71. Which of the following does NOT reduce the potential gross income of a property?

    A. Vacancy rate
    B. Credit losses
    C. Tenants leaving before expiration of the lease term
    D. Income generated by laundry and vending machines

72. Which of the following terms define for an owner and property manager when a property will generate a positive return?

    A. Leverage point
    B. Expense stop
    C. Point of no return
    D. Natural breakeven point

73. Which of the following is NOT an expense in a property operating budget?

    A. Effective gross rent
    B. Debt service
    C. Expenses for insurance and tax
    D. Expenses for utilities and maintenance

74. A capital reserve budget for a property is a(n)

    A. annual budget that includes items of income and expense needed for week-to-week maintenance
    B. projected budget over the economic life of the property including expenses such as repairs and remodeling
    C. forecast of income and expenses as may be reasonably projected over a short term
    D. assessment of the fees for the property manager and his staff over a 12-month period

75. Lydia, a property manager, enlisted her maintenance team to go through the building and assess and repair all items that may need repair or replacement for the calendar year. This is an example of

    A. excessive oversight
    B. due diligence
    C. preventative maintenance
    D. corrective maintenance

76. Which of these types of maintenance is the most difficult to predict and budget for?

    A. Preventative maintenance
    B. Corrective maintenance
    C. Reserve for capital replacement
    D. Construction

77. A rental property shows $425 per month in rental income. The annual expenses of the property are the following: Repairs = $420, Interest = $2,192, Taxes = $621, Insurance = $297, Pest Control = $240, Depreciation = $1,222. What is the annual net rental income for tax purposes?

    A. $108
    B. $1,330
    C. $2,287
    D. $5,100

78. A four-plex is valued at $124,000. To earn 11% on the investment annually, what would the required net monthly income be?

    A. $1,137
    B. $1,240
    C. $13,640
    D. $14,880

79. A leasing agent gets 6.5% commission of the gross rent to be paid. The agent has just negotiated a four-year lease of a 2,400-square-foot space at $1.20 per square foot per month. How much is the commission, which is paid in advance, for the full lease term?

    A. $1,872
    B. $2,246
    C. $7,488
    D. $8,985.60

80. D manages a 20-unit building. Five of the units rent for $1,245, six of the units rent for $2,400, and the remaining units rent for $1,010. If D receives a 3% commission on the gross rental income, what is the fee (rounded) for the first four months of the year?

    A. $2,566
    B. $3,566
    C. $4,578
    D. $4,698

MULTIPLE CHOICE

Identify the choice that best completes the statement or answers the question.

1. Which of the following CANNOT be placed in a broker's trust account?

   A. Tenant security deposits
   B. MLS fees from agents in the office
   C. Earnest money on one of the office's listings
   D. Deposit check on a binder

2. To save on paperwork, broker B decided to combine the office operating account with the deposits obtained with contracts of sale. Broker B is guilty of

   A. nothing at all
   B. accepting money without authorization
   C. the unauthorized practice of law
   D. illegal commingling of funds

3. Deposits for real estate transactions negotiated by real estate brokers may NOT be held by

   A. real estate brokers
   B. attorneys
   C. lenders
   D. sellers

Brokerage Operations and the Practice of Real Estate

4. A broker deposited a buyer's check for earnest money in the amount of $6,000 in his or her escrow account. Before the closing and at the seller's request, the broker withdrew $1,200 from the escrow account to pay for the cost of repairs caused by termites. This expense was necessary so the seller could provide the required termite certificate to the buyer at the closing. Which of the following statements is CORRECT?

   A. Because the $1,200 disbursement from the broker's escrow account was made at the seller's request and benefited both buyer and seller, the broker acted properly
   B. The broker's action constituted an act of conversion and, as such, was improper
   C. The broker's action was unethical but definitely not illegal
   D. The broker's action was proper because brokers manage escrow accounts

5. When agent Yolanda brought a binder signed by the buyer to the sellers for their signature, the sellers informed her that they were taking their property off of the market. What should Yolanda do with the deposit?

   A. Accept the deposit anyway
   B. Accept the deposit for a limited time only
   C. Not accept the deposit
   D. Accept the deposit and place it in her personal checking account until further notice

6. Commingling is illegal and occurs when brokers

   A. take a net listing
   B. publish a blind ad
   C. give legal advice
   D. mix their business escrow account with their office operating account

7. Carole is principal broker of Go-Your-Own-Way Realty. She decides that she needs a vacation and leaves the real estate firm in the hands of two salespersons for three months. While she is gone, one of her deals falls through, but she cannot return the deposit as one of the salespeople inadvertently commingled the deposit with the office operating account and spent the money. Carole

   A. is probably guilty for failure to supervise, but is not responsible for the deposit money
   B. is not at all responsible for any of these activities as she was not there
   C. is only accountable to the state real estate commission and not to the prospective purchaser who placed the deposit with her company
   D. may be vicariously liable for the activities of her salespeople in violation of license law, rules, and regulations, and is guilty of failure to supervise and possible conversion of funds

8. Brokers must maintain their financial records

   A. at the brokerage firm's main office or branch office
   B. at his or her attorney's office
   C. in any safe place
   D. locked in a safe

9. Jane is a real estate broker and accepts a $3,000 deposit. What should she do with the deposit? Place it in her

   A. personal checking account
   B. business operating account immediately
   C. escrow account immediately
   D. safe deposit box

10. Which of the following is a key term used to determine whether a real estate broker is, or is not, legally entitled to a commission?

    A. Acceptance
    B. Accountability
    C. Assignment
    D. Assumption

11. A real estate broker's advertisement for the sale of condominium units or rental apartments containing pictures that show owners or tenants of only one race on the property

    A. may violate fair housing law
    B. is legal if only white people reside in the development
    C. is legal as long as the ad does not appear on the developer or owner's website
    D. is legal as long as the ad is a onetime ad and not used periodically

12. Ads addressing credit terms for consumer loans must follow disclosure requirements under the

    A. Truth in Lending Act
    B. state license laws
    C. state fair housing laws
    D. all of the answers shown

13. Under fair housing laws, owners of multi-unit housing can advertise to

    A. Latino families only
    B. adults only
    C. families without children
    D. older-resident housing if 80% of the units have persons aged 55 or older

14. An example of discriminatory advertising in the sale or rental of residential property would NOT be

    A. "no Puerto Ricans"
    B. "adults only"
    C. "nonsmokers preferred"
    D. "male college students only"

15. Guidelines for Internet advertising for real estate brokers are provided by the

    A. Ethics and Standards Board
    B. Appraisal Standards Board
    C. Association of Real Estate License Law Officials (ARELLO)
    D. U.S. Attorney General's Office

16. Moira, a real estate salesperson, placed an ad that read, "Luxury community in beautiful mountain rural area. Great for 40 something's. Perfect for adult empty nesters that are young enough to still enjoy life." This ad is discriminatory according to the Federal Fair Housing Act because it

    A. discriminates against older people
    B. discriminates against families with children
    C. appeals to affluent people
    D. values youth over old age

17. The most important aspect of the independent contractor relationship is that the

    A. worker is working 40 hours a week
    B. worker earns above $600 dollars a month
    C. employer must file a quarterly Form 941 with the IRS
    D. employer does not have the right to control the details of the worker's performance

18. In order to qualify under the IRS code for the independent contractor relationship, which of the following is necessary? The agent must

    A. be a broker or associate broker only
    B. be licensed
    C. have been licensed for at least one year
    D. work at least 25 hours per week

19. Reuben is an independent contractor who wants to terminate his employment arrangement with his broker. Which of the following is TRUE?

    A. Reuben's broker may refuse to terminate his contract
    B. Reuben must reapply to retake his license exam before he leaves his broker
    C. Reuben may do so at any time
    D. Reuben may do so only with the written permission of the IRS

20. Under IRS rules, a real estate salesperson violates his or her independent contractor status if he or she

    A. becomes an associate broker
    B. has a set salary each week no matter how many sales are produced
    C. works under a written contract specifying independent contractor status
    D. has no specific work hours

21. Which of the following activities is NOT an element of an independent contractor relationship?

    A. Employers withhold federal, state, and social security taxes
    B. There is no compensation based on number of hours worked
    C. There is no specified work place
    D. Either party may terminate the relationship at any time

22. According to the IRS code, real estate licensees can be qualified as which of the following?

    A. Common-law employees
    B. Independent contractors
    C. Statutory employees
    D. Full-time employees

23. Whether a salesperson is associated with a broker as an employee or as an independent contractor is important

    A. for income tax purposes
    B. when applying for a license
    C. when listing property because independent contractors may list in his or her own name
    D. when establishing the escrow account

24. Real estate licensees are classified as independent contractors under

    A. IRS code sections 3508 (a)(b)
    B. common law
    C. local license laws
    D. antitrust laws

25. In the salesperson–broker independent contractor relationship, which of the following characterizes allowable activities in this relationship? The salesperson

    A. is compensated by the number of hours worked
    B. may not engage in outside employment
    C. must work only from the broker's office
    D. commissions are paid without deduction for taxes

26. If a salesperson earns $600 or more, a broker must file

    A. IRS tax form 1040
    B. IRS tax form 1099 misc.
    C. FICA payments
    D. IRS tax form 941

27. Which of the following need NOT be followed to preserve the independent contractor status?

    A. Commissions are directly related to work performed
    B. The licensee must hold a current real estate license
    C. The licensee can be compensated according to the hours worked
    D. The licensee must enter into an independent contractor agreement

28. Although licensees are independent contractors, the broker still has which of the following duties? To

    A. file quarterly employment forms for the salesperson
    B. supervise the activities of licensees in his or her firm
    C. track the hours of licensees and pay them accordingly
    D. provide reasonable vacation and sick pay

29. Which of the following would NOT result in license suspension or revocation? Real estate agents

    A. accepting a commission from their sponsoring broker
    B. accepting compensation from more than one party in a transaction without making a full disclosure to all parties
    C. who are not attorneys giving legal advice
    D. engaging in fraudulent practices

30. Thomas Seaver, a broker associated with Leisure Homes Realty, advised a seller that his property would sell for at least $150,000. Relying on this, the seller listed the property at $150,000. Comparable sales and listings of competitive properties were in the range of $105,000 to $110,000. The seller refused several offers between $106,000 and $112,000 during the 120-day term of the listing. The seller eventually sold his property for $98,000 since expiration of the listing with Leisure Homes. Which of the following is TRUE?

    A. Seaver has done nothing wrong and thus is not liable for any damage
    B. Because Seaver is an agent of Leisure Homes Realty, Leisure Homes is the only party that may be held liable for the seller's damages
    C. Seaver committed an act of misrepresentation and may be liable for the resulting financial loss the seller incurred
    D. Because the seller did not sell the property during the listing period, Seaver is entitled to a commission

31. A brokerage firm receives an order from the court to immediately stop soliciting listings in a certain geographic area. This order is called a(n)

    A. rescission
    B. reformation
    C. injunction
    D. assignment

32. A real estate broker who convinces a party to a contract of sale to break the contract in order to substitute a new contract with another party is guilty of

    A. violating a nonsolicitation order
    B. inducing a breach of contract
    C. failing to disclose his or her interest
    D. commingling funds

33. Mutual agreement by certain states to extend licensing privileges to each other is called

    A. a kickback
    B. market allocation agreement
    C. multiple listing service
    D. reciprocity

34. When brokers improperly pay any part of their compensation to anyone who is not licensed or who is not exempt from the license law, they violate the license law. This payment is called

    A. net listing
    B. breach of contract
    C. commingling
    D. a kickback

35. Noreen, a real estate broker, is about to close a deal on the rental of an apartment in a building that she manages. The deal takes place at the home of the prospective tenant. Noreen has forgotten the preprinted lease agreement, so she hastily writes one up from memory so as not to lose the deal. She has the tenant sign the lease and tells the tenant that the preprinted one can be signed tomorrow and she will throw away the one she wrote. Which of the following is CORRECT?

    A. Noreen's quick thinking saved the deal and there is nothing wrong with her actions
    B. Noreen may have engaged in the unauthorized practice of law and is in violation of license law
    C. Noreen's actions are not exactly appropriate, but she will not be held responsible as she intends to replace the lease the next day
    D. The tenant is at fault for signing the lease, which in turn absolves Noreen of all liability for her actions

36. Delia is planning to open her own real estate office. Which of the following activities is NOT necessary?

    A. Clear the new name of the firm with the real estate commission
    B. Find a location that allows proper signage in accordance with zoning laws
    C. Decide what type of business entity would be best for her
    D. Hire sales agents

37. Which of the following activities is NOT allowable with only a real estate license?

    A. Listing real property
    B. Negotiating the exchange of real property
    C. Negotiating the sale of a business in which a substantial amount of real estate is transferred
    D. Drawing an installment land contract

38. A real estate broker is NOT responsible for

    A. acts of sales associates while engaged in brokerage activities
    B. appropriate handling of funds in trust or escrow accounts
    C. adhering to a commission schedule recommended by the local board of REALTORS®
    D. representing property honestly, fairly, and accurately to prospective buyers

39. A false statement regarding an important matter in a real estate transaction to induce someone to contract is called

    A. the unauthorized practice of law
    B. reciprocity
    C. "buyer beware"
    D. misrepresentation

40. Magda's customer is a developer who does not wish to purchase a certain subdivision before the town planning board approves the site for the construction of 12 single-family houses. Magda advises her customer that she has spoken to the board members individually and they intend to approve the site. She advises her customer to purchase the property before the approval so he or she can buy at a lower price. The customer purchases the property and the subdivision is not approved. Which of the following is CORRECT?

    A. Magda committed an act of misrepresentation and may be liable to the developer for any loss the developer may have as a consequence
    B. Magda was simply doing her job as agent to obtain the best deal for her customer and bears no liability
    C. *Caveat emptor* applies, and therefore Magda is not liable
    D. Magda is not liable simply because the information she had was accurate at the time she received it and subsequent acts of the town board were not in her control

41. George, a real estate sale agent, is about to close a deal on the lease of a retail space. His client has questions about the legality of the termination clause in the lease. How should George respond to this question?

   A. If George believes the clause is legal, he should indicate this to his client and encourage him or her to close the deal

   B. George should not give out legal advice and should advise his client to consult an attorney

   C. George should refer this question to his broker as brokers may offer legal advice with respect to commercial deals

   D. George should advise his client to steer clear of any questionable lease arrangements and look for a more favorable deal elsewhere

42. Even though licensees may be paid through a commission arrangement based on sales, the broker is responsible for which of the following?

   A. Tracking and recording the number of hours worked by each licensee for a period of three years

   B. Filing quarterly FICA payments for each licensee with IRS

   C. Maintaining records as to the gross and net profit of all transactions for a period of a time specified by the IRS and state law

   D. Keeping records of outside employment of each licensee

43. Which of the following is FALSE regarding referral fees?

   A. Referral fees are illegal in a real estate transaction without the informed consent of the parties to the transaction

   B. Referral fees are distributed to the licensee who originated the referral

   C. Referrals cannot be offered for relocation

   D. Referrals may involve receiving compensation for services rendered by another party related to the transaction

44. With a corporation, stockholders are liable

   A. to the extent of their investment

   B. for all debts of the corporation

   C. for all debts incurred in the calendar year that stock was purchased

   D. only if the corporation files a Chapter 11 Bankruptcy Petition

45. Which of the following is FALSE regarding a C corporation?

    A. C corporations may be for profit or nonprofit
    B. C corporations are subject to a double tax
    C. C corporations must issue publicly traded shares of stock
    D. Bylaws generally govern the operation and management of the C corporation

46. Which of the following business structures create unlimited liability for the owners?

    A. Sole proprietorship and general partnership
    B. Limited liability companies and S corporations
    C. S corporations and C corporations
    D. Limited liability companies and limited liability partnerships

47. Which of the following is NOT taxed as a partnership?

    A. S corporation
    B. Limited liability company
    C. Limited liability partnership
    D. Sole proprietorship

48. Broker Alvin and broker Kevin from different real estate brokerage firms decide to bring their dispute over a commission split to a neutral third party that would make a final decision. This is best known as

    A. arbitration
    B. mediation
    C. litigation
    D. torts

49. A disadvantage of a C corporation as a form of business organization is that it is

    A. legal only in some states
    B. not allowed as a form of organization for real estate brokers
    C. taxed on both the corporate and the shareholder level
    D. not allowed to hold title to real estate

50. Limited partners in a partnership business organization are

    A. the same as general partners
    B. not a form of ownership that is allowed for real estate brokerages
    C. not a form of business organization
    D. not liable for the debts of the partnership beyond the amount of money they have contributed

51. According to the tax laws, which of the following business organizations is NOT taxed as a partnership?

    A. General partnership
    B. Limited partnership
    C. S corporation
    D. C corporation

52. A prospectus is used in connection with a

    A. stock offering
    B. corporation formation
    C. partnership formation
    D. bankruptcy filing

53. Which of the following describes a trade-name broker? A(n)

    A. form of business organization that is owned by two or more partners
    B. individual doing business under his or her name only
    C. business formed by two or more individuals who are not personally liable for the obligations of the real estate firm
    D. broker conducting business as a sole proprietorship, using a name other than his or her personal name

54. A disadvantage of conducting business as a sole proprietorship instead of a corporation is the broker

    A. always makes less money
    B. cannot access multiple listing services
    C. has to pay higher board dues
    D. is personally financially liable for debts and/or lawsuits against the business

55. The most common form of business organization created by law with separate tax rates that are different from taxes on individuals is

    A. a sole proprietorship
    B. a corporation
    C. an individual under a trade name
    D. all of the answers shown

56. Bankruptcy cases are heard in

   A. federal court
   B. state court
   C. municipal court
   D. local court

57. If a property is part of a Chapter 7 bankruptcy, who must the broker contact before selling the property of the debtor? The

   A. bankruptcy judge
   B. county clerk
   C. bankruptcy trustee
   D. creditors

58. Which of the following is TRUE regarding online listings posted on a brokerage firm's website?

   A. Should be consistent with the property description
   B. Contain the actual status of the listing
   C. Material changes to the listing status should be updated in a timely manner
   D. All of the answers shown

59. Judy, an agent, finds a buyer who is ready, willing, and able to buy a property. When she contacts the principals on the offer, they request information on the national origin of the buyer. What must Judy do?

   A. Under the laws of agency, she must provide the information
   B. She may not lawfully provide this information
   C. She should tell the principals to withdraw their property from the market immediately
   D. She may volunteer this information in a well-meaning manner

60. The Perfectos are willing to give Jennie the listing on their house, but they do not want to sell to a White couple. They claim that the family would not like their long-time neighbors who are African Americans. Jennie

   A. can accept the listing if it is in a nonsolicitation area
   B. can accept the listing without any reservation
   C. cannot accept the listing as it is in violation of federal and state fair housing and human rights laws
   D. can apply for special permission to accept the listing to her board of REALTORS®

61. Individuals posing as prospective home seekers, but who are actually volunteers who investigate equal treatment by brokerage firms, are known as

   A. investigators
   B. testers
   C. facilitators
   D. finders

62. Familial status, a protected class under the Federal Fair Housing Act, is defined as

   A. being married or not
   B. an adult with children under 18
   C. families that are caring for older parents
   D. all those who are not single

63. The Whitley's refuse to rent an apartment in their multi-family dwelling to Belinda Duval, a financially qualified tenant, who is the single mother of two children under 18. Belinda is able to meet all of the lease terms. The Whitley's are

   A. exempt from selling to Ms. Delaney under the Federal Fair Housing Act
   B. not exempt under the Federal Fair Housing Act
   C. protected by the Civil Rights Act of 1866
   D. allowed under the law to rent their home to whomever they please

64. Broker Jerry brought prospective buyers to a certain community because he felt they would be happier due to their ethnic origin. This violation of the Federal Fair Housing Act is called

   A. blockbusting
   B. redlining
   C. steering
   D. harassment

65. Executives of Choice Bank had a meeting and each loan officer at the meeting was shown certain neighborhoods highlighted in a PowerPoint® presentation. The loan officers were told NOT to make mortgage loans to people buying property in the highlighted neighborhoods. This bank is guilty of

   A. blockbusting
   B. steering
   C. redlining
   D. nothing at all

66. Royce owns and lives in a duplex and wishes to rent out the other apartment. Royce

    A. must rent her home to any person who is financially qualified
    B. may not discriminate against individuals because they are of a certain race
    C. must rent her home to families with children, if approached
    D. must place her house for rent in a local newspaper if she does not use the services of a salesperson

67. Fair housing laws contain some exemptions in certain situations. Which of the following is NEVER an exemption?

    A. Rental applications that ask for an individual's race
    B. Restrictions of all rooms in a housing accommodation to individuals of the same sex
    C. Rental of a room by the occupant of a house or an apartment
    D. The sale or rental of housing exclusively to persons 55 years of age or older

68. Which of the following is NOT an example of housing discrimination?

    A. Owners and sellers requesting that only certain types of people be shown their home
    B. Buyers and renters refusing to be shown houses if certain types of people live in that part of the community
    C. Buyers requesting that only two-story housing be shown to them
    D. Placing tenants with disabilities in a separate building

69. Which of the following is NOT an example of steering? Showing

    A. African-American prospects properties only in integrated areas
    B. high-income buyers luxury properties only
    C. prospects properties in only one neighborhood
    D. Latino buyers only properties in primarily Latino neighborhoods

70. A real estate agent calls several residents of a neighborhood to announce that many families of a certain minority group are moving into the neighborhood. This agent is guilty of

    A. steering
    B. redlining
    C. blockbusting
    D. discriminatory advertising

71. Which of the following is NOT a discriminatory question for a lender to ask while granting credit to an applicant?

    A. Familial status
    B. Income
    C. National origin
    D. Racial background

72. If a seller requests that a real estate salesperson not show the seller's property to minorities, the salesperson should

    A. advise the seller to try another broker
    B. report the seller to HUD
    C. follow the seller's instructions
    D. withdraw from the listing relationship

73. Carlos, of Latino origin, and his wife, Jasmine, an African American, live in a predominately lower income section of town and apply for a home improvement loan to Yes Bank. Their mortgage is paid in full, and the couple is an excellent credit risk with steady jobs. The lender refuses to give them a loan. The lender may be guilty of

    A. redlining
    B. discrimination based on national origin
    C. discrimination based on race
    D. all of the answers shown

74. At the end of a lease, a person with disabilities who has made changes to the unit to fit his or her special needs, must

    A. leave the premises with the alterations intact
    B. return the premises to their original condition
    C. be reimbursed for any expenses incurred by the changes
    D. give sufficient time for the owner to return the premises to their original condition

75. A protected class under certain state laws, but not under the Federal Fair Housing Act, is which of the following?

    A. Sexual orientation
    B. National origin
    C. Race
    D. Familial status

76. Protected classes under the Federal Fair Housing Act do NOT include which of the following?

    A. Familial status
    B. Race
    C. Religion
    D. Marital status

77. Under the Federal Fair Housing Act, exemptions exist for

    A. housing for older people
    B. residential condominiums
    C. all residential sales by real estate brokers
    D. buyers under the age of 21

78. A fine that may be imposed through HUD for a first offense for violation of the Federal Fair Housing Act is

    A. $10,000
    B. $15,000
    C. $25,000
    D. $50,000

79. Real estate agent Latice directed her buyers to a property she had listed. She told them to make a right-hand turn at the corner of Main Street and 5th. She told them that a Catholic Church was at the corner and therefore, they could not miss the turn. What is wrong, if anything, with Latice's directions?

    A. Latice has engaged in discriminatory practices
    B. Latice has done nothing wrong
    C. Latice's directions would be okay if the buyers were Catholics
    D. Since Latice's intent is not discriminatory, her behavior is acceptable

80. Under Federal Fair Housing laws, a lender may NOT

    A. refuse a loan to an applicant because the applicant is unemployed
    B. require a credit report from every loan applicant
    C. require an appraisal of the property
    D. offer a different loan interest rate based on minority status

81. Protected classes under the Federal Fair Housing Act do NOT include which of the following?

    A. Disability
    B. National origin
    C. Sex
    D. Lawful occupation

82. Which of the following statements is FALSE regarding the Civil Rights Act of 1866?

    A. All citizens have the same rights to inherit, buy, sell, and lease real and personal property
    B. This statute is interpreted to prohibit discrimination because of race
    C. The 1866 law was declared null and void after the Civil War
    D. The law is in full force today

83. The civil penalty for repeated discriminatory acts in violation of the Federal Fair Housing Act is

    A. $10,000
    B. $15,000
    C. $25,000
    D. $50,000

84. Which of the following is NOT prohibited under the Federal Fair Housing Act?

    A. Testers
    B. Discriminatory advertising
    C. Steering
    D. Discrimination against families with children

85. Dewey, Cheatum, and Howe Savings and Loan would violate the Federal Fair Housing Act by denying a loan to Seymour because of

    A. low earnings
    B. too many loans
    C. too old
    D. Jewish descent

86. The Civil Rights Act of 1866 prohibits discrimination based on

    A. race only, with exceptions
    B. age and disabilities
    C. race, no exceptions
    D. marital status

87. Which of the following Supreme Court decisions stated that separate but equal facilities were unconstitutional?

    A. Plessy v. Ferguson
    B. Brown v. Board of Education
    C. Buchanan v. Warley
    D. None of the answers shown

88. The Federal Fair Housing Act does NOT cover discrimination in the sale or rental of

    A. commercial property
    B. condominiums or cooperatives
    C. planned unit developments
    D. multi-family housing of any kind

89. The Federal Fair Housing Act of 1968 was amended in 1988 to include

    A. religion and sex
    B. race, color, and national origin
    C. familial status and mental and physical disability
    D. pets

90. The Housing and Community Development Act of 1974 added which protected class?

    A. National origin
    B. Sex
    C. Familial status
    D. Race

91. All but one of the choices below are exemptions regarding protected classes defined under the 1968 Federal Fair Housing Act. Select the one that is NOT exempt.

    A. Real estate owners of up to three single-family dwellings at any one time
    B. A private club not opened to the public if the club owns property for non-commercial lodging purposes
    C. Real estate brokers providing brokerage services
    D. A religious organization if properties are owned and operated for the benefit of members for noncommercial purposes

92. Enforcement of the Federal Fair Housing Act through HUD does NOT include

    A. financial penalties of $10,000 to $50,000 by an administrative law judge
    B. revocation of real estate licensure
    C. action by the U.S. Attorney General
    D. civil suit in federal court

93. Fair housing complaints may be referred to

    A. U.S. Department of Homeland Security
    B. U.S. Department of Housing and Urban Development
    C. local zoning boards of appeals
    D. all of the answers shown

94. Individuals with AIDS are

    A. protected under the Federal Fair Housing Act
    B. not protected under the Federal Fair Housing Act
    C. not protected under the Americans with Disabilities Act
    D. not protected under any law as "disabled" individuals

95. Which of the following is not a protected class under the Federal Fair Housing Act?

    A. Age
    B. Disability
    C. Religion
    D. National origin

96. The federal regulatory agency that oversees human rights complaints and legislation is

    A. HUD
    B. FHA
    C. Fannie Mae
    D. USDA

97. The fair housing law that is interpreted to prohibit all racial discrimination with no exemptions is the

    A. Federal Fair Housing Act of 1968
    B. Bill of Rights
    C. Civil Rights Act of 1866
    D. Civil Rights Act of 1964

98. The requirement that sex offenders register when they move into a neighborhood is mandated by

    A. the Federal Fair Housing Act
    B. Megan's Law
    C. the law of filtering down
    D. testers

99. Which of the following activities are allowable under antitrust laws?

    A. Free competition
    B. Tie-in arrangements
    C. Group boycotts
    D. Price fixing

100. The Americans with Disabilities Act does NOT cover

    A. commercial facilities
    B. public accommodations
    C. single-family homes
    D. multi-family apartment buildings

101. A business activity where there is a monopoly or conspiracy that negatively impacts another individual's or company's ability to do business is called a(n)

    A. injunction
    B. fraud
    C. kickback
    D. restraint of trade

102. The supreme law of our country is the

    A. U.S. Constitution
    B. U.S. Supreme Court
    C. U.S. Congress
    D. Articles of Confederation

103. Which of the following is NOT a penalty under the Sherman Antitrust Act?

    A. Capital punishment
    B. A felony charge
    C. Imprisonment
    D. Monetary damages

104. The governmental commission that has the power to declare trade practices unfair is the

    A. Fair Trade Commission
    B. Federal Trade Commission
    C. Federal Commission on Human Rights
    D. Antitrust Commission

105. One major purpose of the license law for real estate salespersons and brokers is to

    A. protect licensees from dishonest real estate investors
    B. protect consumers from dishonest activities by real estate brokers
    C. protect the profitability of the real estate brokerage profession
    D. establish minimum standards for multiple listing services

106. A tie-in arrangement is

    A. an agreement between a party selling a product or service with a buyer that, as a condition of the sale, the buyer will buy another product from the seller or the buyer will not buy a product or use a service of another

    B. an agreement between competitors to divide or assign a certain area a territory for sales

    C. when competitors conspire to charge the same amount for services

    D. a conspiracy in which a person or group is persuaded or coerced into not doing business with another person or group

107. Hometown Realty and Village Realty agreed not to compete in their neighboring towns. Hometown Realty would handle all business in the town where it is located, and Village Realty would handle all business in the town where it is located. This is an example of an illegal

    A. market allocation agreement

    B. tie-in arrangement

    C. price-fixing arrangement

    D. group boycott

108. Two neighboring county multiple listing services agree to set all commission rates for commercial properties at 10% so that consumers do not have to shop around for lower commission rates. This activity is

    A. an illegal restraint of trade

    B. allowable for commercial properties but not for residential properties

    C. helpful to consumers because they do not have to worry about higher commission rates

    D. allowable under the law because the real estate industry is composed of services, not "trade"-type activity

109. A multiple listing service proposed a Uniform Pricing Guide for real estate fees. Which of the following applies?

    A. This is an appropriate exercise of the regulatory power of the multiple listing service

    B. If the guide is published, all licensees would have to abide by its regulations

    C. If the guide is published, only members of NAR would have to abide by the regulations

    D. This is a violation of the Sherman Antitrust Act and is illegal

110. The dollar amount of the federal annual exclusion per person to the federal gift tax is

    A. $5,000
    B. $13,000
    C. $15,000
    D. $20,000

111. Belle Properties Brokerage and Ruby Real Estate decided that since they are the only two companies that offer residential property for sale in a small town, they would both charge the same commission rate. These two firms are guilty of

    A. nothing at all
    B. an illegal group boycott
    C. illegal price fixing
    D. an illegal market allocation agreement

112. Which of the following is TRUE regarding the multiple listing service (MLS)?

    A. Discount brokers cannot use the service
    B. MLS must allow exclusive agency listings and other lawful listings without any restrictions
    C. All member brokers must charge the same amount
    D. There is no fee for using the MLS

113. In addition to the Sherman Antitrust Act, what other important antitrust act also protects the public against the activities of monopolies that may be an unreasonable restraint of trade?

    A. Sherman Antitrust Act
    B. Clayton Antitrust Act
    C. Federal Trade Commission
    D. General antitrust law

114. Zoning laws may NOT be used to

    A. prevent demolition of historic buildings
    B. regulate architectural style of buildings
    C. control growth and development
    D. establish neighborhoods restricted to people of a certain race

115. Greenleaf Brokerage, a buyer brokerage firm, has a clause in its contract that as a condition of purchase, all buyers needing a mortgage must apply to EZ Loan Mortgage Company. If EZ Loan does not grant the mortgage, then the buyers may approach another mortgage company. This activity is

    A. legal only if the mortgage company gives full disclosure and informed consent
    B. an illegal tie-in arrangement that is in restraint of trade
    C. legal, since brokerages may have mandatory tie-in arrangements with other service companies
    D. illegal since financing cannot be discussed until purchasers sign a purchase offer

116. A state's authority to make and enforce license laws falls under

    A. legal doctrine
    B. police power
    C. regulatory laws
    D. civil procedure

117. Which of the following actions does NOT apply to the Americans with Disabilities Act?

    A. A jail sentence for the first offense
    B. A fine of $50,000 for the first offense
    C. A fine of $100,000 for subsequent offenses
    D. Injunctions against operation of a business

118. The Americans with Disabilities Act applies to

    A. owners and operators of public accommodations
    B. owners and operators of commercial facilities regardless of the number of employees or size of the complex
    C. local and state governments
    D. all of the answers shown

119. The Community Reinvestment Act

    A. was enacted to encourage lenders to help meet the credit needs of communities where the bank is located
    B. requires that each lender's record in helping meet the credit needs of its entire community be periodically evaluated
    C. is also called the Fair Lending Law
    D. includes all of the answers shown

120. One of the main purposes of the Sherman Antitrust Act is to

    A. regulate the real estate industry
    B. allow small businesses to compete effectively with larger companies
    C. protect governmental agencies from competition by private business
    D. regulate the banking industry

MULTIPLE CHOICE

Identify the choice that best completes the statement or answers the question.

1. A salesperson earns a commission of $6,000 in a sale of a property worth $100,000. What is the commission rate?

    A. 3%
    B. 6%
    C. 8%
    D. 9%

2. What is the commission rate on a sale of $111,000, if the total commission paid was $7,215?

    A. 6.5%
    B. 7%
    C. 7.2%
    D. 15.4%

3. A leasing agent obtains 3% of the gross rent to be paid. The agent has negotiated a two-year lease of a 3,500-square-foot unheated industrial space at $1.85 per square foot per month. How much is the total commission?

    A. $388.50
    B. $963.20
    C. $2,331
    D. $4,662

Real Estate Math

4. A salesperson and a broker have a 70–30 commission split program (70% to the salesperson). What is the salesperson's commission on a sale of $124,500, with a 6% total sales commission, if there are no other brokers or salespersons involved?

A. $2,241
B. $5,229
C. $7,470
D. $8,715

5. Three co-tenants own a parcel that cost $72,000. All paid pro rata for their interests; that is, they paid the same percentage of the purchase price as they hold in ownership. If co-tenant A paid $36,000, and co-tenant B paid $12,000, what percentage does co-tenant C own?

A. 24%
B. 33.3%
C. 48%
D. 66.7%

6. Seller Hermione lists her house with broker Hernando for $119,900 with a commission of 6.5%. Broker Hernando negotiates a sales contract between seller Hermione and buyer Jermaine for $116,500. Buyer Jermaine is required to deposit $4,500 as an initial escrow deposit and an additional escrow deposit of $5,500 within five days, and to apply for a new mortgage of $106,500. The real estate commission would be

A. $6,922.50
B. $7,143.50
C. $7,572.50
D. $7,793.50

7. Salesperson Jamal sells a property for $85,000. The commission on this sale to the real estate firm with whom Jamal is associated is 8%. Jamal receives 80% of the total commission paid to the real estate firm. What is the Jamal's share of the commission in dollars?

   A. $6,800
   B. $680
   C. $5,440
   D. $1,360

8. A buyer pays $45,000 for a lot. Five years later, he puts it on the market for 20% more than he originally paid. The lot then sells for 10% less than the asking price. What is the selling price of the lot?

   A. $44,100
   B. $48,600
   C. $49,500
   D. $54,000

9. An owner lists a property for sale with a broker. At what price must the property be sold to net the owner $7,000 after paying a 7% commission and satisfying the existing $48,000 mortgage?

   A. $49,354
   B. $56,750
   C. $57,750
   D. $59,140

10. A property is sold for $64,000 by salesperson Simpson at Horseman's Realty. The commission is 8% and Simpson's split is 65% to Simpson and 35% to Horseman's. Simpson's commission is

    A. $1,792
    B. $3,328
    C. $5,120
    D. None of the answers shown

11. A parcel is 0.84 acres. How many square feet are there in this parcel?

    A. 191 sq.ft.
    B. 36,590 sq.ft.
    C. 43,560 sq.ft.
    D. 51,857 sq.ft.

12. The outside dimensions of a rectangular house are 35 feet by 26.5 feet. If the walls are all 9 inches thick, what is the square footage of the interior?

    A. 827.5 sq.ft.
    B. 837.5 sq.ft.
    C. 927.5 sq.ft.
    D. 947.7 sq.ft.

13. How many acres are in a rectangular parcel of land that is 490 feet × 356 feet?

    A. 4 acres
    B. 6 acres
    C. 8 acres
    D. 10 acres

14. An acre of land is 450 feet wide. If the acre is rectangular in shape, what is its length (rounded)?

    A. 85 feet
    B. 90 feet
    C. 97 feet
    D. 99 feet

15. What is the cost of a lot 264 feet × 660 feet at a price of $8.50 per square foot?

    A. $15,708
    B. $20,500
    C. $493,680
    D. $1,481,040

16. If a lender is currently charging 2.25 discount points per loan (1 point = 1% of the loan amount), what would the charges be for points on a sale of $128,000 with a loan-to-value ratio of 90%?

    A. $216
    B. $240
    C. $2,592
    D. $2,880

17. If a $12,500 loan with 9.5% interest per year is paid back six months from the date of loan origin, how much interest will be paid?

    A. $7,125
    B. $197.92
    C. $593.75
    D. $1,187.50

18. The appraised value of a property is $450,000. The purchaser borrows $375,000. What is the loan-to-value ratio (rounded)?

    A. 75%
    B. 80%
    C. 90%
    D. 120%

19. A 10.5% loan has an interest charge of $962.50 this month. What is the principal balance of the loan?

    A. $9,167
    B. $101,063
    C. $110,000
    D. $121,275

20. The purchase price of a property is $86,300, and the purchaser has secured an 85% conventional loan. The lender charges a 1% origination fee, and additional closing costs total $2,625. How much cash must the purchaser bring to the closing, if he or she has already paid an earnest money deposit of $3,000?

    A. $6,586
    B. $12,570
    C. $13,304
    D. $19,304

21. On February 1, a mortgagor makes a $638 mortgage payment, at the rate of 6.5%. The lender allocates $500 to the interest payment. What is the principal balance due on the mortgage on February 1?

    A. $82,450.38
    B. $92,307.69
    C. $97,402.47
    D. $102,344.89

22. A house sells for $165,000. If the seller agrees to pay 5.5% discount points on a $155,000 mortgage, and the broker's fee is 6%, how much does the seller net?

    A. $146,575
    B. $148,275
    C. $156,575
    D. $158,375

23. The purchase price of a property is $128,000. If a lender's maximum loan-to-value ratio is 80% without private mortgage insurance (PMI), but 90% if PMI is charged, what is the down payment required if the buyers want to avoid the PMI?

    A. $12,800
    B. $25,600
    C. $102,400
    D. $115,200

24. Patricia's mortgage payment this month consists of $225 in interest and $70 applied to the principal. What is the annual debt service?

    A. $295
    B. $840
    C. $2,700
    D. $3,540

25. The closing on the sale of a rental property is to be held June 10. The seller has received the rent for June in the amount of $1,200. What entry will appear on the seller's and buyer's closing statements?

    A. $40 credit to buyer
    B. $800 credit to buyer
    C. $400 debit to seller
    D. $80 debit to seller

26. A sale closes on February 12. The buyer is assuming the seller's mortgage that has an outstanding balance of $28,000 as of the closing date. The last mortgage payment was made on February 1. The annual interest rate is 7.75%, and interest is paid in arrears. What interest proration appears in the buyer's closing statement?

    A. $72.36 credit
    B. $77.52 credit
    C. $180.83 debit
    D. $253.19 credit

27. L's closing date is January 15. The taxes for the calendar year begin accruing on January 1. The seller has prepaid the taxes. If the taxes are $5,000 per year, how much is the seller credited at closing (rounded)?

    A. $4,798
    B. $4,800
    C. $4,823
    D. $4,927

28. In the sale of a house, property taxes for the current calendar year amounted to $920 and have been paid in full by the seller. The sale is to be closed on September 22. What is the amount of tax proration to be credited to the seller?

    A. $173.78
    B. $250.44
    C. $669.56
    D. $746.22

29. K rented out 10 apartments at a monthly rate of $780. The property closed on August 18 and K had collected all of the rent. How much is K debited on the closing statement?

    A. $4,800
    B. $3,465
    C. $3,000
    D. $3,271

30. Using a 360-day year for calculation purposes, a lake access property closing occurred on August 1. A boat dockage fee due to the homeowner's association for $240 for a six-month period from July 1 to December 31 cannot be paid until September 1, and will be paid by the buyer. What entry appeared on the closing statement?

    A. Credit to seller $40
    B. Credit to buyer $40
    C. Debit to buyer $40
    D. Credit to buyer $240

31. A building valued at $105,000 is assessed at 35% of its value and taxed at the rate of 66 mills. One mill = 1/10 of one cent. What is the quarterly tax payment?

    A. $606.38
    B. $1,732.50
    C. $2,425.50
    D. $9,187.50

32. A home is valued at $72,000 and is assessed at 70% of value. The annual tax rate is 0.0575%. What is the amount of the annual tax bill?

    A. $725
    B. $2,898
    C. $4,140
    D. $5,914

33. The tax rate is usually expressed by number of tax dollars per $1,000 of assessed value. If a town levy is $5 million and the entire town has an assessed value of $100 million, what would the tax rate be for the town per $1,000?

    A. $500
    B. $200
    C. $50
    D. $20

34. A lot is assessed for 60% of market value and taxed at a rate of $3.75 per $100 of assessed value. Five years later, the same tax rate and assessment rate still exist. However, annual taxes have increased by $750. By how much has the dollar value of the property increased?

    A. $8,752.75
    B. $20,000.00
    C. $33,333.33
    D. $38,385.82

35. A parcel of land sells at market value. The market value and the tax value are the same. If the tax value is 100% of assessment value, the tax rate is $1.50, and the annual tax is $540, what is the selling price of the land?

    A. $24,000
    B. $27,700
    C. $36,000
    D. $81,000

36. If the assessed value of a property is $340,000, and the annual taxes are $4,250, what is the tax rate per $100 of tax value?

    A. $1.10
    B. $1.25
    C. $4.25
    D. $8.00

37. If an investor's rate of return is 13%, and his investment is $390,000, what will be his net annual income?

    A. $30,000
    B. $33,000
    C. $50,700
    D. $62,000

38. A property valued at $200,000 appreciates by 2% each succeeding year. What is the value of the property after two years?

    A. $201,080
    B. $202,000
    C. $204,080
    D. $208,080

39. A building owner's lease allows him to increase the rent on apartments by 2.25% of the cost of improvements upon lease renewal. The owner spends $1,200 per unit for improvements, and then raises the rent from $380 to $415. By how much has the owner exceeded the terms of the lease?

    A. $8
    B. $15
    C. $27
    D. $35

40. A parking lot containing 2 acres nets $12,000 per year. The owner wishes to retire and sell his parking lot for an amount that will net him $12,000 per year by investing the proceeds of the sale at 8½% per year. What must the selling price be to accomplish the owner's objective?

    A. $96,000
    B. $102,000
    C. $120,000
    D. $141,176

Identify the choice that best completes the statement or answers the question.

Property Ownership

1. The words "estate" or "tenancy" generally imply which right to real property?

   A. Possession
   B. Investment
   C. A large property
   D. Leased property only

2. An attribute of land that means that there is a fixed supply of it is

   A. scarcity
   B. location
   C. uniqueness
   D. indebtedness

3. A plat would best be described as a

   A. legal description
   B. deed
   C. map
   D. metes and bounds

Salesperson 100-Question Practice Exam

4. With regard to fixtures attached to residential property, tenants may

   A. never remove any fixtures
   B. keep any of the existing fixtures not placed by them when the lease terminates
   C. remove fixtures placed by them if agreed to with the property owner when the lease terminates
   D. never attach any fixtures to leased property

5. An example of a freehold estate is a

   A. bill of sale
   B. commercial lease
   C. rental of an apartment
   D. home ownership

6. Bart and Bettina have a one week view of blue waters and bluer skies. They are co-owners of a condominium that is based upon prescribed intervals known as a

   A. Real Estate Investment Trust (REIT)
   B. fee simple absolute ownership
   C. planned unit development
   D. timeshare

7. Title to common areas within and without the condominium is held as

   A. tenants in common
   B. a partnership
   C. joint tenancy
   D. in severalty

8. A mortgage is a type of

   A. deed
   B. lien
   C. judgment
   D. writ of attachment

9. Kimberly believed that her neighbor's fence had migrated over the years to inside her property's boundaries. This event is an example of a(n)

   A. appurtenance
   B. easement by necessity
   C. negative easement appurtenant
   D. encroachment

10. Aviva filed a lien on March 2, 2011. Bentley filed a lien on March 3, 2011. Cassandra filed a lien on April 1, 2011. Assuming the liens are of the same types, which lien would mostly likely to be paid first?

    A. Aviva's
    B. Bentley's
    C. Cassandra's
    D. Either Aviva, Bentley, or Cassandra since liens are never paid in any particular order

Property Valuation, Market Analysis, and the Appraisal Process

11. Which of the following is NOT an economic characteristic of land?

    A. Permanence of investment
    B. Location
    C. Nonhomogeneity
    D. Modification by improvement

12. Which type of value is most important to a residential real estate salesperson?

    A. Assessed value
    B. Hazard insurance value
    C. Mortgage value
    D. Condemnation value

13. Which economic principle is the basis for the sales comparison approach to value?

    A. Conformity
    B. Anticipation
    C. Substitution
    D. Contribution

14. Which of the following methods are NOT used for appraisal purposes?

    A. Income approach
    B. Sales comparison approach
    C. Cost approach
    D. Comparative market analysis

15. One major constraint of the sales comparison approach is that it requires

    A. several newly constructed properties
    B. an active market of competitive properties
    C. accurate cost information
    D. accurate information on investor expectations

16. Which of the following items is NOT a consideration for the cost approach?

    A. Financing terms
    B. Depreciation
    C. Site value
    D. Replacement cost

17. One of the most important aspects of marketing a property is

    A. pricing the property at the lowest possible price for a quick and timely sale
    B. ignoring the competition and allowing the property to sell based on its own merits
    C. knowing the competition and adjusting pricing and marketing accordingly
    D. effecting a sale within 18 months of the listing date

18. Generally, with a real estate investment, the greater the risk of loss,

    A. the greater the return on investment
    B. the less the return on investment
    C. the risk equals the return on investment
    D. none of the answers shown

19. Income received on a property after expenses are deducted is called

    A. net income
    B. gross income
    C. net operating income
    D. debt service

20. Under federal law, to become a licensed real property appraiser, one must first become a(n)

    A. licensed mortgage broker
    B. licensed real estate broker
    C. appraisal trainee
    D. licensed real estate salesperson

Land Use Controls and Regulations

21. Which of the following is FALSE regarding deed restrictions? They

    A. take the form of covenants or conditions
    B. run with the land
    C. must benefit all property owners
    D. are never terminated

22. When Yancy bought her house in a new subdivision, she believed that she owned the house and the lot and could arrange items the way she wanted. After moving her lamppost five feet to the right, she received a letter saying she was not allowed to do this and must move it back. What organization has the legal right to have Yancy move her lamppost back?

    A. State attorney general's office
    B. Next door neighbor
    C. County planning board
    D. Her development's homeowners' association

23. The taking of a property under the government's right of eminent domain is

    A. escheat
    B. estoppel
    C. *in rem*
    D. condemnation

24. The town ordinance requires JayCee to construct her house 90 feet from the road. This restriction on her property is called

    A. incentive zoning
    B. doctrine of laches
    C. setback
    D. taking

25. Because the infrastructure to support new housing construction was not available, the town decided to halt all construction for six months. This action is called a(n)

    A. census
    B. moratorium
    C. referendum
    D. injunction

26. Claudia is about to sign a contract to purchase a large estate. She is worried about the presence of radon on the property. What might her agent, Linda, a buyer broker, do?

    A. Advise Claudia to have the property tested for the presence of radon
    B. Ask the sellers to disclose any knowledge they have of radon issues with the property
    C. Tell Claudia not to worry, because radon is a harmless gas
    D. Tell Claudia not to purchase the property if she feels uncomfortable

27. The preparation of a report documenting the effect that a building and development project may have on the environment is called a(n)

    A. property report
    B. environmental impact statement
    C. appraisal
    D. feasibility study

28. Which of the following contains a list of all real property in the jurisdiction with annual information including its assessed value?

    A. Assessment roll
    B. Equalization rate list
    C. Grievance list
    D. *In rem* document

29. If a property owner believes an assessment is wrong, he or she may file a written complaint called a

    A. certiorari
    B. grievance
    C. subpoena
    D. judicial review

30. The tax rate for a taxing unit is set by

    A. a state agency
    B. the local planning board
    C. the municipality
    D. a tax assessor

Contracts and Relationships with Buyers and Sellers

31. Which of the following is FALSE regarding an earnest money deposit? It

    A. shows the sincerity of the buyer
    B. must always accompany an offer to purchase
    C. demonstrates financial capability to raise the money called for in the purchase offer
    D. may serve as possible liquidated damages to the seller if the buyer defaults

32. A precocious 16-year-old college student signs a contract to lease an apartment for one year with a one-year renewal clause. The lessor accepts the agreement. The validity of this contract may be in jeopardy due to

    A. consideration of the lease
    B. reality of consent
    C. offer and acceptance
    D. legal capacity of the parties

33. Belinda signs an exclusive-right-to-sell listing contract with Diamond Real Estate. Four weeks into the contract, Belinda calls her salesperson and states that a friend of hers is purchasing her house. What obligations does Belinda have with Diamond Real Estate?

    A. None, her contract with Diamond Real Estate is void
    B. Belinda still owes Diamond Real Estate a commission on the sale
    C. Belinda must give Diamond Real Estate only one-half of the commission
    D. Belinda's friend has to pay the commission to Diamond Real Estate

34. A seller tells her broker that she wants to net $160,000 from the sale of her property after the broker commission of 7% is deducted from the sale proceeds. For what price must the property be listed (rounded)?

    A. $124,005
    B. $154,035
    C. $165,010
    D. $172, 043

35. The sellers must sign a disclosure and contingency appended to their contract of sale, but only if their residence was built before 1978. This form is a(n)

    A. rider
    B. lead-based paint disclosure form
    C. mortgage contingency
    D. agency disclosure form

36. Bindu has signed a contract in which he has agreed to pay toward the purchase price on a monthly basis. He will take title when the full amount of the purchase price is paid. This contract is called a(n)

    A. option to buy
    B. binder
    C. lease
    D. installment sales

37. When a party purchases an option, the optionee is purchasing which of the following?

    A. Contract liability
    B. Time
    C. Land
    D. Exercise

38. Julius has listed his house for sale for $250,000. Constance makes a written offer of $243,000, which Julius accepts. Under the terms of this agreement,

    A. Julius was the offeror
    B. Constance was the offeree
    C. there was a meeting of the minds
    D. a unilateral contract was created

39. Which of the following is NOT an example of a means of legal discharge of a contract by operation of law?

    A. Statute of Limitations
    B. Bankruptcy petition
    C. Assignment of contract
    D. Alteration of contract

40. Roza, a listing agent, refuses to transmit an oral offer from Marty, a prospective purchaser. Which of the following is TRUE? Roza

    A. is obligated to forward the offer to her sellers
    B. needs to present only written offers
    C. needs to present the offer only if it is greater than the listed price
    D. cannot legally present the oral offer

Financing

41. The mortgagor is an individual who

    A. receives the payments
    B. lends the mortgage funds
    C. holds the mortgage lien
    D. signs the note and gives the mortgage

42. If the monthly interest payment due on a mortgage on December 1 is $570 and the annual interest rate is 6%, what is the outstanding mortgage balance?

    A. $61,560
    B. $63,333
    C. $114,000
    D. $131,158

43. A mortgage clause that allows a lender to declare the balance due if the borrower sells the property is called the

    A. prepayment penalty clause
    B. alienation clause
    C. granting clause
    D. defeasance clause

44. The sellers, the Wintergreens, have transferred title to the buyer in exchange for a promise to pay secured by a lien on the property. The Wintergreens have taken back from the buyer which type of mortgage?

    A. Second mortgage
    B. Installment land contract
    C. Deed of trust
    D. Purchase money mortgage

45. Leverage is defined as the use of borrowed money. The more borrowed funds and the less personal funds, the greater the leverage. Which of the following mortgage loan programs provides the greatest leverage?

    A. Federal Housing Authority (FHA)
    B. conventional
    C. Department of Veterans Affairs (VA)
    D. 95% insured conventional

46. The process in which the lender evaluates all of the borrower's financial data and determines if the borrower will obtain the loan is called

    A. alienation
    B. preapproval
    C. benediction
    D. loan underwriting

47. The federal law that provides for accurate advertising of financial credit terms is known as

    A. the Real Estate Settlement Procedures Act
    B. Regulation Z
    C. the Community Reinvestment Act
    D. the Equal Credit Opportunity Act

48. In the lending industry, loans made to borrowers who have less than perfect credit ratings are known as

    A. subprime
    B. unqualified loans
    C. nonconforming
    D. low equity

Law of Agency

49. An individual who is hired to work on another's behalf and for his or her best interests is called a(n)

    A. customer
    B. client
    C. principal
    D. agent

50. The Walkers did not tell their listing agent, Una, that their roof leaked badly during the wet weather in the spring. Later, agent Una was found liable for not disclosing this information to the buyers and a court ordered agent Una to pay $10,000 to the buyers. In this case, agent Una is entitled to repayment by the Walkers. This repayment is called

    A. reparations
    B. indemnification
    C. implication
    D. verification

51. An agency relationship can be created

    A. unintentionally
    B. by conduct
    C. by written agreement
    D. by all of the answers shown

52. To make agency relationships clear, which of the following documents is used in many states in the marketing of residential property?

    A. Property condition disclosure statement
    B. HUD Form No. 1
    C. Agency disclosure form
    D. Contract contingency

53. Trisha lists her property with Acme Brokerage. She agrees that if she sells the property herself, Acme will not receive a commission. However, Acme is the only broker she is listing with. This arrangement is a(n)

    A. net listing
    B. open listing
    C. exclusive-right-to-sell
    D. exclusive agency

54. An agent's fiduciary duty is to

    A. the client
    B. the customer
    C. the buyer
    D. other agents in the firm

55. Lorraine enters into a contract with Carlyle to sell him certain land that she owns. During the negotiations, Judith, a real estate broker who represents Lorraine, knows many of Lorraine's statements concerning the geography of the site are false but says nothing. Judith has engaged in

    A. unintentional misrepresentation
    B. positive misrepresentation
    C. dual agency
    D. disclosure

56. A sales agent in one office of Martin Realty has a listing. A sales agent in another branch of Martin Realty has a buyer for this listing but does not represent the buyer. Which of these statements is CORRECT about the agency relationships?

    A. The buyer has client status
    B. There is a dual agency since Martin Realty is the agent of both parties
    C. Martin Realty is the agent for the seller
    D. None of the answers shown

57. A disadvantage of a transaction broker is

    A. the buyer and seller do not have access to the services of a real estate broker
    B. there are no negotiations for a property
    C. the transaction broker is not necessarily a licensee
    D. the buyer and/or seller do not receive the fiduciary duties of an agency relationship

58. Termination of an agency relationship may be accomplished by

    A. completion of the objective
    B. expiration of the listing agreement
    C. mutual agreement
    D. all of the answers shown

Property Conditions, Disclosures, and Transfer of Title

59. Shanice, a real estate agent, is listing a property that the owner described as having asbestos and drainage problems. If Shanice does not mention this to the potential buyers or other brokers, she would be

    A. keeping her fiduciary duty of loyalty
    B. guilty of fraudulent misrepresentation
    C. obtaining a better price for the seller
    D. guilty of innocent misrepresentation

60. Whose responsibility is it to make a last minute inspection of the purchased premises before closing to insure that the property is in the same condition as it was when it was sold?

    A. Seller
    B. Buyer
    C. Broker
    D. Appraiser

61. Sales contracts for properties covered under the Residential Lead-Based Hazard Reduction Act must include which of the following?

    A. Nothing different than before the law was enacted
    B. Specific disclosure and acknowledgment language
    C. Approval by an agent of HUD
    D. An attachment indicating the exact age of the property

62. For a deed to be recorded, it must have a(n)

    A. metes and bounds description
    B. *habendum* clause
    C. acknowledgment
    D. covenant of warranty

63. A standard form used by lenders to demonstrate charges paid at closing is called

    A. HUD Form No. 1
    B. a satisfaction of mortgage
    C. a bill of sale
    D. a certificate of title

64. New home warranties are generally provided by which of the following parties?

    A. The builder
    B. Independent companies from whom the builder purchases coverage
    C. Third-party companies contracted by the homeowner that supplement the builder's coverage
    D. All of the answers shown

65. An unbroken transfer of successive titles to real property is called a(n)

    A. abstract continuation
    B. title search
    C. chain of title
    D. abstract of title

66. Under the Real Estate Settlement Procedures Act (RESPA), what document must lenders furnish to a buyer within three working days of receiving a completed loan application?

    A. A copy of the appraisal of the property
    B. The amount of the broker's commission
    C. A good faith estimate
    D. A copy of the abstract of tile

67. A short sale is a sale of real property

    A. that takes only one month to sell from the date of the listing
    B. in which the sale proceeds are less than the balance owed to the lender
    C. valued under $50,000
    D. that does not involve a formal closing

68. Property eligible for a tax-deferred exchange does NOT include a(n)

    A. industrial property
    B. commercial property
    C. personal residence
    D. hotel or motel

Leases, Rents, and Property Management

69. A leasehold that automatically renews unless proper notice is given is a(n)

    A. estate for years
    B. periodic estate
    C. estate at will
    D. estate at sufferance

70. Who has a reversionary interest in a leased property?

    A. Possessor
    B. Tenant
    C. Lessee
    D. Lessor

71. A lease requiring the tenant to pay a fixed rental computed per square foot, as well as the real property taxes, is a

    A. space lease
    B. gross lease with add-ons
    C. net lease
    D. ground lease

72. An apartment tenant's right of quiet enjoyment means that

    A. the owner can never enter the property without the tenant's permission
    B. other tenants in the building must respect rules regarding noise
    C. unless stated otherwise in the contract, the owner must have the tenant's permission to enter the property with the exception of emergencies
    D. the owner must perform upkeep of the premises

73. To legally remove a tenant from possession of the premises is called

    A. eviction
    B. actual eviction
    C. mitigating damages
    D. holdover tenancy

74. If a tenant dies during the term of the lease, which of the following is TRUE?

    A. The lease is null and void
    B. The lease passes to his or her estate
    C. The landlord can immediately lock up the apartment
    D. His or her estate is no longer responsible for the rent

75. The management agreement automatically creates a

    A. specific agency
    B. general agency
    C. joint tenancy
    D. power of attorney

76. A manager's role in public relations does NOT include which of the following?

    A. Effective use of the media
    B. Community involvement
    C. Feasibility studies
    D. Owner–tenant relations

77. Condominium and cooperative property managers' duties mostly involve

    A. physical maintenance of the property
    B. drafting the proprietary lease
    C. developing the offering plan
    D. communicating with the state attorney general's office

78. Property income and expenses for week-to-week operations are computed in which type of budget?

    A. Capital reserve
    B. Variable expense
    C. Stabilized
    D. Operating

79. With regard to maintenance, a property manager must

    A. supervise physical property maintenance
    B. routinely inspect the building
    C. analyze the building's needs
    D. perform all of the answers shown

80. Manuel rents out six apartments in his building for $750 per month and seven apartments for $1,050 per month. Figuring in a 5% vacancy rate, what is the annual projected rent roll?

    A. $135,090
    B. $139,500
    C. $142,200
    D. $185,300

Brokerage Operations and the Practice of Real Estate

81. A broker must maintain a separate trust account, also known as a(n)

    A. earnest money deposit
    B. commingling account
    C. escrow account
    D. conversion account

82. Broker Maurice places an ad that states: *House, 1/2 acre, 3 bedrooms, 1 bath, $126,000. If interested, please call 555-1234.* Which of the following describes this ad?

    A. Legitimate
    B. Blind ad
    C. Violation of fair housing laws
    D. Net listing

83. In a broker's office, the procedures manual for independent contractor/sales associates should not include

    A. how to develop a marketing plan for a listing
    B. how to enter a listing into the multiple listing service computer
    C. the day and time of the mandatory weekly office meetings
    D. floor duty responsibilities

84. Aliyah is a real estate broker whose sales agents are independent contractors. The employment agreement with the sales agent should include

    A. a statement explaining the minimum wage law
    B. the fact that the sales associate will be paid solely on commission
    C. health and unemployment insurance information
    D. the days and hours that the sales associate must be on duty

85. A zoning law in Storyville does not allow a brokerage firm to place a clear sign on his or her business indicating that the business is a real estate brokerage firm. However, the real estate commission requires a clear and readable sign. What must the broker do?

    A. Find another location for his or her office
    B. Refuse to violate license law to comply with other laws
    C. Apply for a variance for the sign
    D. All of the answers shown

86. Richard, a real estate agent, had Kathleen's land listed for sale at $70,000 when he found a developer who would pay $80,000 for the property. Richard purchased the property from Kathleen for the full listed price, but failed to inform her of the higher resale offer. He then sold the land for $80,000 to the developer. Which of the following is TRUE? Richard, the real estate agent, has

A. done nothing wrong since Kathleen received the price she wanted

B. done nothing wrong since he didn't have a completed offer from the developer before the closing on Kathleen's land

C. violated the duty of loyalty to his principal, Kathleen

D. violated the duty of loyalty to his principal, the developer

87. Commission fees for a real estate broker should be decided by

A. negotiation with the principal

B. guidelines published by the local REALTOR® board

C. schedules established by the real estate commission

D. schedules established by the multiple listing service

88. A broker who conducts business as a sole proprietorship under an assumed name is classified as which type of broker?

A. Associate

B. Individual

C. Trade name

D. Corporate

89. A type of organization that avoids a double tax on trust income is known as a(n)

A. real estate investment trust

B. S corporation

C. trust fund

D. limited liability company

90. When a real estate brokerage firm establishes active online communication with a consumer about real estate services with the intent to form a brokerage relationship through e-mail, instant message, webcam, or VON (voice on net), this is called

A. active solicitation

B. passive solicitation

C. privileged solicitation

D. none of the answers shown

91. Broker J brought prospective buyers to a certain community because he believed they would be happier due to their ethnic origin. This violation of the Federal Fair Housing Act is specifically called

A. blockbusting
B. redlining
C. steering
D. harassment

92. Which of the following statements is an example of blockbusting?

A. Manuel showed an African American couple housing in a predominantly African American neighborhood
B. ABC Realty sold a home to a person in a protected class in the attempt to make the homeowners panic and place their property for sale at reduced prices
C. Janet refused a loan to a Latino family who wanted to move into her predominantly white neighborhood
D. Chuck printed an ad for his apartment building that targeted college-age students

93. Under the Federal Fair Housing Act, which of the following must be displayed prominently in the broker's office?

A. Fair Housing Poster
B. All salespersons' licenses
C. A certificate of Fair Housing Compliance
D. The National Association of REALTORS® (NAR) Code of Ethics

94. The Americans with Disabilities Act applies mainly to which types of properties?

A. Duplexes
B. Residential single-family houses
C. Commercial and public facilities and multi-family housing
D. Hospitals and housing for the physically challenged only

95. Broker Betty has lunch with some area brokers to discuss what fees she should charge in her new office. This is considered to be

A. illegal price fixing
B. a good business practice
C. ethical standards
D. a fair housing violation

96. Megan's Law amended the 1994 federal Violent Crime Control and Law Enforcement Act. What effect did this amendment have?

    A. Protects single mothers with more than one child against discrimination
    B. Prevents discrimination against sex offenders while they are seeking housing
    C. Requires a public registry of known sex offenders
    D. Requires sellers to disclose the location of sex offenders in their neighborhood

Real Estate Math

97. A broker's commission is 7% of the first $100,000 of the sales price and 6% of the amount over $100,000. What is the total selling price of the property if the broker receives a total commission of $10,000?

    A. $100,000
    B. $125,000
    C. $150,000
    D. $175,000

98. A lot measuring 128.5 feet × 236.2 feet would be what percentage of an acre?

    A. 30%
    B. 36%
    C. 54%
    D. 70%

99. An 11.75% loan has an interest charge this month of $849.43. What is the balance of the loan when this payment was made?

    A. $7,229
    B. $83,173
    C. $86,750
    D. $99,808

100. If the tax value is 50% and the assessed value is $89,990, what are the annual taxes if the rate is $4.10 per $100 (rounded)?

    A. $1,844.80
    B. $10,822.22
    C. $1,484.44
    D. $5,444.44

MULTIPLE CHOICE

Identify the choice that best completes the statement or answers the question.

Property Ownership

1. Which of the following is not a "stick" in the bundle of rights to real property?

   A. Mineral rights
   B. Profit
   C. Mortgage
   D. Chattel

2. Of all the characteristics of land, which one has the greatest effect on property value?

   A. Uniqueness
   B. Scarcity
   C. Location
   D. None of the answers shown

3. A description of real property used by surveyors that incorporates permanent objects on the land is called

   A. metes and bounds
   B. description by monument
   C. section, block, and lot
   D. reference to a plat

Broker 100-Question Practice Exam

4. Custom draperies or cabinets that are sized for a certain area, even if not attached, are fixtures by

   A. adaptation
   B. agreement
   C. attachment
   D. usage

5. Fiona and Osborn own property jointly. Fiona owns 80% while Osborn owns 20%. Upon Fiona's death, her interest in the property will go to her favorite charity while Osborn's ownership interest will go to his wife. The type of concurrent ownership Fiona and Osborn have is

   A. joint tenancy
   B. tenancy in common
   C. tenancy by the entirety
   D. estate for years

6. The right of survivorship in real estate can be described as the right of

   A. co-owners to automatically receive the interest of the deceased co-owner upon his or her death
   B. heirs to receive the co-owner's share of real estate as provided in his or her last will and testament
   C. two or more people to hold title to a property at the same time
   D. the bank to automatically receive ownership upon the death of the mortgagor

7. Fabian and Frannie, who are brother and sister, own a property jointly. They have equal percentages of ownership in the property, and they received their title at the same time from the same source. They have the right to undivided possession in the property. If Fabian dies, his share will automatically go to Frannie and vice versa. The type of concurrent ownership Fabian and Frannie have is

   A. joint tenancy
   B. tenancy in common
   C. leasehold
   D. estate for years

8. An easement can be defined as a(n)

   A. parcel of land
   B. nonpossessory use of land by another
   C. easier route through a property
   D. structure that facilitates drainage

9. A lien is best defined as

   A. a privilege to do a particular act
   B. the right to enter a parcel of land
   C. a claim that one person has against the property of another for a debt
   D. the money paid for compensation to use one's land

10. A characteristic of a license to use another's land is that it is

    A. similar to a lien
    B. the same as an easement
    C. a temporary privilege
    D. a permanent privilege

Property Valuation, Market Analysis, and the Appraisal Process

11. A local housing market has a surge in new construction driving house prices down. This is an example of the economic principle of

    A. immobility
    B. scarcity
    C. situs
    D. supply and demand

12. The dollar expenditure for labor and materials is known as

    A. price
    B. cost
    C. investment value
    D. mortgage value

13. The gross rent multiplier is NOT used for

    A. large apartment buildings
    B. medium-sized income properties
    C. single-family residential properties
    D. large commercial properties

14. Properties such as schools, hospitals, and government office buildings are generally appraised by using the

    A. gross rent multiplier
    B. cost approach
    C. sales comparison approach
    D. income approach

15. Gilbert is appraising an apartment building in an average-income location. What adjustment is usually made when a comparable sale from a lower-income location is used in the appraisal report?

    A. A plus adjustment to the subject sales price
    B. A plus adjustment to the comparables sales price
    C. No adjustment is made for location
    D. The comparable would never be used

16. A property has recently been appraised. The value derived is

    A. an estimate
    B. the legal value
    C. the lowest amount a seller will accept
    D. the book value

17. One of the most important factors in selecting comparables for a comparative market analysis is to select properties

    A. within a 60-mile radius of the subject property
    B. older than the subject property
    C. as close in location as possible to the subject property
    D. that have inferior curb appeal to the subject property

18. For federal income tax purposes, which of the following CANNOT be used as a depreciable asset?

    A. Buildings
    B. Personal property
    C. Equipment
    D. Machinery

19. A process that calculates the value of an asset in the past, present, and future is called

    A. leverage
    B. the time value of money
    C. debt service
    D. net operating income

20. Truman, a licensed home inspector, wants to become a State Licensed Real Property Appraiser. Under federal law, to become a licensed real property appraiser, he must first become a(n)

    A. licensed real estate broker
    B. licensed mortgage broker
    C. appraisal trainee
    D. licensed real estate salesperson

Land Use Controls and Regulations

21. Subdivision regulations are primarily for the protection of the

    A. purchaser
    B. subdivider
    C. planning board
    D. general contractor

22. Homeowners' associations may use which of the following actions if homeowners do not comply with rules and regulations of the association?

    A. Lawsuit
    B. Eviction proceedings
    C. Fines to the homeowners
    D. All of the answers shown

23. J was forced to sell the state a portion of his front lawn because the roadway was being widened although he was compensated for the property. This is an example of

    A. escheat
    B. eminent domain
    C. voluntary alienation
    D. a grant to the state

24. The difference between police power and eminent domain can best be determined by whether

    A. any compensation was paid to an affected owner
    B. the action was by a governmental agency
    C. the owner's use was affected
    D. the improvements are to be destroyed

25. The planning board grants a nonconforming use for Xavier's property. Xavier can now

    A. zone his property commercial instead of residential in order to increase property value
    B. build a garage that is bigger than his property line
    C. operate a business from his home even though his community is zoned residential
    D. continue to operate a grocery store that existed before the neighborhood was zoned residential

26. A special assessment is

    A. illegal unless special permission is obtained from the state taxing agency
    B. only used where a state of emergency has been declared
    C. is a specific lien against the property until paid
    D. is a specific lien against the property owner until paid

27. The law that gives the Environmental Protection Agency (EPA) the authority to regulate chemicals is the

    A. Superfund Amendment
    B. Comprehensive Environmental Response, Compensation, and Liability Act
    C. Interstate Land Sales Full Disclosure Act
    D. Toxic Substances Control Act

28. So that liability for hazardous substances and other problems are not passed to new owners, lenders and purchasers may conduct certain reviews of the property called

    A. remedial evaluations
    B. due diligence
    C. feasibility studies
    D. highest and best use studies

29. The basis on which property is taxed is

    A. *in rem*
    B. certiorari
    C. *ad valorem*
    D. "as is"

30. Rafe had a mechanic's or construction lien against his property and a lien against his property for back taxes. He wishes to transfer the property. Which of the following applies? Rafe must pay

    A. only the mechanic's or construction lien
    B. only the lien that had been filed first in the county clerk's office
    C. only the property tax lien
    D. both liens

Contracts and Relationships with Buyers and Sellers

31. When the principals in a contract are not related either personally or in a business relationship, the transaction is called a(n)

    A. agency
    B. fiduciary
    C. arm's length
    D. parol evidence

32. The term "meeting of the minds" is synonymous with what essential of a contract?

    A. Consideration
    B. Offer and acceptance
    C. Competence
    D. Legality of object

33. Paulette told agent Lionel he could have the listing on her property. Nothing was put in writing. Later Paulette signed with another agent. Lionel sued Paulette for part of the commission. The court probably ruled that Lionel's contract is

    A. valid
    B. unenforceable
    C. executory
    D. unilateral

34. A developer entered into a contract to purchase a large tract of land for a housing subdivision. Before closing, the municipality exercised its right of eminent domain to take the land for a highway. The developer's contract to purchase can be terminated because of

    A. incompetent parties to the contract
    B. lack of consideration
    C. impossibility of performance
    D. none of the answers shown

35. When is a tax map, plat, or survey generally attached to a contract of sale?

    A. For all property purchases
    B. For the purchase of condos or coops
    C. If tracts of unimproved land or lots are sold
    D. Whenever the purchase price exceeds $1 million

36. At what point is legal title to real property generally transferred to the purchaser under an installment land contract?

    A. Upon execution of the contract
    B. Within 30 days after the contract is signed
    C. Upon the purchaser's full payment of the purchase price
    D. Upon the issuance of a satisfaction of mortgage by the lender

37. Which statement is TRUE regarding an option contract?

    A. An option is an express unilateral contract
    B. The optionee promises to allow the optionor the sole right to purchase the property by a specific date
    C. The optionor pays for the right to purchase by a specific date but does not promise to purchase
    D. Because two parties agree, the option is a bilateral contract

38. Upon receipt of a buyer's offer, a seller accepts all terms except the amount of earnest money. The seller agrees to accept an amount 20% higher than what the buyer has offered. The real estate agent communicates this fact to the buyer. Which of the following describes these events?

    A. The communication created a bilateral contract
    B. The seller accepted the buyer's offer
    C. The seller conditionally rejected the buyer's offer
    D. The seller rejected the buyer's offer and made a counteroffer to the buyer

39. Nigel had to pay Terrence $10,000 because he failed to purchase Terrence's house even though they had a valid contract. This monetary payment is known as

    A. liquidated damages
    B. rescission
    C. assignment
    D. novation

40. Broker Samuru received an offer to purchase after a contract was pending on the property. Although the new offer was lower than the pending contract, the terms for closing were more favorable to his sellers. Looking at a higher commission, broker Samuru decided not to present the new offer. His activity

    A. violates license law
    B. is perfectly acceptable
    C. is acceptable if the sellers are satisfied with the pending contract
    D. is acceptable if the pending contract has an attorney review clause

Financing

41. A financing concept that allows for paying the debt monthly and in which the interest portion of the payments decreases as the principal portion increases is called

    A. underwriting
    B. PITI
    C. loan to value
    D. amortization

42. If an outstanding mortgage balance is $50,000 on the payment date and the amount of the payment applied to interest is $250, what is the rate of interest charged on the loan?

   A. 5%
   B. 6%
   C. 7%
   D. 8%

43. A mortgage clause that allows the borrower to force the release of the lien if the debt is paid in full is a(n)

   A. *habendum* clause
   B. defeasance clause
   C. alienation clause
   D. acceleration clause

44. Paul has $350,000 equity in his building. He wants to free up this equity but retain possession and control of the building since he has his offices there. What type of transaction might meet his objectives?

   A. Gross lease
   B. Net lease
   C. Percentage lease
   D. Sale leaseback

45. The difference between conventional loans and government loans is that

   A. conventional loans involve no participation by an agency of the federal government
   B. conventional loans are not available in many areas
   C. conventional loans are not available for first-time buyers
   D. government loans are only available for single-family home purchases

46. Sheila obtained an FHA mortgage. Which of the following was required at closing to protect the lender in case of default?

   A. Life insurance
   B. Mortgage insurance premium
   C. A current appraisal of the property
   D. A survey

47. Which of the following about Regulation Z is FALSE? It

    A. regulates interest rates
    B. provides specific consumer protections in regard to mortgage loans
    C. does not apply to commercial transactions
    D. applies to loans to purchase real property

48. Which of the following is FALSE regarding subprime borrowers? They

    A. have less-than-perfect credit ratings
    B. have low incomes
    C. only qualify for mortgages below $200,000
    D. may pay a higher interest rate for a loan

Law of Agency

49. A real estate agent is generally a(n)

    A. special agent
    B. general agent
    C. attorney-in-fact
    D. principal

50. What do subagents, listing agents, seller agents, and single agents have in common? They

    A. are all dual agents
    B. all represent the seller
    C. all must belong to a multiple listing service
    D. are all cooperating agents

51. Seller Armand, who does not want to talk to a real estate broker who claims to have a buyer for Armand's land, tells the broker that Jenkins Realty handles all of his real estate dealings. Even though there is no formal agency contract with Jenkins Realty, Armand may have created an agency by

    A. extension
    B. estoppel
    C. authority
    D. misrepresentation

52. Customers Sam and Jeanne receive a referral from the seller's broker, Halite, for a mortgage broker. Broker Halite receives a referral fee from the mortgage broker but does not tell her sellers. Which of the following is TRUE?

    A. Halite has violated her duty of disclosure
    B. Halite may not accept a referral fee under any circumstances
    C. The lender must disclose the referral fee to the sellers
    D. Halite has done nothing wrong

53. Wendy has entered into an agreement with the expectation of buying a lot to build a house. She has only committed to buy the lot within the next six months or otherwise lose her right to buy along with her deposit. She has probably signed a(n)

    A. exclusive agency agreement
    B. exclusive-right-to-sell agreement
    C. open listing agreement
    D. option to purchase

54. The extent of the obligations and responsibilities of one who acts for another in the agency relationship is set forth in the

    A. contract of sale
    B. property condition disclosure statement
    C. agency disclosure form
    D. brokerage contract

55. Mick, a real estate agent, tells his principal, Phil, that the only offer on his property was $5,000 below the asking price. Phil needs to sell his home, and so accepts the offer. The buyer was Mick's brother-in-law, and Mick had avoided telling Phil about other offers. Mick is guilty of

    A. illegal self-dealing
    B. unintentional misrepresentation
    C. implied agency
    D. nothing

56. Broker Blue lists a property and wants to buy it and collect the commission offered by the listing agreement. Broker Blue

    A. is acting as a dual agent
    B. is acting as the listing agent only
    C. is prohibited by law from purchasing
    D. has a defense to liability if he has his wife purchase the property without disclosing their relationship to the seller

57. A type of real estate licensee that represents neither the seller nor the buyer in an agency relationship is a

    A. dual agent
    B. transaction agent
    C. subagent
    D. all of the answers shown

58. When an agency contract terminates,

    A. so does an agent's authority to act on behalf of the principal
    B. an agent can complete unfinished business of the principal
    C. the listing agreement is always automatically renewed
    D. the principal cannot contract with another brokerage firm for a one-month period

Property Conditions, Disclosures and Transfer of Title

59. Neal, a real estate agent who represents the lessees, does NOT disclose to his lessees that the two-family property they are renting was built before 1978 and may contain lead-based paint. The lessees only pay his commission. Which of the following is TRUE?

    A. Neal, as the lessees' agent, does not have a duty to disclose because his commission is being paid by the lessees
    B. Neal has violated the Residential Lead-Based Paint Hazard Reduction Act
    C. Neal only needs to disclose the possible presence of lead-based paint in properties built before 1968
    D. Neal does not have a duty to disclose because the law only applies to home purchase, not rental

60. Due-diligence reviews of a property before title transfer protects which of the following from liability for environmental problems after title transfer?

    A. Seller
    B. Tenant
    C. Lender
    D. All of the answers shown

61. Which of the following laws seeks reimbursement from responsible parties who have caused hazardous waste?

    A. Real Estate Settlement Procedures Act
    B. Comprehensive Environmental Response, Compensation, and Liability Act
    C. Interstate Land Sales Full Disclosure Act
    D. Residential Lead-Based Paint Hazard Reduction Act

62. Jackson buys a new home and receives a deed. Jackson's recording of this deed provides

    A. actual transfer of the deed
    B. protection against any previous liens or claims
    C. constructive notice effective against any subsequent claims
    D. proof of free and clear title for Jackson

63. Which of the following would most likely prevent a closing from taking place?

    A. The imposition of discount points by the lender
    B. The hiring of an attorney by the purchaser
    C. The existence of outstanding unpaid liens against the property
    D. A purchase money mortgage given to the purchaser by the seller

64. When closing on a mortgage, a title insurance policy

    A. is only issued upon receipt of an acceptable abstract or title opinion
    B. is not generally required by lenders
    C. is routinely issued even without an acceptable abstract of title
    D. can only be issued by a state insurance department after an examination of all records pertaining to the property

65. The Travers sell their five-year old house to the Shaws and pay for a one-year home warranty for the Shaws with an option that the Shaws could extend the warranty if they wanted to. Which of the following would be generally covered under this home warranty?

    A. Sprinkler system
    B. Swimming pool
    C. Items in violation of local codes
    D. Furnace

66. The Real Estate Settlement Procedures Act (RESPA) applies to

    A. residential federally financed or refinanced properties
    B. commercial properties
    C. owner-financed properties
    D. all properties purchased since 2001

67. After foreclosure, the bank informed Shannon that she still owed the bank money. The type of judgment taken by the bank against Shannon is a(n)

    A. redemption
    B. construction
    C. deficiency
    D. *lis pendens*

68. Marcus is single, has lived in his house for the last two years, and is in the 10% tax bracket. He sells his primary residence for a profit of $350,000. How much does he owe in capital gains tax?

    A. $52,500
    B. $17,500
    C. $15,000
    D. $5,000

Leases, Rents, and Property Management

69. A type of estate that exists for a fixed period is a(n)

    A. estate for years
    B. estate at will
    C. freehold estate
    D. periodic estate

70. Which of the following is NOT an element of a lease?

    A. Demising clause
    B. Signatures of the lessor and lessee
    C. *Habendum* clause
    D. Description of premises

71. Which type of lease generally contains an option to renew and a right of first refusal?

    A. Most residential leases
    B. A proprietary lease
    C. Office building leases only
    D. Commercial leases

72. The 1988 Amendments to the Federal Fair Housing Act provides that an owner who has a tenant with disabilities must

    A. make minor modifications to accommodate the life functions of the person with disabilities
    B. give permission to the tenant with disabilities to renovate the premises to accommodate his/her life functions at the tenant's cost
    C. grant permission to the tenant to make necessary modifications at the owner's expense
    D. provide whatever adjustments are needed to fit the life functions of the tenant

73. When the owner dies, the lease agreement

    A. is terminated
    B. is binding on the heirs
    C. reverts to a tenancy from month to month
    D. is considered void

74. Patsy had no heat in her apartment for two months, but decided to tough it out because it was a warm spring. Two months later, she moved out claiming constructive eviction, and asked the court to let her out of her lease obligations. Which of the following applies?

    A. The court will probably let Patsy out of her lease obligations
    B. Patsy cannot claim constructive eviction
    C. Patsy did not breach her lease
    D. An actual eviction has occurred

75. A property manager gives a detailed presentation to the owner for his or her plan to acquire new tenants. This is called a

    A. management agreement
    B. management proposal
    C. property management report
    D. marketing plan

76. A property manager's primary function for an owner is

    A. collecting rents
    B. residing on the property if the use is residential
    C. screening and locating tenants
    D. providing the greatest net return possible

77. Cooperative property managers are generally employees of the

    A. cooperative corporation
    B. individual apartment owners
    C. lenders who hold the underlying mortgage on the property
    D. holders of the proprietary leases

78. A type of budget used for forecasting income and expenses over a number of years is a(n)

    A. capital expense budget
    B. operating budget
    C. variable expense budget
    D. stabilized budget

79. To save money in the management of property, a manager should

    A. subcontract individuals for maintenance duties
    B. take a substantial cut in his or her fees or commission
    C. perform less preventative maintenance
    D. perform less corrective maintenance

80. Blair Management purchased an office building for $625,000 and the total rents received amount to $83,500 annually. Annual expenses total $44,000. What rate of return does Blair Management receive?

    A. 6.32%
    B. 7.04%
    C. 7.49%
    D. 13.36%

Brokerage Operations and the Practice of Real Estate

81. A licensee who deposits an earnest money check in his or her personal checking account instead of in the broker's escrow account would be guilty of

    A. conversion
    B. escheat
    C. commingling
    D. prescription

82. Broker Molly placed a clever ad for a property that implies that she was the owner and did not indicate that she was a real estate broker. This ad is

    A. allowable under MLS rules for advertising
    B. a good way to have someone to call on the ad
    C. a violation of antitrust laws
    D. a blind ad

83. A broker's primary duty to his or her independent contractor/sales agents is

    A. issuing W-2s
    B. enforcing strict work hours
    C. paying the agents a base salary
    D. supervision

84. Broker Lately had several salespeople in the firm, all of whom had not renewed their licenses, which had come due last month. Broker Lately

    A. should not allow these salespeople to transact real estate
    B. may allow the salespeople to transact as it is not the broker's responsibility to ensure salespeople renew their licenses
    C. may allow the salespeople to service existing listings but not obtain new listings
    D. may allow the salespeople to discuss listings and negotiate real estate transactions in the office only but not drive buyers around or visit sellers

85. While a broker was listing a property, the owner told the broker that the house contains 2,400 square feet of heated living area. Relying on this information, the broker represented the property to prospective buyers as containing 2,400 square feet. After purchasing the property, the buyers accurately determined that the house had only 1,850 square feet and sued for damages for the difference in value between 2,400 square feet and 1,850 square feet. Which of the following is CORRECT?

    A. The broker is not liable because he or she relied on the seller's positive statement as to the square footage
    B. The seller is not liable because the broker, not the seller, represented the property to the buyer as containing 2,400 square feet
    C. The theory of caveat emptor applies; thus, neither the seller nor the broker is liable to the buyer
    D. Both the broker and the seller may be liable to the buyer

86. Andy, a real estate broker, negotiated the sale of a single-family house. Both buyer and seller signed the contract of sale, the contract was reviewed and approved by attorneys for both parties, and financing was approved. A day before closing, the buyer wanted to back out of the deal. Andy

    A. must now forfeit his commission because it is unearned
    B. take a lesser commission than arranged because of the new circumstances
    C. is entitled to the full commission as originally agreed upon
    D. must forfeit his commission because the deal involves residential real estate, and if it does not close, the broker cannot be compensated

87. The company dollar in a real estate brokerage firm indicates

    A. the costs to operate
    B. the balance of the firm's commissions after deducting the commissions to salespeople
    C. the portion of revenue that belongs to the brokerage firm after deductions for the cost of operation
    D. the firm's profit indicated on the income and expense statement

88. Karli and Jacob are partners in Success Realty. They are both personally liable for partnership debts exceeding partnership assets. What type of partnership is this?

    A. Limited partnership
    B. Dual partnership
    C. Equal partnership
    D. General partnership

89. The name of Camille's real estate firm is Sweet Home Associates, Inc. Her company would be classified as a

    A. sole proprietorship
    B. trade name
    C. corporation
    D. none of the answers shown

90. When advertising on the Internet, brokers

    A. can advertise in any format they want
    B. should obtain legal advice so they are in compliance with local, state, and federal guidelines
    C. should limit Internet use as much as possible
    D. must only show listings but cannot solicit customers

91. The term blockbusting refers to

    A. phone calls soliciting prospective buyers or sellers in certain target areas
    B. offering property for sale only to persons of a certain race
    C. causing panic selling with the goal of obtaining listings
    D. the government's right of eminent domain to condemn and destroy older vacant buildings in a neighborhood

92. The lending department of Money Bank decided not to make home improvement loans to residents of Lonely Heights because a survey completed by the bank showed a higher number of single-parent families living in that neighborhood. Money Bank is guilty of

    A. redlining
    B. steering
    C. blockbusting
    D. nothing at all

93. When testers visit a real estate office, they are mostly looking for evidence of

    A. redlining
    B. price fixing
    C. racial steering
    D. blockbusting

94. Commercial Properties, a large brokerage firm, does not belong to the local board of REALTORS® or multiple listing service (MLS). A notice is sent from the board telling its members not to show any properties listed by Commercial Properties. Which of the following is TRUE?

    A. The board is illegally promoting a group boycott against Commercial Properties
    B. The board has the right to dictate to its members with whom they may or may not do business
    C. Commercial Properties must belong to both a real estate board and an MLS in order to do business with members of the MLS
    D. Even if the board promotes a group boycott, this is legal since it involves intra-state commerce

95. To comply with the Americans with Disabilities Act (ADA), alterations must be made to existing public accommodations and commercial facilities

    A. if food is served
    B. for transportation
    C. if over 50 years old
    D. if readily achievable

96. Which of the following activities by multiple listing services are allowable under antitrust laws? Multiple listing servces

    A. may refuse any listing lower than 7% of the sales price
    B. can dictate commission rates between REALTOR® board members and their clients
    C. may not circulate information regarding the commission that a broker has agreed upon with his or her client
    D. may limit membership to individuals who are licensed real estate brokers and salespersons

Real Estate Math

97. An 11% loan for $95,000 is made with principal and interest payments of $898.93 per month. What is the balance after the first payment?

    A. $10,450
    B. $94,129.17
    C. $94,101.07
    D. $94,971.90

98. A house has an assessed value of $142,000. The property is taxed at 80% of assessed value at a rate of $2.12 per $100. If the assessed valuation is increased by 18%, what is the amount of taxes to be paid on the property?

    A. $2,638.49
    B. $2,841.82
    C. $4,232.50
    D. $4,567.23

99. The net monthly income of a five-unit apartment building is $4,600. The capitalization rate the lender uses is 6%. What is the value of the building (rounded)?

    A. $76,666
    B. $760,000
    C. $92,222
    D. $920,000

100. A percentage lease stipulates a minimum rent of $1,200 per month and 3% of the lessee's annual gross sales over $260,000. The total rent paid by the end of the year is $16,600. What is the lessee's gross business income for the year?

    A. $73,333.33
    B. $260,000.00
    C. $333,333.33
    D. $553,333.33

Answer Section

Topic 1: Property Ownership

1. C
Real property consists of land and everything permanently attached to land, as well as the rights of ownership.

2. A
The bundle of rights refers to all rights an owner may have in real property. Condemnation is an action to take a property after a government's claim of eminent domain. Water rights are one stick or ownership right in the bundle of rights. Chattel is a term for personal property.

3. D
Possession, leasing real property, or occupying real property are part of a leasehold estate and do not necessarily include other ownership rights. Of the choices in the question, only the right to sell is evidence of ownership rights.

4. A
Littoral rights apply to property bordering a stationary body of water, such as a lake or a sea. In contrast, riparian rights belong to the owner of property bordering a flowing body of water.

5. B
Real property is the land and improvements, and all legal rights, powers, and privileges of real estate ownership. Personal property is readily movable. A license is a personal privilege to do a particular act or series of acts on the land of another. Subsurface rights of a property include the right to the area below the ground.

6. B
Personal property is everything that is not real property, and not attached to land. Real property is a term for land and its legal rights and that does not have readily movable attachments. Real estate is the land and all of its improvements and is not readily movable.

7. B
Sales contracts and purchase offers are used in the sale of real property. H will most likely use a bill of sale to sell personal belongings such as household furnishings.

8. C
The gradual building up of land in a watercourse over time by deposits of silt, sand, and gravel is called accretion. Alluvion is increased soil, gravel, or sand on a stream bank resulting from the flow or current of the water. The sudden loss or gain of land because of water movement or shift in a river bed used as a boundary is called avulsion. Accrual is an accounting term.

9. D
Because of the quarry, Isaac possesses subsurface and mineral rights. Riparian rights also belong to the owner of property bordering a flowing body of water such as a river.

10. C
Lis pendens is legal notice that a lawsuit is pending affecting title or possession of a specific property. Transcript of judgment is a legal record of the judgments of a debtor. An involuntary lien occurs through a legal proceeding in which a creditor places a claim on real and/or personal property to obtain payment of a debt. A general lien is a claim against a person and all of his or her property.

11. B
Chattel is another name for personal property. Real property is the land, improvements to the land, and the rights of property owners. Rights to the area above the earth are air rights.

12. C

Riparian rights belong to the owner of property bordering a flowing body of water. Percolating water is underground water drawn by wells. Littoral rights apply to property bordering a stationary body of water, such as a lake or sea.

13. C

A formal legal description of the land such as a metes and bounds description or reference to a plat, lot, or block is necessary for a deed.

14. D

A description by reference in a deed refers to a description that is in another document. Therefore, the description is not always repeated in a document such as a deed but refers to another already recorded document. Therefore, all of the statements in the question apply.

15. C

A reference to a lot and block number is generally found on municipal tax maps and various forms of deeds. A mortgage is a written instrument used to pledge title to real property to secure payment of a promissory note. A closing statement is a description and outline of the debits and credits due to the buyer and seller at settlement. A contract of sale is a contract between parties to purchase a property.

16. B

A metes and bounds description on a deed can be recognized by the fact that the description starts at a point of beginning. The number of degrees in a direction may be in a metes and bounds description, and also the size of the property, but is not the describing factor. The placement of monuments is another type of property description.

17. D

A metes and bounds description is created from a survey of the property by a licensed surveyor.

18. B

Trade fixtures are items of personal property that a business owner installs in rented building space, and they are presumed to remain personal property. Estates in land are divided into two groups: freehold estates and nonfreehold estates. A stick in the bundle of rights refers to tangible and intangible rights that come with real property. Common elements are the space that all residents have in common to use.

19. B

Application is not a method by which items become fixtures in real property. Attachment refers to the physical connection of objects to the real estate. For example, lumber to build a structure is personal property when delivered to the building site. By attachment and intent of the builder, the lumber becomes a building on the land. Adaptation refers to how an object fits the real estate. Custom draperies or cabinets that are sized for a certain area, even if not attached, are examples. Agreement refers to those items specified by an owner that include part of the real estate and those that are not included.

20. D

Personal property that attaches permanently to the land or improvements and becomes part of the real property is a fixture. Chattel is another name for personal property. Attachment is one way in which a fixture becomes part of the real property. Common elements refer to those areas available to all owners in a condominium such as the elevators, yard, or roof.

21. A

A fee simple defeasible estate is similar to a fee absolute except that there are conditions of ownership as in the question. A life estate is only owned for the owner's lifetime. Tenancy in common refers to two or more people holding title to a property at the same time. In a partnership, a business is owned by two or more people.

22. C

A life estate is only owned for the owner's lifetime. Fee simple absolute ownership is the most complete form of inheritable property ownership. Joint tenancy is ownership between two or more people in which each owner has the right of survivorship. A cooperative is a type of property ownership in which the owner receives shares of stock in a cooperative corporation.

23. D

With tenancy in common, there is no right of survivorship. Joint tenancy is ownership between two or more people in which each owner has the right of survivorship. A life estate is only owned for the owner's lifetime. There is not enough information in the question to know if Telly and Michael have formed a corporation.

24. A

A freehold estate is ownership for an undetermined length of time until, for example, the owner sells the property. Nonfreehold or leasehold estates define possession with a determinable end because they are rental estates. A life estate is ownership or possession for someone's lifetime.

25. B

A reversionary interest occurs if the possession of the property reverts back to the owner at the end of the life estate. Dower describes a life estate that is passed to the wife after her husband dies. A remainder interest occurs if the conveyance from the grantor is to the grantee for life, and then passes to another upon the grantee's death. An act of waste occurs when the life tenant abuses or misuses the property he is granted.

26. A

When a property is in the name of only one person or entity, it is an estate (ownership) in severalty. Joint tenancy is a form of co-ownership with the right of survivorship. A partnership is an ownership between two or more people or entities. Sole proprietorship refers to a sole owner of a business.

27. A

Unity of occupation is not a unity required between co-owners to be recognized as a joint tenancy. For a joint tenancy to be formed, certain unities must exist. The unity of time exists when co-owners receive their title at the same time in the same conveyance. The unity of interest exists if the co-owners all have the same percentage of ownership. The unity of possession exists if all co-owners have the right to possess or access all portions of the property owned, without physical division. This is called the possession of an undivided interest.

28. D

The estate of fee simple absolute provides the most complete form of ownership and bundle of rights in real property. This type of estate is called fee, fee simple, or fee simple absolute. Stacy's ownership includes all of the rights listed in the question.

29. D

An estate for a fixed time period is called an estate for years. An estate at sufferance occurs when a person does not leave the property after a lease has expired. An estate at will can be for any time frame. A freehold estate is an ownership estate.

30. C

A tenancy in common is defined by two or more owners who own a property together at the same time but do not have the right of survivorship. Ownership in severalty is ownership in the name of one person only. Joint tenancy is ownership by two or more individuals who have the right of survivorship. A leasehold estate is not an ownership but a rental estate.

31. B

Tenants in common do not have the right of survivorship. This means that upon the death of one owner, the remainder of the property does not automatically pass to the other owner or owners. The right of survivorship is a right of joint tenancy. In severalty is a type of ownership by one person. An estate at sufferance occurs when an individual continues to occupy property after lawful authorization has expired and is a form of leasehold estate.

32. C

A leasehold or rental estate implies possession but not ownership. A freehold estate is a type of ownership estate. A life estate is ownership of a property for one's life or the life of another. The estate of fee simple absolute provides the most complete form of ownership and bundle of rights in real property.

33. D

This question is an example of a life estate in remainder in which certain persons or entities, called remaindermen, are designated to receive the title upon termination of the life tenancy. A fee simple absolute estate is complete title to a property. A leasehold estate is not ownership but a rental estate. A joint tenancy is a type of ownership with the right of survivorship.

34. B

Fee simple on condition, fee simple defeasible, and life estates, although ownership estates, do not offer the most complete ownership as does fee simple absolute. A fee simple defeasible estate is an ownership estate that can be defeated if certain conditions of ownership are not met. A fee simple on condition is a type of a defeasible fee estate recognizable by words "but if." A life estate is a freehold ownership estate created for the duration of the life or lives of certain named persons.

35. B

The words "as long as" denote a qualified fee simple estate that is a defeasible estate. The estate can revert to the owner if certain conditions are not met. A fee simple absolute estate is complete title to a property. A life estate is a freehold (ownership) estate created for the duration of the life or lives of certain named persons. A nonfreehold estate is a leasehold estate that is not ownership but a rental estate.

36. A

Freehold estates describe ownership for an undetermined length of time, such as fee simple and life estates. A leasehold estate, created by a lease, is a nonfreehold estate of limited duration. A periodic estate or tenancy is a type of leasehold estate that renews itself automatically if no notice is given.

37. D

Fee simple ownership does not have to be conveyed as an estate in severalty (to one party). It can be conveyed to joint owners or tenants in common. Fee simple does allow the owner to dispose of the property at any time, is the most comprehensive title, and is a type of freehold estate.

38. B

A life estate, in this example, is a freehold estate that provides ownership, possession, and control for the life of the named individual(s). A defeasible estate, often used when someone wishes to donate land to a church or school for a specific purpose, is a fee simple estate with a condition or limitation attached. An estate for years has to do with tenancy for a specific time. An estate in severalty is ownership by one party.

39. B

Beverly and Jeff are perfect candidates for a home equity loan as they have complete equity in their home and full ownership. One must own the property to obtain a home equity loan although the mortgage need not be paid in full. Should Beverly and Jeff default on the home equity loan, the lender can bring forth foreclosure proceedings jeopardizing their ownership of the property.

40. C

In this example, Tony is a tenant in common with the other owners because he can go outside the tenancy and leave his share of the property to his brother. This cannot be accomplished with joint tenancy where the other co-owners have the right of survivorship. A remainderman is the party who inherits a life estate according to the terms of the estate. A life tenant is one who has a life estate in a property.

41. D

All of the answer choices apply. A life tenant must preserve and protect the property for the benefit of the reversionary interest or the remainderman and has the right to possess and enjoy the property. The life tenant may have a right to lease the property and receive income. This depends on the wording of the life estate.

42. A

A tenant in common may bring legal action to have the property partitioned. A partition allows each tenant to have a specific and divided portion of the property exclusively. If this action can be done equitably with a piece of land, each would receive title to a separate tract according to his or her share of interest. If it cannot physically be done, the court may order the sale of the property. The court then orders the appropriate share of proceeds distributed to the tenants in common.

43. C

Although no longer recognized in many states, the wife has a life estate called dower while the husband has curtesy rights. The term dowager refers to the woman herself and not to the life estate. The term courtesy means good manners. The term life tenant refers to one who owns a life estate in real property. Remainder refers to the type of ownership of a life tenant, which could be broadly used to describe the husband or wife in this situation.

44. A

A life tenant who "wastes" the property by not taking care of the property or by being irresponsible in its use is violating the right of estovers. Alienation refers to the transfer of property. The term reversion refers to a life estate returning to the original grantor. Encumbrance describes any lien or restriction on a property.

45. D

Periodic estates and estates for years are types of leasehold or rental estates and of limited duration. An estate for years exists only for a fixed time while a periodic estate automatically renews itself unless notice is given. A life estate is not limited by calendar time but is based on ownership, possession, or control for someone's lifetime. Dower rights refer to a widow's rights of ownership. Periodic estates and estates for years are not ownership or freehold estates.

46. C

Jeremy and Melissa are tenants in common because they do not share the unities of time and possession required for a joint tenancy to exist. They own the property so they do not possess a leasehold or rental estates. A *pur autre vie* estate is a type of life estate created for the duration of the life of a person other than the life tenant.

47. C

A *pur autre vie* estate, in the question, is a type of life estate created for the duration of the life of a person (Jack) other than the life tenant (Raul). *Caveat emptor* is a Latin term for "buyer beware." An unencumbered property is property free from any liens. An estate in severalty is ownership by one party.

48. C

The grounds, roof, hallways, elevators, and pools in a cooperative and condominium development are called common elements because all of the owners have access to them. Chattel is a term for personal property. A life estate is ownership for the life of certain named persons.

49. A

The right of occupancy to a cooperative is evidenced by a proprietary lease and not a deed as in other transfers of real property. The articles of incorporation are created when the cooperative corporation is formed. A bill of sale is for the sale of personal property.

50. D

The person receiving the title upon the death of the life tenant is called the remainderman; therefore, Jennifer has a life estate in remainder. A reversionary estate is created when a life estate returns to the original grantor. The term recession could be used to describe an economic downturn. A rescission is a cancellation.

51. B

   A cooperative apartment purchase is different from other types of property transactions because a cooperative purchase involves purchasing an interest in a corporation and receiving shares of stock as evidence of ownership of part of the cooperative corporation. Cooperative purchases are not necessarily more expensive than other real property purchases. A cooperative can be sold by a real estate licensee. Cooperative purchasers do not necessarily have to commit to a five-year lease term but may have to commit to some ownership time frame for some cooperatives.

52. A

   Covenants, conditions, and restrictions are rules that govern condominium ownership. Chattel, another name for personal property, is conveyed by a document called a bill of sale. Shares of stock are used to transfer cooperatives.

53. A

   Condominium purchasers receive a deed for the purchase of their condominium. Shares of stock and a proprietary lease are evidence of a cooperative purchase. A mortgage is not evidence of a purchase but a promise to pay a debt using the property as collateral.

54. B

   Cooperative purchasers receive a security interest in a cooperative corporation. Therefore, at closing, they receive a certain amount of assigned shares of stock to the unit they are purchasing. Cooperative purchasers do not receive a deed to their unit. A bill of sale is used for the sale of personal property.

55. B

   Financing for condominums is as readily available as other types of property and depends on borrower qualifications and economic conditions. Condominium ownership applies to both residential and commercial property. The owner owns the individual unit exclusively and the tenants use the common areas together.

56. A

   The reversion of an intestate (no will) decedent's property to the state is the power of escheat. The term appurtenance refers to the rights that an owner may have to sell or allow another to use his or her property. An owner can give someone a license to use his or her property, allow another to profit from the soil or other component of the property, and allow another water rights to the property. Note that these rights might be limited by government laws.

57. B

   Any object that intrudes on another's boundary line, such as a satellite dish, is an example of an encroachment. Appurtenances are ownership rights in real property. A license is a type of appurtenance and is permission to do something on the property of another.

58. B

   A deed restriction, that is, a limitation on property appearing on the deed, is not a lien, but an encumbrance that affects the property owner's use. A mortgage, judgment, and property tax are encumbrances and liens, because they are claims against another's property. An encumbrance is anything that lessens the bundle of rights in real property, but a lien is a special type of encumbrance.

59. A

   An encroachment is a trespass on land or an intrusion over the boundary of land. A survey of a boundary provides evidence of an encroachment. An encumbrance is a claim, lien, charge, or liability attached to and binding upon real property. An easement is a nonpossessory right of use in the land of another. Profit describes the right to take products of the soil from someone else's land, including soil, minerals, or timber.

60. B

   Ramon owns mineral rights to the property. Air rights are the ownership rights to the airspace above the property. Littoral rights are a type of water right and refer to the rights of a property owner whose land borders a stationary body of water such as a lake or sea.

61. A

A survey determines whether physical encroachments exist. A vendor's affidavit is a document that states that the seller has done nothing since the original title evidence to adversely affect title. Title insurance is a policy guaranteeing marketable title. A perc test determines whether the soil will support the proper functioning of a septic system.

62. D

Title is what the owner receives, generally through a deed, which gives him or her ownership to the property. An appurtenant right is a right that an owner gives to another to use his or her land through a license or another type of right such as a right to use water on the property or profit from the soil or land in some way.

63. A

An easement by necessity, and not an encroachment, is necessary when there is no access to roads from the property. Encroachments are created by the intrusion of a structure or object across a boundary line. The encroaching owner may be responsible for removing the encroachment. Encroachments, such as a fence dispute, may be determined by a survey of the property and sometimes disputes may lead to legal action.

64. C

An easement owner has the right to use and access the land. However, someone who owns an easement right does not own or have possession to the land where the easement lies. An easement can terminate under certain conditions and can be used for commercial purposes.

65. B

An easement is defined as a nonpossessory interest in land owned by another. The right a landlocked property owner has to cross his or her neighbor's property to the road is an example of an easement. The intrusion of driving into another's land is an encroachment. A landowner has the right to the crops produced on the land because the crops are personal property and having nothing to do with easements.

66. B

An easement by prescription is obtained by use of land without the owner's permission for a legally prescribed length of time. An easement by necessity exists when land has no access to roads and is landlocked.

67. D

An easement created by the government's right of eminent domain is called easement by condemnation. Easement by necessity exists when land has no access to roads and is landlocked. Easement by prescription is obtained by use of land without the owner's permission for a legally prescribed length of time. Easement by grant is created with the written express agreement of the landowners.

68. A

An easement in gross refers to a type of commercial easement; therefore, a utility pole would be an example. The other items are types of easement appurtenant such as a party wall, shared driveway, and right-of-way agreement.

69. D

The easement in gross is the most common form of easement, not the least used form of easement. An easement or right-of-way can be created by need, law, or use, and can be negative or affirmative. With an affirmative easement, the dominant tenement or estate has the right to physically cross the servient tenement. When a negative easement appurtenant exists, the dominant tenement does not have the right to enter the land of the servient tenement. Instead, the dominant tenement has the right to restrict some activity or use of the servient tenement. An easement may be commercial in nature and owned by the government, a government agency, or a public utility.

70. B

The land that benefits, in this case, B's property, from the easement appurtenant, is called the dominant tenement or estate. The land that serves the needs of the other property (allows the use) is called the servient tenement, in this case, A's driveway. The term easement refers to the nonpossessory use of the land. An easement appurtenant is the term used to describe all easements that are not commercial.

71. A

When an easement appurtenant follows the transfer of title to land from one owner to another and attaches to the land, this is called running with the land. Not enough information is given in the question to determine if the easement appurtenant is an easement by prescription, an easement in gross, or an easement by implication.

72. B

Easements by necessity may be granted by the courts when a property owner has no access to roads and is landlocked. Easements by condemnation are created by the government's exercise of the right of eminent domain. Encroachments are unauthorized use of another's property. Easements by grant are created by written agreement of the landowners.

73. D

Authorized use of another's property is called an easement. Encroachment would indicate Odetta is using the driveway without John's permission since encroachment is unauthorized use. A sublease would be taking place if Odetta were renting the driveway from John and then re-renting it to another party. An implied easement allows one to believe that there is an agreement regarding the driveway but no verbal or written language.

74. C

Easements by condemnation are created by the exercise of eminent domain for projects like road widening. Through this power, the government takes title to land and the right to use land in the future. An easement by prescription is obtained by a hostile use of another's land for a legally prescribed length of time. An easement by necessity may exist when a landowner has no access to roads and is landlocked. An easement by grant is created by the express written agreement between landowners.

75. A

General liens, in this example, are claims against a person (Casey) and all of her property. A specific lien, such as a mortgage, is a claim against a specific and readily identifiable property. A mechanic's or construction lien is a type of specific lien filed by a person who provided labor on a property. A mortgage lien exists when property has been used as collateral for a debt.

76. B

Mechanic's or construction liens receive priority because of the time and date of the filing. Mechanic's or construction liens do not receive preferential treatment because of the type of documentation required to record the lien, the amount of the lien, or any penalties assessed if they are not paid.

77. B

The mechanic's or construction lien refers to a specific lien filed by a supplier of labor or improvement to a building. "Laborer's" is not a type of lien. *Lis pendens* refers to notification of pending litigation on any number of liens. *In rem* does not refer to a lien, but to a legal proceeding that occurs when an action is brought against the property directly and not against an individual or his or her personal property.

78. A

A party wall is a type of cross-easement. A lien is claim against the property of another. An appurtenance is an ownership right such as a water right. A *lis pendens* is notice that a lawsuit is pending.

79. D

The term egress is the right to leave a parcel of land entered (ingress) by law. State income tax liens are liens against taxpayers who are delinquent in paying income tax. Mechanic's or construction liens are liens against suppliers and laborers who do not deliver supplies or finish contract labor. Real property tax liens are against property owners who are delinquent in paying property tax.

80. C
An unpaid lien can trigger foreclosure proceedings if the property transfers to the new owner and the lien remains unpaid.

Topic 2: Property Valuation, Market Analysis, and the Appraisal Process

1. D
The present use, the market value, and the use that best suits the neighborhood do not necessarily define highest and best use. It is the feasible use that will produce the highest present value.

2. A
Market value is generally the appraised value, and market price is what the property will sell for eventually. Replacement cost is the cost to rebuild a property. It is not generally the same as the market price. Value in use is the value a specific owner has for a particular property because of its uniqueness or function. This is not the same as market value. Buyers pay a market price; not necessarily the market value for a property.

3. D
$325,000 × 0.03 = $9,750
$325,000 + $9,750 = $334,750 = 1st year appreciation
$334,750 × 0.03 = $10,042.50
$334,750 + $10,042.50 = $344,792.50 = 2nd year appreciation
$344,792.50 × 0.03 = $10,343.775
$344,792.50 + $10,343.775 = $355,136.27 = 3rd year appreciation

4. D
Value in use is the uniqueness of a particular property to an owner and is not considered in highest and best use studies. Possible use considers the physical characteristics of the property. Permissible use is the use that is legally available for the land. Feasible use refers to the physical characteristics of the property and the legal controls that make the land appropriate for the market, neighborhood, and economic conditions. These three items are all part of a highest and best use analysis.

5. A
Valuation is the actual determination of a probable price while evaluation is not. A license is required for appraisals (valuations) for most lending purposes. There is no such thing as legal value. A comparative market analysis (CMA) and a valuation are similar, but not the same. An evaluation is not a formal appraisal.

6. B
If there are construction problems and time constraints, the cost of the property may exceed the market value. One reason is that time is money.

7. A
Evaluations do not necessarily produce an estimate of value, as does an appraisal or a comparative or competitive market analysis. (Both terms essentially mean the same thing.)

8. C
A property will probably not sell for market value if the buyer and seller are related to one another. The sale should be an arm's-length transaction in which the buyer and seller are not related in any way—personally or professionally.

9. C
Depreciation of real property is a loss of value from any cause. Economic obsolescence is a loss in value caused by events such as changes in surrounding land use patterns and failure to adhere to the principle of highest and best use. This can be one cause of property depreciation.

10. A

A front foot is defined as a linear foot of property frontage on a street or a highway. A fixture is personal property that has become real property by having been permanently attached to real property. An acre is a measurement for a plot of land containing 43,560 square feet.

11. A

100 ft. × 150 ft. = 15,000 sq. ft. (An acre is 43,560 sq. ft.)

12. B

Highest and best use is defined as the use that will bring the greatest return from the property to the owner. Highest and best use studies generally take community development goals into consideration. Value in use is specific to an owner and has nothing to do with the highest and best use of the property.

13. B

Surveyors' and appraisers' fees in relation to property development are indirect costs. Hard or direct costs are costs for labor and materials. Impact fees are made to the municipality by a developer for infrastructure and other requirements.

14. C

The only physical force in the choice of answers is climate. Plottage is the combining of two or more parcels of land into one tract that has more value than the total value of the individual parcels. Zoning regulations are laws enacted by local government.

15. D

An arm's-length transaction means that the parties are not related as relatives, friends, or business associates.

16. D

The profit on real property will decrease when competition occurs because there will be more housing choices on the market, which tend to drive prices down. The principle of contribution states that each portion of a property contributes to the property's ability to produce income.

17. C

Plottage refers to the combining of two or more parcels of land into one tract that has more value than the total value of the individual parcels.

18. B

The term for the value of a particular property for a certain investor is investment value. Insured value estimates the value of property as a basis for determining the amount of insurance coverage necessary to protect the structure adequately against loss by fire or any other casualty. Value in use is the value that a particular owner ascribes to the property. This value may not be the same for everyone.

19. D

Market analysis surveys the competition or supply and demand in the market place that a property will face upon sale attempts. The principle of anticipation is based on expectations or hopes of the future benefits of ownership.

20. B

The principle of anticipation is based on expectations or hopes of the future benefits of ownership. This is the underlying principle of the income approach as the appraiser attempts to analyze both the current and future income of a property. The principle of conformity states that general conformity among properties in a neighborhood produces maximum value for these properties. The principle of substitution states that, all other things being equal, a buyer will purchase a property that is offered at the lowest price. The principle of contribution states that each portion of a property contributes to the property's ability to produce income.

21. C

Topography is defined as the physical features and contours of land. How a property situates on a plot of land or how a subdivision is designed depends a great deal on the natural topography of the land.

22. B

The principle of anticipation is based on expectations or hopes of the future benefits of ownership. This is the underlying principle of the income approach as the appraiser attempts to analyze both current and future income of a property.

23. D

Population growth in an area is one social consideration that an appraiser analyzes to value a property. To analyze race, religion, or national origin in an appraisal report or any kind of market analysis violates fair housing laws.

24. A

The assessed value of a property is most relevant to a city or county budget official as it is used to determine the taxable base of property that is used to raise tax revenue. Insurance value is used to determine the amount of hazard insurance to be carried. Value in use reflects the value to an owner. Mortgage value is what a lender believes a property will bring at foreclosure.

25. D

Highest and best use analysis attempts to find the purpose of a site that brings the highest monetary return for the property.

26. A

A seller's market implies that there are not many available properties on the market and buyers' choices are fewer. Sellers can ask more money for their properties because they do not face stiff competition. This might lead to new construction, which in turn gives buyers more choices.

27. C

An appraisal is an unbiased estimate of value. The word, estimate, is important because the appraiser cannot find an exact value. The appraiser bases his findings on supported data from the market.

28. A

If the comparable has an item that is better than the subject property, the appraiser must subtract a certain dollar amount from the comparable. Although comparable properties are not exactly like the subject, the appraiser can still use them in the appraisal.

29. D

Because both the sales comparison approach and the comparative market analysis (CMA) compare properties that are similar to the subject, the CMA is most closely related to the sales comparison approach.

30. A

The cost approach values a property according to the cost to reproduce it. The income approach and appraisal by capitalization are the same and are used to value income-producing properties. The sales comparison approach uses comparables that are similar to the subject. These approaches do not consider the reproduction price for the property.

31. C

The most applicable approach for appraising single-family residential properties is the sales comparison approach. The sales comparison approach to value takes other very similar properties and adjusts their value to derive a value for the subject property. The cost and income approaches to value are used to value other types of properties.

32. A

The appraisal approach that considers the cost to replace a property that is similar to the original property but that uses modern building methods and materials is the cost approach-replacement cost. The income approach and appraisal by capitalization are the same and are used for income-producing properties. The sales comparison approach uses comparables that are similar to the subject. The cost approach-reproduction cost is an approach to value that estimates the cost of producing an exact replica of an existing building.

33. D

The principle of substitution states that, all other things being equal, a buyer will purchase a property that is offered at the lowest price. An appraiser uses this principle in comparing properties to one another to arrive at a value for the subject property using the sales comparison approach. Reconciliation occurs when an appraiser selects the most significant information from a variety of data and uses it to arrive at a value conclusion in the appraisal report. The principle of conformity states that general conformity among properties in a neighborhood produces maximum value for these properties. Demand is the level of need for a property in the market place.

34. D

The income approach to value is based on the principle of anticipation; that is, the prediction of future benefits or earnings. The approach looks for the potential gross income of the property and includes an estimate of the net operating income for the property. The sales comparison approach is not used to value income-producing properties.

35. B

Because there are few, if any, comparables and the properties are not income producing, the cost approach is generally used to appraise schools, hospitals, and other public buildings.

36. A

Reproduction cost and replacement cost may both be analyzed in the cost approach to value. The cost to produce an exact duplicate is the reproduction cost. The cost to produce a similar property is the replacement cost. Neither one is more or less accurate than the other. The choice depends on the property being appraised and the needs of the client.

37. A

Feasibility studies, highest and best use studies, and land utilization studies are all forms of evaluation studies. An appraisal of a single-family home is an estimate of value.

38. D

Federal and state laws including fair housing laws must be considered in the appraisal report. In addition, the Uniform Standards of Professional Appraisal Practice (USPAP) and the Appraisal Board Advisory Opinions, which are created and updated by the Appraisal Foundation, the government body that governs appraisal practice, must be followed.

39. A

The rental income for the property and the comparable sales price are the two elements that are used to derive the gross rent multiplier (GRM).

40. D

Functional obsolescence results from defects in the efficiency or functioning of a property such as a two-story residential property with only one bathroom. Conformity refers to properties in a neighborhood being the same or similar. External obsolescence is the effect on the value of a property from a problem nearby such as a toxic waste site. Physical deterioration is a loss in value of a property caused by wear, tear, age, and use.

41. D

The cost approach depends on the replacement or reproduction value of a property. The gross rent multiplier (GRM) is used in appraising income-producing properties. The GRM is multiplied by the annual gross rental of a property to yield an estimate of value. The income approach is based on the income-producing capacity of a property. The sales comparison approach compares similar property values to render an estimate of value for the subject property.

42. C

The principle of contribution states the each portion of a property contributes to the property's ability to produce income. The principle of conformity states that general conformity among properties in a neighborhood produces maximum value for these properties. The principle of substitution states that, all other things being equal, a buyer will purchase a property that is offered at the lowest price. The theory of supply and demand means that the price for goods varies depending on the relationship of the supply and the demand for the product.

43. A

In using the sales comparison approach to value, the appraiser makes adjustments to the comparable properties to make them like the subject. These comparables are selected because they closely, but usually not exactly, resemble the subject property.

44. B

Of primary importance in the appraisal report is that any adjustments made in the report must be supported from known and current market data. The appraiser obtains data from a variety of sources including multiple listing services, census data, and tax records.

45. A

Although all of the given choices are steps in the appraisal process. The first step is to define the purpose of the appraisal and the type of value estimate. Reconciling the data, arriving at a value estimate, and preparing the written appraisal report are later steps in the appraisal process.

46. A

An appraisal is an estimate or opinion only. There is no such thing as the legal value of a property nor does an appraisal address the amount a seller will accept. Book value is a value derived through accounting methods.

47. B

Properties to be built are generally not considered for a comparative market analysis (CMA) because they are not currently on the market. Similar properties that were recently sold, properties listed for sale, and expired listings that are not too old are all part of the CMA.

48. C

A real estate agent must be able to adjust the listing price according to the market. Pricing the property at the lowest possible price for a quick sale should only be done with the permission of the seller.

49. C

An expired listing that is over six months old is generally too outdated to give any valid information on the current real estate market. Sales, listings, and pending offers of similar properties are all valid items that can be considered in analyzing data for comparison.

50. A

A listing price is the price stated in the listing agreement. This price can be modified by agreement between broker and seller. The mortgage value is what a lender is willing to lend. The market position refers to the competition in the market place. The highest possible use is the use of a property that would produce the greatest return in value but is not necessarily the current use of the property.

51. D

An appraisal estimates the value of the subject property. A credit report determines a borrower's ability to pay. A sales contract is an agreement between a buyer and a seller. A title search is research of a property's title (transfers) to verify the condition of the title before closing.

52. C

The comparative market analysis (CMA) is generally used by real estate agents to find a listing price for a property. The sales comparison approach is an approach to value used by appraisers as one method of valuing residential property. Although similar to the CMA, the sales comparison approach adjusts comparables to match the subject. This adjustment is generally not performed for a CMA.

53. C

Expired listings are properties that were not sold during the term of the listing agreement for one reason or another. Often, they are priced above market value. They are often used in a comparative market analysis (CMA) if they are not too old because they help to indicate a market value that may be too high for the subject property.

54. D

Favorable financing terms are extremely important to a flourishing real estate market. When market prices fall below the cost of construction, then building tends to decelerate. Income levels have a great influence on housing demand. Government regulation greatly impacts housing as the government has the right to lower interest rates.

55. C

Most agents do not like to use comparables that date back more than six months. This is because of changes in market value over time.

56. C

The multiple listing service (MLS) pools information on all properties that are entered into its system, and is available to all of its members. The sales comparison approach is an appraisal approach to value. The URAR (Uniform Residential Appraisal Report) is a residential appraisal report form required by Fannie Mae (Federal National Mortgage Association). The CMA is short for comparative market analysis.

57. D

The price obtained in the sale of a property is not always equivalent to the market value of the property. It may be more or less.

58. A

The use of borrowed funds is called leverage. The investor will want to make the least possible down payment and obtain the lowest possible interest rate over the longest period. This allows the investor to accumulate the maximum amount of real estate with the minimum amount of personal funds. However, for the investor expecting a cash flow, the expenses and mortgage costs may well exceed the returns if too much leverage is used.

59. C

$140,000 \div \$1,166,666 = 0.12 = 12\%$

60. A

Land investment *can* be as profitable as any other investment. Disadvantages of land investment include the fact that unimproved land cannot be depreciated for tax purposes, money must be invested in approvals when the land is developed, and, generally, the investor must wait longer than other types of investments for profits.

61. B

Rent roll refers to the number of rental units that are currently occupied multiplied by the rental amount per unit.

62. D

Property taxes may be deducted from all types of property.

63. C

In the sale of a real estate investment, the taxpayer is taxed only on the profit, or gain, from the sale and not on the price or net proceeds. The time value of money calculates the value of an asset in the past, present, or future and is based on the premise that the original investment will increase in value over a certain time.

64. C

Value in use is based on the property's usefulness to an investor and not necessarily for its market value. Investment value is the amount of return on a certain dollar investment a property will produce. Insurance value estimates the value of property as a basis for determining the amount of insurance coverage necessary to protect the structure adequately against loss by fire or other casualty.

65. C

The rate of return is the percentage of income that the investor receives back on an investment. The loan-to-value ratio compares a lender's loan amount to the property value. The time value of money calculates the value of an asset in the past, present, or future. Interest is payment for the use of another's money.

66. B

The result of deducting operating expenses is net operating income. Debt service is mortgage and interest payments. Mortgage principal is the amount owed on the mortgage. Gross income is income received without deducting expenses.

67. A

G did have good fortune, but the use of other people's money is called leverage. The example does not discuss G's cash flow. Depreciation is an accounting concept that deducts certain monies from net income of property when arriving at taxable income.

68. C

Many times, an investment property will not yield the income expected to cover operating costs, and make a profit for the investor. This is known as decreasing returns. The principle of anticipation is based on expectations or hopes of the future benefits of ownership. The theory of supply and demand means that the price for goods varies depending on the relationship of the supply and the demand for the product.

69. C

$68,500 cost + $12,000 air-conditioning + $7,500 bathroom = $88,000 adjusted basis

70. C

A second mortgage on an investment property would further encumber the property and reduce the owner's equity position.

71. B

Tax depreciation is a tax-deductible paper loss that allows investors to show less income for tax purposes. The adjusted basis includes the price paid for the property, expenses incurred in acquiring the property, and the cost of any capital improvements (less depreciation if applicable).

72. A

Accrued depreciation is the total loss in the value of a property that takes place over time. The breakdown method is an appraisal method for measuring depreciation. It is derived by dividing depreciation into its three separate components: physical deterioration, functional obsolescence, and external influences or obsolescence.

73. C

Tax depreciation is a provision of the tax law, applicable to certain types of assets, that permits a property owner to take a business deduction for annual depreciation. Depreciation due to physical deterioration is economic depreciation. Capital loss occurs when investment is sold at a loss. The adjusted basis consists of the price paid for the property, plus expenses incurred in acquiring the property, plus the cost of any capital improvements (less depreciation if applicable).

74. C

Advertising, utility costs, and insurance may all qualify as deductible expenses for a business property for tax purposes. Mortgage principal is not tax deductible although mortgage interest is.

75. B

In this case, the lender, by asking Anthony to turn in a lower valuation no matter what his true findings, is violating fair housing and fair lending laws. Anthony must refuse the appraisal assignment.

76. A

Properties that have a transaction value of $250,000 or less, even though they are federally related (lender-financed transactions), do not require that an appraisal be performed on the property according to federal law.

77. D

A Certified General Real Property Appraiser is licensed to appraise any type of real property.

78. B

The Licensed Real Property Appraiser, the Certified Real Property Appraiser, and the Certified General Real Property Appraiser are all levels of appraiser licensure. There is no such category as the FDIC-Certified Appraiser.

79. D

Helen still has a form of appraisal license even though she cannot work without the supervision of a licensed or certified appraiser. She must follow all fair housing and fair lending laws and any other laws, codes, and regulations applicable to the profession including the Uniform Standards of Professional Appraisal Practice (USPAP).

80. C

If Miranda draws an unsupported conclusion that the ramps, widened doorways, and other accommodations for the disabled enhance or detract from the value of the property, she may be violating fair housing laws.

Topic 3: Land Use Controls and Regulations

1. B

The study of the social and economic statistics of a community is called demography. The services of a community such as roads, hospitals, police, and fire departments are known as the infrastructure. Geography is the study of the location of cities, countries, and waterways. Topography refers to the physical features and contours of the land.

2. B

Enforcement of the covenants is not restricted to the original owners but runs with the land to all subsequent owners. Private land use control is enforced by public law, an injunction can prevent a use contrary to the restrictions of record, and failing to enforce restrictions in a timely manner may result in the loss of the right to enforce them at all.

3. D

Deed restrictions limit the use or appearance of a given property and are an example of private control of land. Eminent domain is the power of the government to take private property for public use with just compensation to the owner. Escheat is the power of the government to take a property that has no heirs after the owner's death. Police power is government's regulation for the benefit of the public.

4. D

Certain restrictions may appear on individual deeds that do not appear on others. In Cameron's case, for example, a building in her yard may block some kind of view of the subdivision that the developer did not want blocked.

5. D

Streets, highways, and parks belong to the public and are governed by city, state, or federal regulations. A residential subdivision is privately developed and condominiums and shopping malls are privately owned.

6. B

Covenants and conditions are privately imposed land use controls. A restriction (generally found on deeds) is also a private land use control. A variance is a permitted deviation from specific requirements of zoning ordinance, which is a form of public land use control.

7. D

A moratorium imposed by a municipality is a delay in allowing development of property that is imposed only for public welfare. A variance is permission to use the land in a way that is not normally allowed by the dimensional or physical requirements of the zoning ordinance. Spot zoning occurs when a property does not conform to the other zoning in the area and is illegal in many states. A nonconforming use allows existing businesses to be "grandfathered in," even though rezoning occurs. These businesses can then keep the original use they had before the rezoning.

8. A

Nonconforming use occurs when a preexisting use of property in a zoned area is different from that specified by the current zoning, which does not apply in Zane's case. Zane might be required to submit plans to the planning board. He may be subject to a government-ordered stoppage or moratorium on all buildings. He may also have to contribute fees for construction for some of the infrastructure, which is known as impact fees.

9. B

Police power enables governments to legislate for the public good and includes all inherent powers of government including escheat, eminent domain, and the power to create and enact laws including IRS regulations.

10. B

Escheat is the power of the government, after proper legal notice, to take the property of a deceased owner who has left no will or heirs.

11. A

The Interstate Land Sales Full Disclosure Act regulates developers of subdivisions of 25 or more lots sold across state lines.

12. B

Intestate is a term that refers to an owner who dies without leaving a valid will. A testate decedent dies leaving a will. *Pur autre vie* is a term referring to ownership for the term of "another's life." Bankruptcy does not necessitate property reverting to the state by escheat.

13. D

Restrictive covenants are private restrictions on ownership and may be found on deeds or plat maps. Taxation is the government's power to levy property and income taxes. Eminent domain is the government power to take private property for public use with just compensation. Police power is the government's right to legislate for the public good.

14. C

When property is condemned under eminent domain, the property owner is compensated. *Caveat emptor* is a term meaning buyer beware. In the use of police power, such as zoning, property owners must generally file suit to be compensated for losses to the property value. In a court action regarding restrictive covenants, an injunction is sought from the court, not compensation.

15. C

Cluster development occurs when buildings are built closer together to preserve open space. One of the main purposes of cluster development is to preserve open space so that it can be enjoyed by the community. This could take the form of parks, trails, swimming pools, and other forms of recreation.

16. D

Building codes are rules set by government to regulate building and construction standards. Zoning ordinances are regulations for the use of property and restrictive covenants regulate a specific property or all properties in a given area. Deed restrictions regulate property use of a private owner.

17. B

The certificate of occupancy is issued after a satisfactory final inspection of a property by the building department or other government agency, which permits occupation of a property. A property report is a disclosure required under the Interstate Land Sales Full Disclosure Act that gives specific information about the land offered for purchase. A declaration of restrictions, usually found in a deed, lists the rules an owner must follow for a specific property or properties in a given area. Enabling acts are laws passed by state legislatures authorizing cities and counties to regulate land use within their jurisdictions.

18. A

The federal Interstate Land Sales Full Disclosure Act regulates interstate sale of unimproved lots. The sale of lots may be regulated on a local level but does not require HUD (Department of Housing and Urban Development) documentation. The Superfund Amendment regulates the disposal of hazardous waste. The Truth in Lending Act deals with matters related to finance.

19. D

The question illustrates a type of preexisting or nonconforming use. Even though rezoning occurs, existing businesses may be "grandfathered in" and can keep the original use as long as they are there. Once they move out or change the use, the current owner or new occupants must comply with current zoning. A variance is permission to use land in a manner that is not normally allowed by the dimensional or physical requirements of a zoning ordinance. Cluster zoning is a type of configuration used to allow open space in subdivisions. Spot zoning allows a use that does not match existing uses in a given area and is illegal in many states.

20. A

The first step in community planning is to develop a master plan for the community. The decisions for the community are based on this initial plan. These decisions include zoning ordinances, the type of structures that will be allowed in certain zones, and infrastructure requirements to handle the plan (police force, for instance).

21. A

Along with the master plan, planning boards, based on community input, decide on zoning requirements.

22. A

Variances are permitted when the deviation is minimal and would not affect the neighborhood and where strict compliance to the restriction would cause undue hardship to the owner. A nonconforming use occurs when a preexisting use of property in a zoned area is different than that specified by the zoning code. A PUD creates a neighborhood of cluster housing and supporting business establishments. Subdivision regulations protect property owners.

23. B

Special use permits must be granted with special permission by the planning board or legislative body. Nonconforming use occurs after an area is rezoned but owners may continue their existing use. Variances allow a deviation from the dimensional or physical requirements of current zoning. Spot zoning is a use that does not conform to current zoning and does not necessarily benefit the public.

24. D

Termination of a restrictive covenant may be an application of the Doctrine of Laches that states that if landowners are lax in protecting their rights, they may lose them. The Statute of Frauds requires all documents that create an interest in real estate be in writing. Articles of incorporation are included in the documents that form a corporation such as a cooperative. Zoning regulations are part of the community zoning ordinance.

25. A

Lead-based paint disclosure is only necessary for homes built before 1978 when lead-based paint was in use. The other choices in the question may be part of the building process. A variance is permission to use the land in a way that is not normally allowed by the dimensional or physical requirements of the zoning ordinance. Building permits allow building to occur and certificates of occupancy are given by the building department if the structure meets code requirements.

26. B

Teri would have to apply for a variance. A nonconforming use is one that already had existed before the zoning was changed. Illegal spot zoning occurs when property does not conform to the other zoning in the area.

27. C

While planning and zoning proposals may be presented to property owners in a community, unanimous consent of all owners is not typically required. Planning and zoning do provide for the orderly growth and social benefit of the community. Police power is the basis of legislation and regulation for the public good.

28. D

All of the choices may be considerations when converting apartments into condominiums as there may be additions and changes made to both the exterior and interior of the building. There may also be changes to the landscaping (green space), zoning compliance issues such as setback requirements, and consideration for increased traffic and accessibility to the condominium.

29. C

Changes to a community's master plan are generally voted for and decided by a majority referendum of a community's residents.

30. D

A zoning map divides the community into various designated districts, and the text of the zoning ordinance sets forth the type of use permitted under each zoning classification. A planned unit development may be included on a specific zoning map for a certain project. Nonconforming use, spot zoning, and cluster development are zoning issues.

31. C

The zoning board of appeals interprets zoning policy but does not make policy. Drafting a policy is often accomplished by the planning board.

32. B

If zoning of a property is solely for the benefit of the property owner and increases land value, the rezoning is considered illegal spot zoning in most states. A nonconforming use occurs when a preexisting use of property in a zoned area is different than that specified by the zoning code. A variance is a permitted deviation from the specific requirements of the zoning ordinance.

33. C

In this example, the nonconforming use is violated. After the street is zoned as residential, the warehouse may be allowed a nonconforming use since its use existed before the rezoning. Once the warehouse converts to a retail store, it loses it nonconforming use status. The retail store must apply for a special use permit or variance to continue in the residential zone.

34. A

An outlot is a parcel of land that is outside the main area of development. Sometimes, this land is used for landscaping.

35. C

Asbestos is a fibrous mineral found in rocks and soil that is also friable and can cause lung cancer when released into the air. Formaldehyde is a substance often used for preservation. Radon is a radioactive gas, and PCBs are synthetic liquid organic compounds used in the insulation of electrical transformers.

36. D

When the Superfund Amendment was passed, the innocent landowner defense was also added to the Comprehensive Environmental Response, Compensation, and Liability Act (CERCLA). The purpose of the Amendment was not only to find persons responsible for the contamination but to identify innocent landowners who might not be liable for cleanup.

37. D

Radon is a radioactive gas measured in picocuries. Electromagnetic waves are high frequency radio waves in which the electric and magnetic fields are inseparable. Formaldehyde can be toxic and is often used for preservation. A PCB is a manmade, odorless, liquid organic compound and a carcinogen that is found in groundwater and soil. The substance was used in electrical transformers as a cooling and insulating medium.

38. D

The purchaser may be liable for environmental contamination on a property, so a due-diligence review by the purchaser before title transfer is necessary to protect the purchaser from liability problems later.

39. B

The Comprehensive Environmental Response, Compensation, and Liability Act (CERCLA) defines persons liable for hazardous waste cleanup costs. The Real Estate Settlement Procedures Act has to do with lender disclosure of closing costs. The Interstate Land Sales Full Disclosure Act covers disclosure requirements for certain properties sold across state lines. The Residential Lead-based Paint Hazard Reduction Act provides disclosure requirements for the presence of lead-based paint.

40. A

Plans must be submitted to the appropriate government agency for approval to construct on or near a wetland. If plans are approved, construction may take place. Construction on or near a wetland is allowed with permission in some areas. In most places, wetlands are protected areas.

41. A

The federal organization that oversees navigation, flood control, and dredging projects is the Army Corps of Engineers. The Environmental Protection Agency (EPA) oversees a variety of environmental concerns. HUD administers funding for projects related to housing. State and local departments of health address drinking water and disease issues.

42. D

Generally, a pest inspection is required in all residential real estate transfers, and the sale is contingent upon the inspection and remediation of any problem. If a licensee knows of any termite infestation, this information must be shared with the prospective purchasers.

43. B

Mold is a type of bacteria that grows freely in high humidity and high moisture areas. In the sale of real estate, mold can be a big issue for purchasers since mold is difficult to remediate in many areas. PCBs are a chemical compound that is toxic and was used as an insulation medium in electrical transformers. Asbestos is not currently used in building materials but can be found in older buildings. The crumbled particles of asbestos can cause illness when inhaled. Formaldehyde is a preservative that was used in home insulation but is no longer used.

44. C

The Environmental Protection Agency (EPA), oversees the regulation of underground storage tanks. The Federal Housing Administration (FHA) is the U.S. agency that insures mortgage loans to protect lending institutions. The Department of Housing and Urban Development (HUD), is a federal agency that administers funding for projects related to housing. Fannie Mae, the shortened name for the Federal National Mortgage Association (FNMA), is a privately owned corporation that purchases FHA, VA (Department of Veterans Affairs), and conventional mortgages.

45. C

Environmental considerations, easements running through the property, and zoning surrounding the site must all be considered in the development of the site plan. The power of escheat allows government to take the property of persons who die without a will or heirs and does not generally affect the site plan.

46. B

Not all property transfer and/or development is typically subject to an environmental review and corresponding environmental impact statement. When an entity applies to transfer or develop land, usually a government agency on the local or state level decides whether an environmental review and impact statement are necessary.

47. A

Generally, once an environmental impact statement is completed, a public comment period and then a public hearing on the development take place. An impact statement may have been prepared by a variety of experts and a number of agencies including state and local government agencies and personnel. The public needs time to study these issues to assess their effect on the community.

48. D

If there is contamination, the owner would need to remove the product from the tank. Older tanks, worn by age, corrode due to their chemical content or from a reaction between the tank and the soil. This is a cause of leakage. Owners must periodically inspect the tank, must repair or replace leaky tanks, and must restore any contaminated soil around a leaky tank.

49. D

Because Wayne is planning to expand or change the plant, he may be subject to both lender and government approvals and inspections. Because of due-diligence requirements that mandate that the property owner is responsible for cleanup if a property is environmentally threatened or damaged, the lender will probably require an environmental assessment. Because Wayne is expanding the property, he will probably be required to have an environmental impact statement. If any problems are found, the existing tanks may be inspected for leakage.

50. C

In the example in the question, both the sellers and the broker may be liable. Agents must disclose what they know or should have known. A court of law would make the final decision as to liability.

51. D

In this example, Tanisha, the buyers' broker, and the buyers' attorney may be liable. Although a radon testing contingency is not mandatory in some states, the clients requested that the property be tested for radon. This request, along with generally accepted practice in many states to test for radon, would be in favor of the clients against Tanisha and the attorney.

52. C

Under the Comprehensive Environmental Response, Compensation and Liability Act (CERCLA), programs exist to identify sites with hazardous substances, seek reimbursement from responsible parties, and ensure cleanup by the responsible parties or the government. Under the Superfund Amendment to CERCLA, innocent landowners who purchase property not knowing about contamination have a defense against liability for cleanup and fines under the law.

53. D

Knowledge of appropriate contingencies is very important, especially in areas where the agent initially fills in the contract of sale. In the example, the property was built after 1978 so a lead-based paint contingency and disclosure is not necessary. A contingency is needed to inspect the well condition and water flow and the septic system. The radon levels should also be checked since radon can seep into the house from the well.

54. D

The danger of radon gas lies in its radioactivity. Friability is a crumbling quality of asbestos that occurs when it is moved and can cause lung damage. Magnetic strength is a characteristic of electromagnetic fields that is given off by power lines.

55. D

All of the choices in the question are applicable to building near tidal waters or wetlands. This type of project requires a number of considerations including the extra cost of construction, paying for special government permits, and building according to regulatory specifications. Among other issues is the approval of the plans for private drinking water and wastewater systems since public systems may not be available near tidal waters or wetlands.

56. A

The only true and impartial standard for setting assessments is the market value standard. Market value can be defined as a property's worth in terms of price agreed upon by a willing buyer and seller when neither is under any undue pressure and each is knowledgeable of market conditions. The cost approach to value calculates a substitute structure to which depreciation is deducted and land value added. The income approach is the primary method for estimating the value of properties that produce rental income. A uniform percentage is a percentage of value used as a basis for assessing.

57. A

An *in rem* legal proceeding occurs when an action is brought against the real property directly and not against an individual and his personal property. *Ad valorem* means "to the value." There is no such thing as an *ad valorem* legal proceeding. *Caveat emptor* is Latin for "buyer beware." The Doctrine of Laches refers to the loss of legal rights because of failure to assert them on a timely basis.

58. A

The amount that the municipality must raise by taxes on real property is called the tax levy. The tax levy determines the tax rate. An assessment is a percentage of a property's market value. A property tax lien creates an encumbrance against the property. A tax exemption allows taxpayers relief from paying certain school or property taxes either completely or in part.

59. C

A homestead is a type of property where people live. A warehouse used for commercial or industrial purposes would not be classified as a homestead property. All other choices in the question would be classified as a homestead property.

60. A

assessed value $\times$ tax rate = annual tax
$89,990 \times 0.5 = $44,995
$44,995 \times (4.10 \div 100)
$44,995 \times 0.041 = $1,844.80

61. A

The two items that determine a tax bill are the property's taxable assessment and the tax rates of the taxing jurisdiction in which the property is located.

62. D

Religious organizations are the only properties listed in the question that always have full exemption from property taxes.

63. B

Serena paid $325,000 for a house that may not have been reassessed in eight years. Therefore, the assessed value may be $200,000. The assessment does not change upon purchase, however. The house must still be equitably compared to other similar houses. So if the tax assessor has to raise Serena's assessment based on $325,000 (which may be the fair market value of the house), the assessor would technically have to increase the assessment on other similar houses to that amount. This may not happen right away.

64. D

Depending on the locality, full or partial exemptions for school and property taxes are available for senior citizens, veterans, and people with disabilities. There are varying levels of exemptions and certain requirements to obtain the exemptions. For example, for the senior citizen exemption, an individual may have had to own and reside in the property for a specified time.

65. A

Assessments are computed and decided upon by the local assessor.

66. C

rate = tax dollars required/taxable assessed value
rate = $5 million $\div$ $100 million = 0.05
$0.05 \times $1,000 = $50 per $1,000

67. A

Appropriation occurs when a government agency sets aside funds for a certain purpose.

68. B

A tax lien attaches to the property if the taxpayer does not pay his property taxes. This is an encumbrance against a property filed by the taxing jurisdiction. A judgment is a court order. Foreclosure is the legal procedure of enforcing payment of a debt secured by a mortgage or by any other lien. Equity of redemption is a borrower's right to redeem the title conveyed in a mortgage or a deed of trust after default and before a foreclosure sale by paying the debt in full.

69. C

Generally, the owning of back taxes will not affect the reassessment of a property.

70. A

A map, drawn to scale, showing all of the real property parcels within a city, town, or other assessing unit is a tax map. A plat is property map recorded on the public record. The assessment roll lists all real property in the taxing jurisdiction, including information about each parcel and its assessed value and exempt status. A "homestead diagram" is a fictitious term.

71. C

rate × value = assessed value
0.70 × $100,000 = $70,000

72. A

There would be no need for equalization if all municipalities assessed all property at 100% of market value each year. This is because all properties would be taxed equally at full market value.

73. B

$200,000 × 0.90 = $180,000
assessed value × tax rate = annual taxes
180,000 × 0.06 = $10,800

74. A

assessed value × tax rate = annual taxes
9,500 ÷ 0.045 = $211,111

75. A

Apportionment is the division of property and school tax monies so that school districts, counties, towns, and cities in the different municipalities all pay their fair share of the tax levy. Appropriation occurs when a government agency sets aside funds for a certain purpose. Assessment is a percentage of a property's market value. This figure is used for property tax purposes and ultimately determines how the total tax is shared among property owners. Equalization is the use of an equalization rate as a common denominator to apportion or appropriate taxes fairly. This is because various municipalities throughout a state use different uniform percentages for assessments.

76. C

$150,000 × 0.15 = $22,500
$150,000 + $22,500 = $172,500 increased valuation
$172,500 × 0.75 = $129,375 new tax basis
$129,375 × (4.5 ÷ 100) = 0.045
$129,375 × 0.045 = $5,821.88

77. B

The amount that the municipality must raise by taxes on real property is the tax levy. Tax rates sometimes cannot be set until the tax levy is apportioned, or divided, among various municipalities. A special assessment is a specific lien for an improvement to a property or properties that do not affect the entire taxing unit. The tax rate is the amount of money needed by a municipality to meet budgetary requirements divided by the taxable assessed real property within that jurisdiction.

78. B

0.75 × $80,000 = $60,000
assessed value × tax rate = annual taxes
0.032 per $1,000 × 60,000 = $1,920 annual tax

79. B

$94,000 × 0.40 assessment ratio = $37,600 assessed value
assessed value × tax rate = annual taxes
$37,600 × 0.017 = $639.20

80. B

rate = tax dollars required ÷ taxable assessed value
rate = $1.5 million ÷ $75 million = 0.02
0.02 × $1,000 = $20 per $1,000

Topic 4: Contracts and Relationships with Buyers and Sellers

1. B

Consideration is the giving of something of value as an inducement to contract. Quiet enjoyment has to do with uninterrupted possession of one's property. A power of attorney gives a person authority to act for another in legal matters.

2. B

The mortgage contingency clause states that the contract is contingent, or dependent upon, the purchaser's receipt of a mortgage commitment. If the purchaser does not obtain a commitment by a certain date, the contract may be canceled and the deposit returned to the seller.

3. A

A deed is a legal document that conveys real property from one party to another and is not a contract. A lease and mortgage are both bilateral contracts where parties make promises to each other. An option is a unilateral contract where one party makes a promise to another.

4. C

A bilateral contract, in which two parties make promises or perform acts, is the correct answer. In a unilateral contract, only one party makes a promise or acts. A void contract has no legal effect. An option contract is a type of unilateral contract because a promise is made by one party.

5. C

An attorney review clause is a condition that makes the contract subject to approval by each party's attorney, and can help avoid the unlawful practice of law. In many states, a broker can fill in a contract but cannot make any changes to the actual form. If it is reviewed by an attorney, the practice of filling in the blanks is acceptable. A rider covers supplemental issues of the agreement, and can actually be unlawful if prepared from scratch by the agent. The right of first refusal allows the holder a right to purchase a property if the seller decides to sell or another purchaser comes along.

6. B

In real estate, the most typical example of liquidated damages is forfeiture of earnest money should the buyer be unwilling or unable to execute the sales contract. Penalties for extremely bad behavior by a party and for fraudulent advantage taken by one party over another are punitive damages. Compensation for money actually lost is compensatory damages.

7. A

A valid contract is a contract that legally obligates all parties to abide by its terms and conditions. A void contract has no legal effect because it is impossible to be completed or its purpose is illegal. A voidable contract may or may not be enforceable because one of the parties cannot/will not perform as agreed. An executed contract is one that has been completed.

8. B

At 15, Carolanne is considered a minor. Minors do not have the legal capacity to contract. Therefore, with minors such as Carolanne, the contract is voidable at her option. A void contract has no legal effect because it is impossible to be completed or its purpose is illegal. With a unilateral contract, there is a promise made by one party to perform a specific action. An implied contact is one created by the conduct of, rather than from the direct words of, the parties.

9. D

An earnest money deposit should accompany a contract because it shows the sincerity of buyer, demonstrates financial capability to raise the money called for in the purchase offer, and may serve as possible liquidated damages to the seller if the buyer defaults.

10. B

Mutual mistake of a material fact by both parties causes the contract to be voidable but not void. Fraud is intentional deceit. Misrepresentation is the unintentional misstatement of facts. Legality of object requires the contract to be for legal purpose.

11. C

An earnest money deposit is *not* used to buy down the interest rate of the mortgage loan. "Points" are paid for this purpose. Although earnest money is not required by law, it is offered as evidence of the buyer's sincere offer to purchase and demonstrates the buyer's ability to raise the agreed-upon funds. Earnest money may be used as liquidated damages should the buyer willingly default on the contract terms.

12. C

An executed contract is one that has been fully performed meaning that all of the parties to the contract have performed their duties.

13. B

Because C does not have any land to sell, the contract has no legal force or effect and is void. It cannot be enforced. An executed contract is one that has been fully performed, which is not the case in this example.

14. D

Value of comparable sales, a method appropriate for estimating the value for marketing purposes, is not an essential element of a contract. Capacity of the parties means that those involved have the right to convey and accept the terms of the contract. Legality of object means that the purpose for which the contract exists is legal. Consideration is the giving of value for the property for which the contract is created. All of the foregoing are essentials of a valid contract.

15. D

The mortgage contingency clause is generally part of a clause in a contract of sale, but it is not an actual form of contract. The condominium contract of sale, option to buy, and installment sales contract are all forms of real estate contracts.

16. D

A back-up offer occurs when a contract is signed and is pending and another contract comes in. An assignment is the giving over of a contract and its obligations to another. Novation is the substitution of a new contract for an older contract. A counteroffer is a new offer made by an offeror rejecting an offer.

17. D

A valid contract is binding and enforceable on all parties. A contract may be bilateral with both parties making a promise, or unilateral; with one party making a promise to induce a second party to do something. It need not be filed with the county clerk, and is sometimes breached by one or both parties.

18. C

Under an express contract, the parties to the contract have definitely agreed on all of the contract terms. A promissory (note) is the written promise of one person to pay a certain sum of money to another at a specific time in the future. An executed contract is one that is fully performed. An implied contract exists when the parties signify through conduct or actions, but without express agreement, that a contract exists.

19. A

An order from the court requiring specific performance means that the contract is to be completed as originally agreed. Rescission means to take back, remove, or annul, and may occur when a contract is not performed by either party or when a party breaches it. When a party breaches a contract, one or more other parties usually suffer monetary damages. The amount of money actually lost is the amount of compensatory damages that the court awards. Instead of compensatory damages, the parties to the contract can stipulate an amount of money to be paid upon certain breaches of the contract and are called liquidated damages.

20. C

The portion of the money paid to purchase a property that is paid in cash and is not part of the mortgage loan is called the down payment. The down payment is determined by the lender and depends on the loan amount. The upfront or earnest money deposit accompanies the offer to purchase and shows the buyer's sincerity. Boot is the cash received in a tax-deferred exchange. A contingency is a condition in a contract relieving a party of liability if a specified event occurs or fails to occur.

21. C

The example in the question is an assignment. The contract is assigned from Frank's daughter to Frank's son who has assumed all contract obligations. A counteroffer is a new offer made by an offeror rejecting an offer. An installment contract or contract for deed is contract of sale and a financing instrument in which the seller agrees to convey title when the buyer completes the purchase price in installment payments. A contingency is a condition in a contract relieving a party of liability if a specified event occurs or fails to occur.

22. B

A contract expresses the rights and duties of the parties and is an agreement between the parties to do some legal act or to refrain from doing some legal act in exchange for consideration. The contract involves an offer and acceptance—a promise made to comply with the contract terms upon acceptance of that offer. An application is a form of request supported with qualifications for the request.

23. D

A person's competence or mental and emotional ability to enter into contracts determines legal capacity. Contracts entered into by parties lacking legal capacity are voidable by the party lacking capacity. With minors, the contract is voidable at the minor's option. Individuals or other entities may give a person a power of attorney to act for them in legal transactions such as real estate contracts.

24. D

Although a contract may be assigned to another, it is not necessary for validity. Consideration includes anything of value, such as money, and some kind of consideration must be present for a contract to be valid. Lawful objective means that the contract is for a legal purpose. Mutual agreement means that the parties to the contract agree to and understand its terms.

25. D

Deposits for real estate transactions may be held by real estate brokers, attorneys, or lenders. The seller does not generally hold the deposit if the transaction is negotiated by a broker.

26. D

The listing contract is typically owned by the brokerage firm.

27. C

An injunction is a stop order from a court to cease an activity. Rescission means to take back, remove, or annul and may occur when a contract is not performed by either party or when a party breaches it. Upon suit for rescission, the court orders the parties placed back in their original positions as if the contract had never existed. Reformation allows the court to rewrite a contract that may, for example, have a clerical mistake. Assignment is the giving of contract rights to another.

28. C

An exclusive agency listing selects only one broker as the only agent but the owner reserves the right to sell the property himself without obligation to the broker. An open listing, also called a nonexclusive agency, permits the owner to list with many brokers individually. An exclusive-right-to-sell listing engages the services of only one broker, who must produce the ready, willing, and able buyer acceptable to the seller.

29. C

In all of the responses except for answer "C," part of the tests that entitle a broker to compensation is missing. A broker producing a ready, willing, and able buyer or presenting an offer that meets the terms and conditions of the listing contract acceptable to the seller are the tests entitling the broker to compensation. Either test is sufficient.

30. A

It seems from the example in the question that Jacob has earned his commission. The closing is taking place and the sale is complete. To collect the commission, Jacob will most probably have to sue unless he can reach an agreement with the sellers. A *lis pendens* is a notice that a lawsuit is pending regarding a property. A real estate commission generally hears complaints from consumers.

31. C

The listing contract between the seller and agent is executory because a buyer has not been found and the contract is not complete. An implied contract is one inferred from the conduct and actions of another without express agreement. A void contract has no legal force or effect. An unenforceable contract is one that appears to meet the requirements for validity but is not enforceable in court.

32. C

An open listing, the correct answer, describes a listing that allows the owner to list with several brokers and to compensate the broker who produces the ready, willing, and able buyer who is accepted by the seller. With an exclusive-right-to-sell listing, the property is listed with only one broker. A contract for deed allows the buyer to pay in installments and the seller to convey title when full payment is received. An option is a contract in which the optionor sells the right to the optionee to act at some particular time.

33. C

An unenforceable contract is one that appears to meet the requirements for validity but is not enforceable in court. The parties can still go forth with the contract even if the "time is of the essence clause" has been violated. An executed and fully performed contract has been completed according to its terms. An implied contract is one that is made by the actions of the parties.

34. C

The law that requires all contracts that create an interest in real estate be in writing to be enforceable in court is the Statute of Frauds. The Statute of Limitations has to do with the statutory time limit to bring a legal action against a party. Regulation Z has to do with truth in advertising credit terms. The Real Estate Settlement Procedures Act deals with lender disclosures in making mortgage loans.

35. C

The buyer *does* begin the contractual process as the offeror, and not the offeree, so that statement is true. A buyer's agent represents the buyer and the seller's agent or seller's attorney generally holds the deposit. Lead-based paint disclosure applies only to properties built before 1978.

36. C

A contract of sale is binding when the attorneys for each party approve the contract.

37. A

It is customary for a purchaser to deposit a percentage of the purchase price to be held, in escrow, as an initial earnest money deposit. The amount varies depending upon the nature of the transaction and the area in which it takes place. In many areas, it is an amount equal to 10% of the purchase price.

38. B

    sales prices × rate of commission = total commission
    $90,000 × 0.06 = $5,400
    $5,400 × 0.60 = $3,240

39. B

    A binder is a written outline of the scope of the transaction but does not generally contain the elements of a valid contract. In some areas, it is used in place of the offer to purchase. A proprietary lease is given to the purchaser of a cooperative apartment. A deed of trust and a mortgage are financing contracts.

40. C

    The principals do not form an agency relationship with each other. The agency relationship is between agent and principal. However, it is true that a purchase contract is a bilateral express contract, that the parties are assumed to be in equal bargaining positions, and have equal ability from opposing viewpoints.

41. C

    A contract stating "time is of the essence" means that the contract must be performed on or before the date stipulated on the contract.

42. B

    In this example, it looks like the couple did not have the down payment, which is a portion of a property purchase price that is paid in cash and not a part of the mortgage. Being college graduates, we can assume they are over the age of 18 and have legal capacity to contract. A right of first refusal allows the holder a right to purchase a property if the seller decides to sell or another purchaser comes along. A mortgage commitment is a lender's promise to loan a certain amount of funds that is evident, in this example, by the lender's promise of $275,000.

43. C

    sales prices × rate of commission = total commission
    $12,000 ÷ 0.06 = $200,000

44. D

    Contingency clauses, addenda, and riders are all possible additions to the contract. A codicil is an addition to a will.

45. B

    Generally, the purchaser signs the offer to purchase first because he or she is making the offer and earnest money deposit, and the seller wants to verify that the purchaser is serious about the offer.

46. B

    This agreement is now voidable by either party since the pest damages exceed the agreed-upon sum for repairs. The contract is not void until the buyer and seller decide to terminate their relationship. At this point, either party may agree to pay the excess amount. It would not be described as executed, since it is not fully performed nor is it unenforceable. Until the parties agree that the contract is definitely void, it is still enforceable.

47. A

    Because the contract is in writing, it is express, not implied. The contract is bilateral, not unilateral because there are two parties making promises. The closing has not yet taken place, so it is not executed or fully performed.

48. A

    Pet restrictions and repair obligations are disclosed in a condominium's bylaws. A letter of intent is a document that expresses mutual intent but without liability or obligation of the parties. It is sometimes used when a party wishes to purchase a condominium that is not yet constructed or converted. The condominium contract of sale is the document that details the terms of the sale of the condominium. The deed contains the legal description of the property.

49. D

    The proprietary lease is given to a shareholder of a cooperative upon purchase of the unit. The declaration is the document that creates a condominium. It is also called a master deed. The prospectus is included in the declaration and describes the scope of the condominium project and a description of the corporate setup as required by law. The initial declaration, prospectus, and price of the units are included in the condominium offering plan.

50. C

    Although a board package addresses a number of issues, some of them personal, it mainly consists of financial data.

51. A

    A contract of sale, specifically for the transfer of cooperatives, is generally used for the sale of cooperative property. The proprietary lease documents the interest and regulations of the owner's interest in the cooperative. An installment sales contract is the document used when a seller receives the sale price over a specified period of time. A letter of intent is a document that expresses mutual intent but without liability or obligation of the parties.

52. C

    An installment land contract *can* be used on any type of property and is sometimes called a "contract for deed." An installment land contract does provide equitable title to the buyers, must be in writing to be enforceable, and is binding on the heirs of the parties.

53. B

    A right of first refusal clause allows the holder a right to purchase (or lease) a property if the seller decides to sell or another purchaser (or lessee) comes along. In a right of first refusal, the owner must have first put the property up for sale or lease. Second, he must have an offer from another party. A binder is an agreement to purchase a property. The "time is of the essence clause" is a phrase indicating that closing must take place on or before the exact date stipulated in the contract. An injunction is an order by a court to stop an activity.

54. A

    A written option agreement is a contract that specifies a time limit within which the optionee may choose to purchase or lease a piece of real property. Written option agreements are enforceable in court, include a sales price, and do not convey title upon signing of the option contract.

55. B

    The best choice is an option contract that requires the optionor (owner of the property) to comply with the agreement, but does not require the optionee (the nephew) to perform. A bilateral contract requires each of two parties to make promises to one another. An unenforceable contract is one that appears to meet the specified requirements of a contract but would not hold up in court. An executed contract is one that has been fully completed.

56. D

    An assumable mortgage, home equity loan, and FHA loan are types of lending financing. A purchase money mortgage is a seller financing contract in which a seller holds all or part of a mortgage for the purchase.

57. B

    A counteroffer is a new offer made by an offeror rejecting a previous offer. A contract is void if it has no legal force or effect. The sellers do not have a fiduciary duty to the agent as they are entitled to counteroffer. Breach of contract is failure to perform under the contract.

58. B

    A contract for an illegal purpose is void. Brad and Donna are both old enough to enter into a contract.

59. A

The correct answer is novation, which is the substitution of a new contract for a prior contract and not a remedy for breach of contract. Legal remedies for a breach of contract might include a request for specific performance, compensatory damages, and liquidated damages.

60. A

Novation is the substitution of a new contract for a prior contract. Injunction is a court order requiring the party to stop an act. Full performance means that the contract is complete. A release allows one or both of the parties out of the contract.

61. A

Kickbacks are payments by a broker of any part of his or her compensation from a real estate transaction to anyone who is not licensed or who is not exempt from license law. Commingling occurs if a broker mixes the money of others such as earnest money deposits with his or her personal or business operating funds. A net listing is not really a type of listing. In this commission arrangement, all money above a specified net amount to the seller would go to the broker as a commission. This method is illegal in many states.

62. B

A broker may not interfere with a lease or contract of sale that a principal has with another broker. The example is not a violation of license law. Failure to disclose his interest in the real estate would also be a license law violation. Brokers may not commingle the funds of others with their business or personal accounts.

63. C

Agents should not accept deposits from purchasers if they have some reason to believe the seller cannot perform on the contract.

64. D

A false statement regarding an important matter in a real estate transaction to induce someone to contract is called misrepresentation. Reciprocity refers to licensure arrangements between certain states. "Buyer beware" refers to prudent acts by the buyer to protect himself or herself from fraudulent activities.

65. A

Whether the homeowner has used a real estate agent or not, all discrimination based on race violates the Federal Fair Housing Act.

66. B

In this example in the question, broker B is engaging in illegal self-dealing. Real estate brokers must disclose to prospective purchasers any interest they have in the real estate transaction.

67. B

This arrangement is called a net listing and is illegal in many states. A net listing is not really a type of listing. In this commission arrangement, all money above a specified net amount to the seller would go to the broker as a commission. Net listings can be unfair to a seller if the seller's property sells for more than the listed price. A net listing may allow a broker to take advantage of a property owner by putting the broker's own interests above the interests of the principal.

68. B

Brokers must pass on what they know or should have known about a property to all others involved in the transaction including other licensees.

69. D

Generally, brokers cannot advise on matters such as legal wording in a real estate contract and should advise their clients to consult their attorneys. In this question, Raphael's advice regarding the "as is" clause in the contract may constitute the illegal practice of law.

70. A

If a broker spends a client's deposit money, he or she is guilty of conversion. Self-dealing occurs if a broker fails to disclose his or her interest in a property for sale. Specific performance is a court order for payment on a contract.

71. A

Misrepresentation through one agent to another is a violation of license law.

72. A

In most areas, in advertising residential properties, the ad must indicate that the licensee is in the real estate business.

73. C

Should a salesperson receive a deposit check, he or she must turn it over to his or her broker. The accepted practice in many areas is for the broker to hold a purchaser's deposit in his or her escrow account until closing. In other areas, the real estate broker turns over the deposit to the attorney for the seller where it is kept in the attorney's escrow account until the closing.

74. A

The broker's actions in this case are an example of undue influence that is any improper control or influence by one person over another. Duress is the threat of violence or placing a person in fear of his or her safety. Misrepresentation is the unintentional misstatement of facts. Fraud is the intentional misstatement of facts.

75. A

In disclosing confidential information to the buyer, broker B violated her fiduciary duties to the seller.

76. C

Generally, a broker is entitled to the commission if he or she produces a ready, willing, and able buyer and/or the terms have been accepted by buyer and seller.

77. B

Brokers must present all offers to the seller.

78. A

A broker *is* entitled to a commission if he or she produces a buyer who is ready, willing, and able to complete the terms of the transaction. Antitrust laws *do* prohibit competing brokers from collaboration on a commission percentage to charge collectively. The brokerage firm does own the commissions and can charge different commissions for various properties.

79. B

Generally, in most states, brokers cannot give out legal advice. In this example, the broker is telling his clients that he does not agree with the wording of the contract, a legal document. This could constitute the illegal practice of law on the part of the broker.

80. A

Full performance takes place when the parties carry out their contract promises as agreed upon. The closing exemplifies the full performance of the contract. An executory contract is one that is not yet fully performed. Meeting of the minds refers to the offer and acceptance necessary for a contract to exist. The substitution of a new contract for a prior contract is a form of contract termination called novation.

Topic 5: Financing

1. B

A mortgage is a two-party instrument between the lender and the borrower. A cash sale does not involve a mortgage. Banks are not the only lending institutions.

2. D

Depression is the lowest possible point in the economic cycle. The cycle encompasses all facets of the economy, including real estate and business. Recession is a moderate and temporary decline in economic activity that occurs during a period of otherwise increasing prosperity. Stagflation occurs when economic growth is at a standstill but inflation still exists. Inflation is an increase in money and credit relative to available goods, resulting in higher prices.

3. D

The mortgage requires the borrower to pay real property taxes and assessments, keep the buildings in good condition, and have the buildings insured against loss.

4. A

The interest is the money paid for using someone else's money.

5. A

EZ Pay Mortgage Company is the *mortgagee* because it is receiving a mortgage from Barry. Barry is the *mortgagor* because he is giving a mortgage to EZ Pay Mortgage Company. The trustor and beneficiary are parties to a deed of trust, not a mortgage.

6. C

The mortgage principal is never tax deductible.

7. D

Redlining is an illegal practice on the part of a lender in which certain neighborhoods are "redlined" or considered off limits in making a mortgage loan. This practice violates the Federal Fair Housing Act. The most important factor the lender will consider is the borrower's ability to repay the loan that takes into account the borrower's income. After that, the credit history is considered.

8. B

The mortgage represents the security or collateral for the note that is typically the property. The loan is the money paid to the mortgagee by the mortgagor. The note is the evidence of the mortgage debt. Defeasance is the right of the borrower to have the lien removed upon full payoff of the debt.

9. B

"In arrears" means "at the end of the period." The interest paid is for use of the money for the previous month and not for the upcoming month. Foreclosure, late charges, or additional funds have nothing to do with the concept of arrears.

10. C

The lender of mortgage money is the *mortgagee*. The borrower of mortgage money is the *mortgagor*. This can be best understood if one views the mortgagor as the giver of the mortgage or promise to pay and the mortgagee as the receiver of the mortgage payments. A trustee and trustor are parties to a trust, another type of legal arrangement.

11. D

In making a mortgage loan, the lender requires that the borrower sign a promissory note or bond. The acceleration clause permits the lender to declare the entire principal balance of the debt immediately due and payable if the borrower is in default. The defeasance clause allows the mortgage loan to be "defeated" upon full payment. A power of attorney is a legal agreement allowing a person to act for another in legal matters.

12. A

The numbering of liens is for convenient identification of priority in case of default of any or all of them. The purpose of recording a lien is to provide notice. The lien is perfectly valid against the mortgagor without recording, but it is ineffective against third parties without notice to them.

13. B

The right of assignment provides liquidity to the lender because it enables the lender to sell the mortgage at anytime and obtain the money invested.

14. **B**

   The original amount of money loaned is the principal. Interest is the "rent" for the use of the money. The mortgage and note are documents involved in the transaction that define the loan amount, terms for repayment, and promise to pay.

15. **D**

   The monthly mortgage payment generally consists of principal, interest, taxes, and insurance. This payment is known in the mortgage business as PITI. **P** is the principal that is the portion of the monthly payment applied to reduce the mortgage amount. The amount of the principal payment applied to the mortgage payment increases over time as the interest amount decreases. **I** is the interest that is the largest part of the mortgage payment. It is the lender's fee for the loan. In the early stages, the major portion of the payment goes toward interest. Over time, as the principal decreases, the interest payment decreases, and more of the payment credits toward the principal. **T** is taxes that are government charges to the public for services for public welfare. **I** is the insurance that can include mortgage insurance and flood insurance.

16. **A**

   The ratio of the loan amount to the property value is the loan-to-value ratio. The relationship of income producing value to mortgage value indicates the value of the income stream in relationship to the mortgage. Sales value to listing value indicates the percentage of listing price obtained at a given time in the market. Interest value to remaining balance generates a ratio pertaining to debt service.

17. **C**

   loan ÷ value = ratio
   $475,000 ÷ $500,000 = 95%

18. **B**

   The note or bond is the document that is the borrower's promise to pay back the loan. The mortgage alienation clause allows the lender to declare the balance due if the mortgagor sells the property during the mortgage term. The borrower's ability to pay is put in writing by the note.

19. **B**

   The loan-to-value ratio establishes how much the borrower will pay from his or her personal funds toward the purchase of the property. This is the down payment. The appraised value of the property determines the property value that assists the lender in determining the mortgage amount.
   The interest rate is determined by prevailing rates at the time of the loan.

20. **A**

   A request by a purchaser to reserve a certain loan interest rate for a specified time is called a rate lock. A commitment is a promise by a lender to make a mortgage loan. A rate cap is a limit on an interest rate.

21. **D**

   The grace period allows a window of time in which a loan can be made without the borrower being in default. Most mortgage loans are set up for the interest to be paid in arrears rather than in advance. The lender sometimes escrows taxes and insurance.

22. **A**

   Interest rates for fixed rate mortgages remain constant throughout the life of the loan. This would be a likely choice for Kathy because she can lock in a favorable rate for the life of her loan. Adjustable rate mortgages use floating interest rates set by a predetermined index and are subject to fluctuation. The other choices in the question refer to mortgages. A graduated payment mortgage has lower monthly payments in the early years that increase at specified intervals. A growing equity mortgage has monthly payments increasing annually.

23. **A**

   Creditor A will be paid first since he filed the lien first. Liens are generally paid according to priority of the date and time of recording.

24. C

The acceleration clause allows the lender to claim the entire balance due and payable immediately should a borrower default on his or her loan obligations. A granting clause is found in a deed. The alienation clause is a statement in a mortgage or deed of trust entitling the lender to declare the entire principal balance of the debt immediately due and payable if the borrower sells the property during the mortgage term. The defeasance clause protects the borrower in having the lien released upon full payoff of the debt.

25. D

Because the balance is being paid off early, the lender may be entitled to or is exercising its right to a prepayment penalty. Not all lenders charge this penalty should the loan be paid off early. An acceleration clause enables the lender to declare the entire balance remaining due if the borrower is in default. Discount points are fees charged by a lender and are a percentage of the loan amount. A defeasance clause gives the borrower the right to remove the mortgage lien by paying the indebtedness in full.

26. C

The alienation clause is also called a due-on-sale clause that allows the lender to make the loan due when the property is sold. The acceleration clause allows foreclosure upon default. The reconveyance clause in a deed of trust requires the trustee to reconvey the property upon full payoff of the indebtedness. The assumption clause is a provision in a mortgage contract that allows the seller of a home to pass responsibility to the buyer of the home for the existing mortgage.

27. B

The alienation clause (making the mortgage debt due on sale) may provide for release of the original borrower from liability if an assumption is permitted. This release is referred to as a novation. A defeasance gives the borrower the right to remove the lien by paying the mortgage debt in full. Equity of redemption occurs before foreclosure, giving the borrower the right to redeem his or her property by paying the debt.

28. D

A blanket mortgage contains a "release clause." After a parcel is sold and a portion of indebtedness paid off, the loan balance is reduced. An installment contract or contract for deed require a purchaser to pay the mortgage indebtedness to a seller before title is transferred. A shared appreciation mortgage allows a lender to share in the profits of the mortgagor. A commercial mortgage is any type of mortgage loan used for a business or investment property.

29. C

An amortized mortgage is one in which uniform installment payments include payment of principal and interest. A balloon mortgage is an amortized mortgage that calls for a final large payment at the end of the term. A balloon mortgage does not fully retire the debt during the duration of the loan. A subordinate mortgage is one that is second in priority to another. Gap financing is short-term financing until permanent financing is in place.

30. B

Bridge loans are not generally long-term loans, are legal, and based upon arrangements between a borrower and lender. A bridge loan is a legal short-term loan used to obtain interim financing for projects before a long-term loan is in place. A home equity loan uses the security in one's home for the mortgage debt.

31. B

A junior mortgage may be a second, third, or fourth mortgage, but is always subordinate (lower in priority) to another mortgage. A term mortgage allows interest only for a specific term and then a principal payment when that term is completed. An amortized mortgage retires the debt through interest and principal payments throughout the entire mortgage term. Adjustable rate mortgages float the remaining balance of the mortgage at changing rates according to a standard index.

32. D

A deed of trust is a financing instrument that it is used in many states. It is made up of three parties: the trustor who is the borrower; the trustee, which is an entity that holds "bare or legal" title; and the beneficiary, which is the lender.

33. A

The title theory is an actual conveyance of the title to a disinterested third party during the payment term. This is the basis for the deed of trust, a financing instrument used in many states. The lien theory would not require this transfer of title. The lien theory is one in which the loan constitutes a lien against the real property. This is a basis for mortgage lending that is used in states that do not use a deed of trust as the financing instrument. A contract for deed would find the seller retaining title. A nonrecourse note would not transfer title.

34. B

Negative amortization occurs when the index rises while the payment is fixed, causing payments to fall below the amount necessary to pay the interest required by the index. This shortfall is added back into the principal, causing the principal to grow larger after the payment. Amortized payment provides for interest and principal to be paid simultaneously. Growing equity payment permits monthly payments to increase annually with the added amount going directly to the principal. A balloon payment is the final payment of principal and remaining interest on a balloon mortgage.

35. B

A wraparound mortgage is a subordinate mortgage that includes the same principal obligation secured by a superior mortgage against the same property. This mortgage "wraps around" the existing first mortgage that stays in place. The seller of the property makes a wraparound loan to the buyer, who takes title to the property subject to the existing first mortgage. The seller continues to make the payments on the first mortgage, and the buyer makes the payments to the seller on the wraparound. A bridge loan is a type of interim or gap financing that is usually not secured by a mortgage. A blanket mortgage consists of two or more parcels of real estate that are pledged as security for payment of the mortgage debt. In a straight-term mortgage, the borrower pays interest only for a specified term and then pays the principal.

36. D

A blanket mortgage is one in which two or more parcels of real property are pledged to secure payment of the mortgage debt. A shared appreciation mortgage allows the lender to participate in the appreciation of property value in exchange for a lower interest rate. A bridge loan is a short-term loan. An installment contract allows for the title to pass to the borrower once the mortgage obligations are fulfilled.

37. C

A swing loan is a type of interim loan in which a borrower uses the equity in one property to obtain the funds necessary to buy another property. The purchase money mortgage, including the wraparound, is a type of seller financing. A package mortgage is one in which personal property as well as real property is pledged to secure payment of the note.

38. A

The interest is taken out of the payment first and any remainder applies to reduce the principal. Taxes and insurance are calculated only when there is an impound, escrow, or reserve account for this purpose, and these figures remain the same for a given period.

39. C

A loan that does not meet the Federal Bank's loan criteria for funding is called a nonconforming loan. A straight term loan is one that may have interest-only payments in the early stages of the loan.

40. D

An adjustable rate mortgage rate floats based on a standard index as opposed to a fixed rate loan in which the interest rate stays the same throughout the mortgage term. A straight term mortgage allows interest-only payments for a specified time.

41. A

    $155,000 \times 0.055 = \$8,525$
    $165,000 \times 0.06 = \$9,900$
    $\$9,900 + \$8,525 = \$18,425$
    $\$165,000 - \$18,425 = \$146,575$

42. D

    The construction loan made to a developer is disbursed in progressive installments to finance each portion of the project completed. Disbursements are often made in stages based on the percentage of work in place instead of completed structures. A construction loan is generally a short-term loan and not based on the appraised value of the property. Home equity loans are against a homeowner's equity in the home and are not a construction loan.

43. D

    A package mortgage pledges personal property such as furniture in addition to the real property. The purchase money and wraparound mortgages are types of seller financing. The home equity loan is a loan using one's home as a security for the debt.

44. A

    A borrower who has hypothecated collateral does not give up possession of the collateral. The mortgage is the document securing these pledged properties. In some states, the deed of trust is the document securing the pledged properties. Liquidity refers to how readily an asset can be converted to cash.

45. A

    An open-end mortgage is a mortgage in which the mortgagor (borrower) is allowed to re-borrow against principal that has been paid so far. This mortgage allows Royale to avoid the paperwork and expense of a new mortgage each time he requires funds. When two or more parcels are pledged as security for the mortgage debt, it is called a blanket mortgage. A bridge loan is a short-term loan used to obtain interim financing. A mortgage given by a buyer to the seller to cover part of the purchase price is known as a purchase money mortgage.

46. D

    Junior, secondary, and subordinate mortgages all describe a priority of mortgage, not a type of mortgage.

47. A

    In a straight term mortgage, the borrower pays interest only for a specified term and then the borrower is required to pay the principal. With an amortized mortgage, the borrower pays principal and interest together until the loan has been repaid. With an open-ended mortgage, the balance may be refinanced without rewriting the mortgage. With a graduated payment mortgage, the monthly payments are lower in the early years and increase at specified intervals.

48. C

    The wraparound mortgage "wraps around" the first mortgage, which stays in place and continues to be paid. A participation mortgage is one in which a lender participates in the profits generated to secure payment of the mortgage debt. A growing equity mortgage supports a loan in which monthly payments increase annually. A blanket mortgage is for two or more parcels of land pledged as security for payment of the mortgage.

49. B

    Used by older people who need additional income and want to take advantage of the equity in their homes, a reverse annuity mortgage allows homeowners to draw upon the equity in their homes during their lifetime. A balloon mortgage is an amortized mortgage that calls for a final larger payment at the end of the term. A straight term mortgage calls for an interest-only payment for a specified term. A deed of trust is a financing instrument that transfers title to a trustee.

50. D

A sale-leaseback is a transaction in which a property owner sells a property to an investor who immediately leases back the property to the seller as agreed to in the sales contract. In a sale leaseback arrangement, as owner and lessor, the owner obtains income tax benefits of ownership. Because the seller is now a lessee and no longer owns the property, he or she must pay rent, and maintain possession and control of the property.

51. D

The question describes a balloon mortgage in which payments of principal and interest may be lower in exchange for a large payment at the end of the mortgage term. In a straight term mortgage, the borrower pays interest only for a specified term and then the borrower is required to pay the principal. A growing equity mortgage supports a loan in which monthly payments increase annually. The blanket mortgage is for two or more parcels of land pledged as security for payment of the mortgage.

52. D

Fannie Mae (short for Federal National Mortgage Association) is part of the secondary mortgage market where mortgage loans are purchased from the primary mortgage market. The VA (Department of Veterans Affairs) and FHA (Federal Housing Authority) are government-backed agencies and are part of the primary mortgage market. HUD is a federal housing organization.

53. C

A conventional loan involves no participation of a federal government agency such as FHA and is not always amortized. An amortized loan is one in which uniform installment payments include payment of principal and interest. An FHA (Federal Housing Authority) loan is a type of government-insured loan.

54. D

Conventional loans involve no participation by an agency of the federal government. The Department of Veterans Affairs (VA), the Rural Housing Service (RHS), and the Federal Housing Authority (FHA) are government agencies. The RHS, part of the U.S. Department of Agriculture, offers direct loans and limited grants. The VA guarantees a home loan amount of $36,000 for loans below $144,000 (as of March, 2011) in case a borrower defaults. For loans above $144,000, the VA will guarantee up to 25% based on county limits. The FHA insures a loan in case of borrower default.

55. B

Because a primary mortgage is sold to the secondary market, the money invested in the mortgage is freed from the original lender without the lender waiting for the borrower to repay the debt over the long mortgage term. This process keeps funds flowing back into the primary market, providing liquidity, so the funds can be loaned to others. Loans to first-time buyers are made through the primary lender. The primary lender then sells its mortgage debt to secondary institutions that collect the mortgage debt.

56. A

The Department of Veterans Affairs (VA) may loan 100% of the loan amount to qualified mortgagors. As of March, 2011, a VA mortgage limits the maximum loan amount with no down payment to $417,000. The Federal Housing Administration (FHA) insures loans to buyers who meet certain criteria. The Rural Housing Service (RHS) makes loans to qualified buyers in rural areas. All of these are government agencies.

57. B

Ginnie Mae (short for Government National Mortgage Association) is a federal agency and is limited to purchasing FHA (Federal Housing Authority), VA (Department of Veterans Affairs), and RHS (Rural Housing Service) loans on the secondary market. FHA, VA, and RHS are all government-backed agencies that are part of the primary mortgage lending process.

58. B

FHA does not make mortgage loans but insures loans in case of borrower default. Its mission is to make home ownership more available. FHA does allow lenders to make high loan-to-value ratio loans and is an agency of HUD.

59. C

The FHA (Federal Housing Authority) insures loans to protect lenders against financial loss. The FHA does not make mortgage loans or target low-income housing.

60. D

Secondary mortgage market activities are regulated through three large national institutions: Federal National Mortgage Association (Fannie Mae), Government National Mortgage Association (Ginnie Mae), and Federal Home Loan Mortgage Association (Freddie Mac). Because a primary mortgage is sold to the secondary market, the money invested in the mortgage is freed from the original lender without the lender waiting for the borrower to repay the debt over the long mortgage term. This process keeps funds flowing back into the primary market so the funds can be loaned to others. Second or junior mortgage loans may be obtained through the same lenders as first mortgage loans.

61. A

loan balance $\times$ rate $=$ annual interest
$\$350,000 \times 0.06 = \$21,000$ annual interest
$\$21,000 \div 12 = \$1,750$ monthly interest
$\$1,750 \times 2 = \$3,500$

62. D

Even though the property has been taken in a foreclosure, there may be a deficiency judgment for any monies still due the lender. Nonrecourse debt or loan is a debt secured by collateral such as real property, but for which the borrower is not personally liable. If the borrower defaults, the lender/issuer can seize the collateral, but the lender's recovery is limited to the collateral. A redemptive right gives a borrower a right to redeem his or her property generally by paying the mortgage debt in full before foreclosure. A purchaser may volunteer to pay discount points to buy down or reduce a mortgage interest rate at the time of making the loan that has nothing to do with foreclosure.

63. A

A mortgage broker is one who negotiates a mortgage loan between a borrower and a lender for a fee. A mortgage broker who represents a purchaser in negotiating a mortgage loan has a fiduciary relationship with the client and is the client's agent.

64. B

A cash flow projection or forecast is for income producing or commercial business or property only. It is an estimate of the timing and amounts of cash inflows and outflows of a business or commercial property over a specific period; typically one year. This projection shows if a company needs to borrow money, the amount of money, and how it will repay the loan. A lender evaluates the financial strength of the borrower, the condition of the property, and generally has an appraisal performed for both residential and commercial loans.

65. C

A mortgage broker who represents the purchasers in negotiating a mortgage, while also representing the sellers as a real estate broker in the same transaction, is acting as a dual agent.

66. A

The right of assignment addresses the lender's right to assign the loan to a new lender. Foreclosure enforces payment of a debt secured by a mortgage. Acceleration enables the lender to declare the mortgage balance due if the borrower defaults. The alienation clause provides for release of the original borrower from liability if an assumption is permitted and is called novation.

67. B

$\$4,200$ gross income $\times 0.29$ maximum housing expense ratio $= \$1,218$ maximum housing expense

68. B

A mortgage commitment is a lender's promise to loan a certain amount of funds. A contract is an agreement between competent parties upon legal consideration to do, or abstain from doing, some legal act. A rate lock occurs when a purchaser obtains a promise from a lender for a specific interest rate available for a specified time. A bond is a contract to pay money, indicating one party's indebtedness to another.

69. B

   Once all information has been verified and the loan documentation assembled, the loan processor submits the loan to underwriting.

70. D

   The lender must take location, condition, and comparable values into consideration before granting a loan.

71. B

   30 years × 12 payments per year = 360 payments
   360 × $984.21 per month = $354,316 (rounded) total principal and interest
   $354,316 – $128,000 principal repaid = $226,316

72. C

   loan × number of points as percentage = dollars in points
   $325,000 × 0.05 = $16,250

73. B

   TILA is the Truth in Lending Act and addresses the informed use of consumer credit. The Act requires disclosures regarding credit terms and costs included in Regulation Z. TILA requires four chief disclosures: annual percentage rate, finance charge, amount financed, and total amount of money to be paid toward the mortgage in both principal and interest payments. RESPA is the Real Estate Settlement Procedures Act and regulates activities of lending institutions in making mortgage loans for housing. MIP stands for mortgage insurance premium that is calculated on the base loan amount and is paid on FHA mortgages. APR stands for annual percentage rate.

74. C

   Regulation Z, which is a section of the Truth in Lending Act (TILA), does not cover commercial loans.

75. B

   The Equal Credit Opportunity Act (ECOA) prevents discrimination in the lending process. ECOA applies to discrimination toward any person who participates in a credit decision, and includes banks, retailers, credit card and finance companies, and credit unions. The Truth in Lending Act addresses the informed use of consumer credit and requires disclosures regarding credit terms and costs. The Real Estate Settlement Procedures Act addresses lender's disclosure of borrower costs in obtaining a mortgage. The Community Reinvestment Act encourages lenders to meet the credit needs of communities.

76. C

   The Community Reinvestment Act seeks to address discrimination in loans made to both individuals and commercial endeavors from low- and moderate-income neighborhoods. It is also called the Fair Lending Law as one of its purposes is to abolish the discriminatory practice of redlining in which lenders do not loan money in certain low-income communities. A lender's records are evaluated by the government to ensure that the lender is fairly meeting the needs of the community.

77. A

   Because a cooperative purchase involves the transfer of shares of stock (personal property), the transaction is governed by the Uniform Commercial Code (a code adopted in some form in nearly all jurisdictions). The Real Estate Settlement Procedures Act is a federal law regulating the activities of lending institutions in making mortgage loans. HUD is a federal agency that administers funding for projects related to housing. Local zoning ordinances have no jurisdiction over the financing of a cooperative.

78. C

   When a lender solicits a mortgagor to refinance a loan for no apparent reason, this practice is called loan flipping. This tactic greatly increases the debt because fees (often very high) are tacked on to each loan transaction. The borrower may pay a higher interest rate than with the original loan. The acceleration clause is a provision in a mortgage or deed of trust that permits the lender to declare the entire principal balance of the debt immediately due and payable if the borrower is in default. Redlining is refusal of lending institutions to make loans for the purchase, construction, or repair of a dwelling or business because property is in a low-income, and/or an integrated, or culturally diverse area.

79. D

Loans based on the borrower's ability to pay are not a predatory lending practice. Predatory lending takes advantage of the consumer making unaffordable loans based on the assets of the borrower, rather than on the borrower's ability to repay an obligation ("asset-based lending"). Making loans to unqualified buyers, increased interest rates due to borrow default, and taking kickbacks are all examples of predatory lending practices.

80. C

Subprime lenders are companies that provide loans to homebuyers who do not have adequate credit histories or are risky candidates for repayment because of income and previous debt.

Topic 6: Law of Agency

1. C

The principal selects an agent to act on his behalf. The agent is a fiduciary whose job is to bring a customer to purchase a property.

2. B

Another term for the principal is the client. The client or principal hires an agent to work on his or her behalf. A supervising broker is one who oversees the activities of the sales agents.

3. B

If the buyer is represented by the agent, he or she is the principal, not the customer. A subagent works for the seller possibly through a multiple listing service (MLS). A third party could be a customer whom an agent brings to a seller.

4. C

A buyer's broker is a special agent for the specific purpose of finding a property for the buyer. A power of attorney, a general agency, or an attorney-in-fact has more authority to work for a client and his or her affairs than the special agency described in the question.

5. D

A seller, buyer, or lessor of real property may all be clients or principals who are represented by an agent in a real estate transaction.

6. C

A real estate agent who lists a property to sell is a special agent who has narrow authority only for the specific real estate transaction. A general agent, such as a property manager, may perform many tasks for the principal.

7. B

Brokerage is the business of bringing buyers and sellers together and assisting in negotiations for the sale of real estate. A single licensed broker (sole proprietor) may own a brokerage firm. In addition, more than one licensed person, such as a partnership or a corporation, may own the firm. A listing occurs when a seller contracts with the brokerage firm to sell or lease his or her property.

8. B

A general agent is someone authorized to handle all affairs of the principal concerning a certain matter or property, usually with some limited power to enter into contracts. An example of a general agent is a property manager. The property manager may collect rent, evict tenants, enter into leases, and perform many activities for the principal concerning the specified property. A dual agent is a real estate agent who represents the buyer and seller in the same transaction. A special agent has narrow authority to represent a seller or buyer in a one transaction.

9. C

The customer, in this case, Dominique, is the party whom the agent brings to the principal as a buyer of the property. The client or principal is whom the agent represents, which in this case, is Perry. A fiduciary is a person who is in a position of trust.

10. **B**

A listing agreement does not automatically permit subagency. The principal must agree to it. In addition, many brokerage firms do not allow subagency outside of the firm. A multiple listing service (MLS) is based on the concept of subagency in which many agents working for the seller may market a property and share in the commission. But a listing seller does not have to allow subagency just because his agent belongs to the MLS. In certain cases, the seller may be liable for the acts of subagents.

11. **D**

A subagent is an agent who works through a listing agent in marketing and selling a property. Subagents do not work for buyer clients.

12. **B**

At the point described in the question, Gregory is acting under an implied authority only as the seller has allowed him to take a prospect through the property. An express agreement would be a written listing agreement or a definite verbal agreement to market the property.

13. **B**

The listing agent is the primary agent who is hired by the principal. Other agents work through the primary agent who is the listing broker as subagents including salespeople. The buyer and seller are not agents.

14. **C**

The multiple listing service (MLS), if one is available in the community, would publish the share that a buyer broker would receive from the listing broker. In addition, some buyer brokers require an upfront or separate compensation from the buyer. In all transactions, the commission is fully negotiable and may be paid by either party to the transaction.

15. **D**

Cooperating agents are agents from the same or different offices who participate as agents to buyers or sellers in a real estate transaction. Dual agents are agents who represent the buyer and the seller in the same transaction. Subagents are agents of the principal under the agency relationship with the broker. Seller agents are agents who work for the best interests of the seller.

16. **C**

Generally, the broker receives compensation at closing and apportions the salesperson's share. The compensation to a salesperson does not generally come directly from the client or customer.

17. **D**

Because of Joyce's conduct, it would seem that Joyce is representing the seller. However, since the agency relationship has not been discussed or put in writing, it is implied. The activities described do not fall under a general agency relationship that would cover more than one activity. Dual agency occurs when an agent represents the buyer and the seller in the same transaction. Express agency requires an oral or written agreement between the parties.

18. **C**

Subagents must deal fairly and ethically with the buyer-customer. However, their loyalties are with the seller.

19. **D**

Broker Clarice's statement of buyer agency would negate any subagency. Wong's sales agents are subagents of the principal, Peterson. The agents in the local multiple listing are also subagents of the principal. An out-of-state broker, who refers a buyer, is also a subagent working in the best interests of the seller.

20. **C**

Melissa can contact the sellers and discuss the matter with her broker. She can show the buyers the property if her broker and the sellers allow her to show it. She may not want to show the property if the sellers are unwilling to compensate her should the buyers purchase the property. Agents do not have a fiduciary relationship with all sellers, just those with whom they have an agency relationship.

21. A

The real estate broker usually is hired by a seller as an agent through a document known as a listing agreement. A binder is a form of contract that is generally accompanied by a deposit for the purchase of real property. An option to buy is a type of contract that is an offer. The seller is the offeror. If the buyer exercises the option, he accepts the offer. The option is for a particular price for a specified time.

22. D

Contracts (expressed) and conduct (implied) may be separately or jointly responsible for establishing an agency relationship. The fact that an agent has a real estate license does not automatically create the agency relationship. It is created by the action of the parties to the agency.

23. D

Because the property is listed by broker Green as stated in the question, broker Green represents the seller. Broker Green has an agreement to market the property for the seller. Broker White is bringing a buyer or customer to the listing agent, Broker Green. Because broker White has a customer, he does not represent the buyer, but represents the seller. Brokers do not represent each other. Broker White is a subagent of broker Green, because broker Green is the listing broker.

24. B

In a listing arrangement, the principal has an agency relationship with the agent and broker. Even though a sales agent may list a property, the listing belongs to the brokerage firm, and the broker is the primary agent. All other agents in the firm work through the primary broker agent.

25. D

Under the usual commission split agreement, a portion of the fee goes to the primary broker, a portion goes to the agent who listed the property, and a portion to the sales agent who sold the property. If a sales agent sells a listed property, the agent receives both portions. Some brokers use an incentive program, raising the proportion paid to the sales agent according to the dollar volume produced by that sales agent.

26. A

An agency relationship is always consensual. Both the principal and agent must agree to the terms of the agreement. A customer is the party the agent brings to the principal as a buyer of a property and is not a part of the agency relationship.

27. C

A written listing agreement is an example of an express agency. Express agency is an agency relationship created by an oral or a written agreement between the principal and the agent. Single agency is an agent who works only for the buyer or the seller. Implied agency occurs by the words or actions of the principal and agent that indicate that they have an agreement. Cooperative agency occurs when agents work together to sell real property.

28. D

A multiple listing service pools the listing of all member firms and allows extensive marketing of member firms' properties through multiple offices. A corporation is a form of a business organization. A brokerage is a firm that brings together buyers and sellers for a fee and markets real property. A franchise is an umbrella organization that lends its name and expertise to member firms that carry the franchise name.

29. C

Sometimes, a seller is reluctant to list a property with the multiple listing service (MLS) because the seller may be liable for the actions of subagents who work through MLS. These subagents may not be members of the brokerage firm that the seller initially listed his property with. It should be noted that some brokerage firms will not list a property through the MLS as well because of liability and other issues. MLS does allow greater exposure, a larger inventory for buyers, and may effectuate a faster sale through its marketing and number of agent members.

30. B

An agency relationship occurs upon signing of a listing contract that states the employment terms for the broker who will act as agent for the principal. A sales contract details the actions of a buyer and seller regarding the sale of property. Transfer of title occurs upon the completion of the terms of the contract. A license is permission to do a particular act upon certain property.

31. C

Although there are other reasons for agency disclosure laws, the overall reason is to protect the consumer and make them aware of the available agency choices. Many times, parties to a real estate transaction are not sure whom the agent they are working with represents. For example, buyers working with an agent may believe that an agent showing them property represents them when the agent may actually be representing the seller. A buyer, not knowing whom the agent represents, may divulge information to the seller agent that can be used against him or her in the negotiations. Agency disclosure and the use of agency disclosure forms help to clarify agency relationships.

32. A

Generally, if a real estate broker receives compensation from more than one party in the transaction, the broker must disclose the fact and receive the consent of all parties to the transaction. A broker who mixes his or her operating account with the office escrow account is guilty of commingling the funds. The escrow account is generally for deposit money and is not legally the broker's. Should a broker spend any monies held in escrow, the broker is guilty of conversion.

33. D

A seller broker must disclose to a prospective buyer, information about any defects in the structure. Matters such as the amount of her or his commission, the seller's financial status, and reasons for selling are private issues and part of the fiduciary relationship between the seller and the agent.

34. B

Although many properties listed for sale have material defects, the agent has a duty to disclose the defects to all interested parties.

35. A

Agent Regina has committed an act of misrepresentation because she has made a statement about the property, when in fact, she does not know whether the statement is true or false.

36. B

An agent must disclose any material defects he or she knows about to a prospective buyer. Reporting information to the multiple listing or elsewhere does not let the agent off the hook.

37. A

With an exclusive-right-to-sell contract, the broker receives a commission no matter who sells the property. An open listing allows an owner to list with one or more brokers. A net listing (illegal in many states) offers the seller a set price with the broker keeping any funds over that price for his or her commission. In an exclusive agency agreement, if the owner sells the property, the broker is not entitled to the commission.

38. D

The listing contracts are typically owned by the brokerage firm.

39. C

In an open listing agreement, the property is shown by more than one broker and the one who concludes the sale is entitled to the commission. An exclusive-right-to-sell agreement means that only one broker lists the property, and the broker is entitled to the commission no matter who sells it. In an exclusive agency agreement, if the owner sells the property, the broker is not entitled to the commission. In an option to purchase, the property owner contracts the right to purchase his property to a prospective buyer.

40. A

A broker must present every offer to the seller. It is ultimately up to the principal to choose the offer. Brokers cannot legally give legal advice to their clients or customers.

41. A

Real estate agents may not receive compensation directly, but through their sponsoring brokers.

42. C

Most commissions are calculated as a percentage of the final sale price of the property. Flat fees are far less common than percentage calculations. A fee for a broker is negotiated between the broker and the principal. Commission rates established by real estate boards violate antitrust laws.

43. A

Real estate agents may not receive compensation directly from other parties to the transaction, but through their sponsoring brokers. In this case, with the knowledge and consent of all parties to the transaction, broker Jack can forward the bonus to Kerry's broker.

44. D

A net listing, which is illegal in many states, is one in which the agent specifies a certain price for a property, and takes the amount above that price for the commission. This type of arrangement takes advantage of sellers who may not fully understand the value of their property. With a net listing, the agent may receive a higher commission percentage than is fair to the seller.

45. A

In a net listing, the seller specifies a net amount of money he or she wants to receive upon the sale of a property. All monies above this net amount are the broker's commission. This type of commission arrangement is illegal in many states. Net listings can be unfair to a seller if the seller's property sells for more than the listed price. A net listing may allow a broker to take advantage of a property owner by putting the broker's own interests above the interests of the principal. In an exclusive agency agreement, if the owner sells the property, the broker is not entitled to the commission. In an open listing agreement, the property is shown by more than one broker and the one who sells is entitled to the commission. An exclusive-right-to-sell agreement means that only one broker lists the property, and the broker is entitled to the commission no matter who sells the property.

46. D

sales prices × rate of commission = total commission
$100,000 × 0.06 = $6,000 total commission
100% – 70% = 30%
$6,000 × 0.03 = $1,800 firm's share of the commission

47. A

The fee or commission rate payable to a real estate broker is strictly negotiable between the broker and the seller or buyer.

48. A

Confidentiality is part of the fiduciary relationship. Disclosure of a seller's personal circumstances would be a violation of a broker's fiduciary duties to the principal.

49. D

Giving legal advice to principals or customers may constitute the unauthorized practice of law by real estate agents. Agents should refer legal questions to an attorney. Loyalty, reasonable care, and confidentiality are all common law fiduciary duties of an agent to the principal.

50. D

A broker must obey reasonable and lawful instructions from the principal. The broker must disclose material defects to the buyer even though the buyer is a third party outside of the fiduciary relationship between the broker and the principal. A broker must also obey all human rights laws and must present all offers to the sellers.

51. C

The agent does not have the duty of protection to the agent. Full disclosure, loyalty, and obedience to the principal are all common law fiduciary duties of the broker to the principal.

52. B

In offering services to the principal, brokers must assert reasonable care. Brokers must demonstrate that they possess the necessary skills and training to perform the requested services including providing trained and competent sales agents to market a property. Accountability, another fiduciary duty, refers to financial accountability. Brokers must account for and promptly remit, as required, all money or property entrusted to them for the benefit of others. Because of the fiduciary relationship, brokers owe the principal trust and confidentiality. Brokers must also act with obedience and obey reasonable and legal instructions from the principal.

53. D

Buyers agents owe complete loyalty and other fiduciary duties to the buyer and cannot negotiate for the sellers without giving up their role as a fiduciary to the buyer. Buyer agents can help the buyer to negotiate a price and perform a market analysis of any properties that the buyer is considering.

54. C

Because of the fiduciary relationship, the agent owes the principal trust and confidentiality. Should a seller need an agent to reduce his or her commission, this can be negotiated. However, commission reduction is not part of the fiduciary relationship between the broker and principal. The fiduciary duty of loyalty means that the agent must serve the best interests of the principal under the terms of the agency contract. Accounting of funds through a trust account is the agent's fiduciary duty of accountability. An agent must disclose any property defects he or she knows about to a customer or any other third parties. The agent may not work for personal interest or for the interest of others adverse to the principal's interest.

55. A

The principal has a duty to disclose all information to the agent bearing on the agency relationship and also not hinder the agent in his or her efforts to market the property. If the agent is found liable to third parties for the principal's misrepresentation, the agent is entitled to repayment from the principal. The repayment is indemnification to the agent and makes the agent financially whole.

56. C

A broker may not betray the confidence of the seller by telling the buyer that the seller is anxious to sell because of a job transfer. This is a violation of the broker's fiduciary duty of confidentiality. A broker may advise a seller on price, negotiate on the seller's behalf, and represent both buyer and seller in the same transaction with disclosure and informed consent.

57. C

Broker Bert may sell a property he owns through proper disclosure of his interest, and the fact that he is a real estate broker, to all parties to the transaction.

58. B

Brokers must keep adequate records about the deposit and disbursement of funds. Brokers should have at least two accounts: an office escrow account for client deposits and an operating account for business expenses in an insured bank. If brokers use deposit money that is not yet theirs, place it into the operating account, and spend it, they may be guilty of conversion. Conversion occurs if brokers use other people's money for their personal use.

59. C

An unintentional misrepresentation occurs when the seller broker makes a false statement to the buyer about the property and the broker does not know whether the statement is true or false. The broker is liable to a customer who suffers a loss because of acting or failing to act in reliance upon the misrepresentation. Brokers are liable for what they know from disclosure by the principal, what they should know because of their skill and training, and by an inspection of the property. The principal Bob, the salesperson Tom, and Tom's broker may be found liable for the misrepresentation.

60. C

The duty of accountability requires that brokers must account for and promptly remit as required all money or property entrusted to them for the benefit of others. Brokers are prohibited from commingling or mixing the funds of others with their business or personal funds. They must keep adequate records about the deposit and disbursement of funds. Brokers should have at least two accounts: an office escrow account for client deposits and an operating account for business expenses. The fiduciary duty of disclosure refers to communication of material information to the client. The duty of loyalty requires diligent work in the client's best interests. The duty of care, skill, and diligence refers to brokers having the necessary skill and training to perform services required under the agency relationship.

61. C

The principal cannot require the agent to perform any illegal acts, such as violating fair housing laws. If the principal insists that the broker commit an illegal act, the broker must withdraw from the relationship.

62. C

A positive misrepresentation may occur by omission of facts about the property even if the buyer does not ask. The agent has a duty to disclose what he or she knows or should have known about the property being marketed. The buyer could sue the agent and the agent might be found liable for the misrepresentation.

63. D

To avoid misrepresentation concerning a property being marketed, brokers are responsible for what they know from the disclosure by the principal, and should know because of their skill and training and through an inspection of the property. Brokers may be liable, and have to pay damages, should a misrepresentation be challenged in court.

64. A

This form of exaggeration in the real estate business is called puffing and is a form of misrepresentation of the facts.

65. B

By sharing confidential information with the buyers, the agent may have created an undisclosed dual agency and has betrayed her fiduciary position of confidentiality and trust to the sellers. This can occur when a subagent or seller agent is working with a buyer customer and negotiates or gives information regarding an offer to the buyer customer rather than working in the best interests of the other client, the seller. Price fixing occurs when two or more brokers conspire to charge certain commission rates to listing sellers.

66. B

A dual agent is an agent who is acting as a buyer's agent and a seller's agent in the same transaction. Dual agency can occur when one sales associate is involved with both buyer and seller. It can also occur when the sales agent representing the seller and the sales agent representing the buyer work for the same broker. In such cases, only one firm (one agent) is involved despite the fact that two separate agents are working independently with the two parties. Generally, dual agency is legal with disclosure and informed consent of both parties. Dual agency can occur in residential and commercial transactions. In many states, an agency disclosure form is presented to and signed by the parties to the transaction. This form outlines the choices for representation and what they mean to the buyer or seller. This form is generally used for certain residential transactions and not commercial transactions. Some states do not permit dual agency.

67. C

With dual agency, one brokerage firm or one agent represents both buyer and seller in the same transaction. Under a dual agency relationship, the agent has no duty to disclose all confidential information from one party to another. However, an agent's fiduciary responsibility of undivided loyalty is forfeited in a dual agency relationship.

68. B

Agency coupled with an interest occurs if the agent has interest in the property that is the subject of the agency relationship as is the case with salesperson Hersh. An arm's-length transaction means that the parties to the transaction are not related by business interest, friendship, or familial relationship. Exclusive agency is a type of listing in which a seller lists with one broker but does not receive a commission if the seller sells the property.

69. A

Although separate sales agents are representing the buyer and the seller, the brokerage for which both sale agents work is representing both buyer and seller, thus creating a dual agency. Double agency is not a real estate term and ostensible agency is a type of implied agency.

70. C

The desire of the sales agent to purchase a listing that belongs to the brokerage firm creates a dual agency relationship. The parties to the transaction, the seller and the sales agent, can agree to the dual agency with disclosure and informed consent. However, the seller would be giving up the fiduciary duty of undivided loyalty from the broker.

71. D

An alternative for handling a dual agency in a brokerage form, in many states, is the designated agent. With disclosure and informed consent of the buyer and seller, one sales agent in the firm is designated to represent the buyer. Another agent is designated to represent the seller. A designated agent is an agent, supervised by a broker, who is assigned to represent a client when a different client is also represented by such real estate broker in the same transaction. Both buyer and seller give up the fiduciary duty of undivided loyalty. The agent can still offer each the duties of reasonable care, obedience, and accountability.

72. C

Under a dual agency relationship, the agent has no duty to disclose all confidential information. However, the parties to the transaction must forfeit the fiduciary duty of undivided loyalty as this is impossible to achieve if both parties are represented by the same agent or the same brokerage firm.

73. B

Dual agency can occur when one brokerage firm or one sales agent represents both buyer and seller in the same transaction. Subagency occurs when a seller and broker agree that other agents will work in the best interests of the seller. Buyer agency occurs when the agent represents the buyer as principal and enters into an agency agreement with the buyer. Undivided loyalty is a fiduciary duty of the agent to the principal.

74. C

Although the sales agents are from different branch offices, they are still members of the same brokerage firm. If one sales agent from one office represents the seller and another sales agent from another office represents the buyer, then a dual agency has arisen.

75. B

In many states, an alternative for handling a dual agency in a brokerage firm is the designated agent. With disclosure and informed consent of the buyer and seller, one sales agent in the firm is designated to represent the buyer. Another agent is designated to represent the seller. A designated agent is an agent, supervised by a broker, who is assigned to represent a client when a different client is also represented by such real estate broker in the same transaction. Buyer agents are agents who represent buyers as clients in an agency relationship. General agents are agents who represent another in a number of different matters in an agency relationship.

76. C

As another choice for representation and to avoid dual agency, in certain states, some agents will work as transaction agents. Transaction agents do not represent either party and do not protect the interests of the seller or the buyer. They facilitate the transaction. A transaction agent helps to fulfill the obligations of the purchase contract and provides the necessary paperwork for each side.

77. A

In the question, Hannah is a single agent working for the seller and a subagent under the agency of her broker. Hannah is not a dual agent because she is only working for Sean in this transaction.

78. D

A transaction agent is an agent that works with both parties in a transaction. The transaction agent has no agency relationship with either party to the transaction but serves as the manager of the transaction, communicating information between the parties. A transaction agent does not promote the interests of one party over the interests of the other party and cannot advise or counsel either party as to how to gain an advantage at the expense of the other party. The role of a transaction agent is to locate qualified buyers for a seller or properties for a buyer. The agent then works with both parties to arrive at an agreement for the rental or sale of the property. A designated agent, seller agent, and dual agent are types of agency relationships that do not apply to a transaction agent.

79. B

An exclusive-right-to-sell agreement means that only one broker lists the property, and the broker is entitled to the commission no matter who sells the property including the owner. Seller Martin must pay a commission to broker Gerald, and if he does not, he is in breach of contract. Reformation permits a court to rewrite a contract perhaps to make it clearer. Injunction is a court order to stop an act. Assignment is the signing over of a contract to another party.

80. C

A listing contract generally terminates if the brokerage's license is revoked. This is because the brokerage is the primary agent on the contract and cannot do business if the license is revoked.

Topic 7: Property Conditions, Disclosures, and Transfer of Title

1. C

For much of the twentieth century, lead was a toxic component in most paint and was banned for that use. It can still be found in the water supply and in soil because it can chip and mix with soil from aging buildings that used the paint. Both radon and formaldehyde are gases. Radon seeps into the property generally from the ground and is radioactive. Formaldehyde is a type of preservative formally used in spray-in foam insulation and also can be found in furniture. Asbestos is a friable substance, which, when disturbed, possibly causes lung disease and is generally not found in soil or water.

2. A

Underground storage tanks may corrode over time and therefore leak their chemical content into the ground.

3. D

Radon is a radioactive gas that can seep into a property through cracks in the structure and through any soil or water that enters the property. Although all radon gas is believed to be unsafe, if tests show radon levels greater than four picocuries per liter of air in livable areas of the home, the Environmental Protection Agency (EPA) suggests a follow-up test. There are risks at very low levels. Electromagnetic waves are high frequency radio waves in which the electric and magnetic fields are inseparable. Formaldehyde can be toxic and is often used for preservation. PCBs are a toxic synthetic liquid organic compound that was used to insulate electrical transformers. PCB production is currently banned.

4. C

Total dissolved substances (TDS) are the number of different minerals in the water. Corrosive water is hard water with a high pH and a large number of TDS. One of the biggest concerns about water safety is that highly corrosive water may contain dangerous amounts of lead. The other pollutants—bacteria, radon, and PCBs—may be found in water, but are non- or less corrosive compounds.

5. A

The land mass added to property over time by accretion is called alluvion. It is owned by the owner of the land to which it has been added. Avulsion is the loss of land when a sudden or violent change in a watercourse results in its washing away. The gradual buildup of land in a watercourse over time by deposits of silt, sand, and gravel is called accretion. The right of accession refers to the right of property owners to all their land produces or all that is added to their land.

6. A

Theresa will be required to purchase flood insurance. In many areas throughout the country, properties may fall within the distance of the 100-year flood plain (the distance likely to be flooded over the next 100 years). The Federal Emergency Management Agency (FEMA) administers the National Flood Insurance Program (NFIP). The NFIP helps those in Special Flood Hazard Areas (SFHAs) to obtain coverage. Federally regulated lenders must require borrowers in SFHAs to buy flood insurance as a condition of their mortgage. Flood insurance is often not included in a homeowner's insurance plan.

7. C

The presence of underground storage tanks (USTs), often used to store home heating fuel, must be disclosed when a property is transferred. New owners obviously might not know USTs are on the property if not disclosed and have a duty to oversee and maintain them once they purchase the property.

8. C

Accession rights are property owners' rights to all the land produces or all that is added to the land, either intentionally or by mistake. Avulsion is a sudden loss or gain of land because of water movement or a shift in riverbed that may have been used as a boundary. Reliction is a withdrawal of water leaving a land mass. These events are accession rights that give Jaqueena rights to the land that forms on the waterside of her property. Escheat and eminent domain are the loss of property by government action. Adverse possession is a method of acquiring a title after compliance with certain statutory regulations over a long time period.

9. B

Real estate agents have a duty to disclose problems or potential problems that they observe on a property or that they find out about through the sellers or elsewhere. If Jeffrey does not disclose his observation to the purchasers, he may be committing an act of misrepresentation. Should there be a problem with the UST, he and his broker may be liable for the nondisclosure.

10. C

In this example, both the seller and the broker may be liable. Agents must disclose what they know or should have known regarding any defects concerning the property. If the dispute is not settled out of court, a court of law would make the final decision as to liability.

11. B

B must disclose what she knows about the property to any and all prospective buyers. Disclosure applies to both residential and commercial properties. In many states, a property condition disclosure form, mostly used in the sale of residential properties and completed by the seller, assists in disclosing property defects and other issues to prospective buyers.

12. C

If zoning changes are imminent, the seller and/or the seller's agent should share this information with the purchasers and not attempt to hide it from them or close the property before the change takes place and the buyers find out. If the agent or seller does not disclose this information, they are guilty of misrepresentation. Before closing, a home inspection is generally performed and should be performed in a timely manner because a closing date has been set. A real estate contract may be contingent upon the outcome of the home inspection and buyers may make their final decision to purchase depending on its results.

13. D

Latent defects may be structural or other problems that a seller may know about but are not obvious to the purchaser. Examples are hidden water damage or faulty wiring. If the seller fails to disclose this information to the agent, legal action may be brought by the buyer against the broker. The broker may then bring legal action against the seller for failure to disclose. Should an agent find out about any latent defects, the agents should disclose the information to the purchaser.

14. D

Most of the time, the buyers accompany the home inspector on an inspection of the property they intend to purchase. The home inspector can point out current and potential problems along with favorable features of the property. The home inspector is also on hand to answer questions from the purchaser about the property that he or she is qualified to answer.

15. A

Property condition disclosure forms must be completed by the seller who is best able to evaluate the property. In many states, the seller must complete a property condition disclosure statement outlining the status of his or her residential one-to-four-unit property. The form is provided to the buyer or buyer's agent before the seller's acceptance of the purchase offer. The statement may include a pre-scribed number of questions related to the property's condition, latent defects, structure, and location in a flood plain.

16. C

A property condition disclosure form discloses and reports various issues that a seller knows about the property. A seller has a duty to disclose problems or defects regarding the property with or without the form. A seller and/or real estate agent may be responsible in cases of misrepresentation. If there is a problem with the property, the seller cannot ignore the problem, but may negotiate with a buyer on its resolution.

17. B

The Residential Lead-Based Paint Hazard Reduction Act of 1992 sets forth the procedures in disclosing the presence of lead-based paint for sales of target properties built before 1978. Seller disclosure, distri-bution of an EPA lead hazard pamphlet, and a lead paint assessment all apply to the Act. The law does not apply to commercial properties. Target properties include most residential housing for sale or lease including cooperative apartments. Certain types of residential housing are exempt, such as senior citizen housing.

18. B

In the sale of large tracts of land or other types of commercial property, because of possible liability, lenders, purchasers, and tenants often conduct due-diligence reviews of the property. The parties to the transfer of property evaluate these reviews. A private engineer or consultant can conduct these assessments or audits. The assessments may go through four phases. These phases are not always uni-form. Phases may depend on what parties (lender, purchaser, or tenant) ask for in the assessment. Feasibility studies and highest and best use studies are types of property valuation studies.

19. C

Penalties for noncompliance to the Residential Lead-Based Paint Hazard Reduction Act may include the payment of up to three times the amount of damage incurred by a purchaser or lessee, up to a $10,000 fine, and criminal penalties for repeat offenders.

20. C

Removal of all lead-based paint before a property is leased or sold is not a mandate of the Residential Lead-Based Paint Hazard Reduction Act. Parties to a contract under covered properties are entitled to a 10-day period for lead paint assessment, disclosure of lead-based paint information if available, and must receive a lead hazard pamphlet. These pamphlets are published by the EPA.

21. B

The Residential Lead-Based Paint Hazard Reduction Act applies only to target residential properties built before 1978. The law does not apply to commercial properties. Target properties include most residential housing for sale or lease including cooperative apartments. Certain types of residential housing are exempt, such as senior citizen housing.

22. D

Although property may be transferred that requires cleanup, CERCLA does not prohibit the transfer, but does mandate that the party responsible for the waste clean it up. Because of the problems that may ensue should a contaminated property be transferred, due-diligence reviews are generally conducted by lenders, purchasers, and other parties to seek information about the property and plan for remediation if necessary.

23. D

A bankruptcy may force the debtor to unwillingly give up his or her property; therefore, it is an example of involuntary alienation. The sale, gift, or dedication of a property is all voluntary transfers and alienation of property.

24. B

The recipient or receiver of title is the *grantee*. The giver or conveyor of the deed is the *grantor*. When a sale of personal property is involved, the vendor (seller) is the "giver" and the vendee (buyer) is the "receiver."

25. D

Oscar is the *grantor*. He is granting title and the property to Yoko. The *grantee*, Yoko, is the receiver of the title and deed. The mortgagee loans money to the mortgagor who gives a promise to pay the mortgagee.

26. D

A quitclaim deed contains no warranties whatsoever. The grantor makes no statement or even implies ownership of the property being quitclaimed to the grantee. A full covenant and warranty deed contains the strongest and broadest form of guarantee of title of any type of deed, and provides the greatest protection to the grantee. Dedication by deed is the deeding of property to the public. A bargain and sale deed with covenants is an implied representation on the part of the grantor that he or she has good title and possession of the property.

27. C

A deed is the document that conveys real property. An affidavit is a sworn statement of any nature. A will is a document to direct distribution of property upon death of the property owner. An abstract of title is a summary of the history of ownership and title to a property.

28. D

Alienation is the transfer of title to real property. Delivery and acceptance is the actual transfer of a title by deed requiring the grantor to deliver and the grantee to accept a given deed. Dedication occurs when transferring property to the public. Execution is the act of signing a legal document.

29. A

The covenants described in the question are some that are contained in a full covenant and warranty deed. In the covenant against encumbrances, the grantor assures the grantee that there are no encumbrances against the title except those as set forth in the deed itself. The covenant of quiet enjoyment is an assurance by the grantor to the grantee that the grantee will have quiet possession and enjoyment of the property being conveyed. The covenant for further assurances states that the grantor must perform any acts necessary to correct any defect in the title being conveyed and any errors or deficiencies in the deed itself. A quitclaim deed or an executor's deed does not contain any and/or all of these warranties.

30. B

Caroline, the grantee on a prior deed who was the former purchaser, now becomes the seller or grantor on the new deed. A vendor is a seller on a contract. The part of the second part is the grantee on a deed.

31. A

A full covenant and warranty deed contains the strongest and broadest form of guarantee of title of any type of deed, and provides the greatest protection to the grantee. A quitclaim deed contains no warranties whatsoever. A bargain and sale deed is an implied representation on the part of the grantor that he or she has good title and possession of the property. Judicial deeds result from a court order.

32. C

Delivery and acceptance is the delivery of a valid deed to the grantee and the grantee accepting the deed. Dedication is an appropriation of land or an easement given by the owner to the public. Probate is the procedure for legally establishing the validity of a will. Adverse possession is the method of acquiring a title to real property by conforming to statutory requirements.

33. B

Constructive notice only requires that a real estate document be recorded generally with the county clerk. Many types of documents can be recorded that are not real estate related.

34. C

Continuous possession, open and notorious possession, and exclusive use apart from Jared are requirements for adverse possession. Dorothy does not need to show Jared's permission. If Jared had given permission, then the use would not be adverse.

35. A

A conveyance by deed is a voluntary transfer during one's lifetime. Involuntary alienation refers to involuntary transfer of title. Eminent domain is the taking of one's property with just compensation for the public good. It is a form of involuntary alienation. Adverse possession is another type of involuntary title transfer in which a party claims the land of another after occupying the land and possessing it for a statutory time period.

36. C

To claim ownership under adverse possession, the possession must be continuous and uninterrupted for a number of years. The statutory time for the possession differs among states. With adverse possession, there is no agreement between the claimant and property owner. A court has to rule on the legality of the adverse possession after the statutory time has passed.

37. A

Deeds must be in writing to be valid. Deeds do not require the signature of the grantee. The grantor signs the deed. Deeds do not need to be recorded to be valid but only to provide notice of the transfer.

38. D

The *habendum* clause, meaning "to have and to hold," describes the estate granted. Consideration is the evidence of value. Acknowledgement is the oath in front of a witness that signing the deed is a voluntary act. Limitation and subject to clauses dictate certain ways the property may or may not be used.

39. D

Calvin, the devisee, is the recipient of a gift of real property by will.

40. D

The judicial determination of a will's validity is called probate. The signing of a will is called the execution of the will. Distribution and descent refer to the passage of property according to state laws when there is no will.

41. D

Personal property given to someone by a will is called a legacy. Real property transferred at death is a devise. Inheritance could address either real or personal property. A gift could be in life or at death and could include real or personal property.

42. B

The term probate refers to the process of court supervision; thus, this term would not describe Lupe. However, Lupe is named as an executrix (executor would be a man). Lupe will be a devisee to the extent of the real property she receives and a beneficiary to the extent of the personal property she receives.

43. B

Intestate means a person has died without leaving a valid will. The term intestate has nothing to do with where the decedent resided or a decedent's assets. The concept of escheat, in which a decedent's assets pass to the state, would occur only in the absence of a will or any heirs.

44. D

Since the executor of an estate is named in the will, the testator (that is, the person who drafts the will) names him or her. The devisee is a recipient of real property left in a will. The trustee is a person appointed to control the assets of a trust. A court names the administrator when there is no will and thus no executor.

45. A

A purchase money mortgage is a type of seller financing in which a mortgage is given by a buyer to the seller to cover part of the purchase price. Therefore, a purchase money mortgage appears on the closing statement as a seller debit and buyer credit. The buyer is credited for the amount of mortgage money owed to the seller.

46. A

An encroachment is a trespass on the land of another as a result of intrusion by some structure or other object. Ensuring that no encroachments exist is a purpose of the survey. Verifying the deed, the chain of title, and preparing an abstract of title are tasks that are performed during a title search to make sure the title is clear.

47. D

A comparative market analysis (CMA) is used by the salesperson to find a listing price before the property is placed on the market. This document is not needed at closing. The contract of sale is the outline of the transaction and would be needed at closing. In addition, the broker would submit a commission statement so his or her commission would be paid. A title insurance policy insures a mortgagee (lender) against defects in a title pledged by a mortgagor (purchaser) to secure payment of a mortgage loan.

48. D

A census statement is not necessary for a closing to take place. A census is a government recordation of the demographics of an area. A survey shows the measurements, boundaries, and area of a property and may be required for a closing. A certificate of occupancy is a local government document allowing the premises to be occupied, and also may be required at closing. The prior deed is needed by the attorneys to prepare the new deed.

49. B

Proration is the division of expense and income between a buyer and seller at closing. The appraisal fee is the fee the lender charges the purchaser for a property appraisal. A survey is the process by which parcels of land are measured.

50. A

$2,581 ÷ 31 = $83.25806 rent per day
13 remaining days × $83.25806 = $1,082.3547 = $1,082 buyer credit (rounded)

51. C

A cooperative is conveyed through the transfer of shares of stock and is evidenced by a proprietary lease. Condominiums and other types of property are transferred through a deed.

52. C

$3,600 ÷ 12 = $300 per month
$300 ÷ 30 days = $10/day
8 months × $300 = $2,400
15 days × $10 = $150
$2,400 + $150 = $2,550 seller payment for property taxes

53. C

The buyer generally pays for the structural inspection of the property. There may be exceptions.

54. A

To protect the title, liens are almost always paid before closing.

55. A

$600 ÷ 30 = $20 rent per day

20 × 15 days not used

$300 unused rent credited to buyer at closing

56. D

An escrow department of a lender, an independent escrow company, or the escrow department of a title insurance company can handle an escrow closing. In addition, the escrow agent can be an attorney. Sometimes, real estate brokers offer escrow services but if the broker is earning a commission, then he or she should not perform the service because the broker would not be a neutral party. Most states require escrow agents to be licensed and bonded for that purpose.

57. B

The HO number does not refer to how long the policy has been in force, the premium discount earned, the number of units in the dwelling, or the number of people in the household. Different HO policies are applicable to different parties and properties.

58. C

An assessment refers to condominium and cooperative monies payable to the homeowners' association for maintenance of the common elements. A condensed history of a property's title is known as an abstract of title.

59. A

An escrow closing is a real estate transaction involving a neutral third party called an escrow agent who organizes and holds all documents for all parties to the closing. The escrow agent receives instructions from the parties to the transaction. A deed in lieu of foreclosure is conveyance of title to the mortgagee (lender) by a mortgagor (borrower) who is in default to avoid a record of foreclosure. Within three working days of receiving a completed loan application, the lender must provide the borrower with a good faith estimate of the likely costs at settlement. A trust is a legal relationship in which title to property is transferred to a person known as trustee.

60. A

$28,000 × 0.0775 = $2,170 interest per year

$2,170 ÷ 12 months = $180.83 interest per month

$180.83 ÷ 30 days = $6.03 interest per day

$6.03 × 12 days = $72.36 buyer credit

61. A

Title examination usually *does* begin with the present public record and works backward. A survey and an examination or inspection of the property are not a title examination. Verifying the last transfer of the property is only part of the title examination.

62. C

Recording the new deed has nothing to do with past claims and interests affecting the quality of title. However, clear title can be verified by an abstract and opinion of title. This document is a condensed history of the transfers and claims affecting the title. Also, a title insurance policy insures a mortgagee (lender) against defects of title of regarding the property.

63. A

An abstract of title is a condensed history setting forth any matters of public record affecting the title. The sales contract, which outlines the real estate transaction, does not present evidence of marketable title. A survey determines physical defects and not title defects. The settlement statement sets forth the expenses at closing.

64. D

A marketable title is one that is reasonably free and clear of encumbrances. Marketable title is not perfect title and is not necessarily free of all liens. For example, with a mortgage assumption, the buyer accepts the seller's title with the present mortgage as a lien on the title.

65. D

Since Peggy and Sue are not obtaining a mortgage loan, they will not receive any of the items mentioned in the question. These items are required according to the Real Estate Settlement Procedures Act (RESPA) for people who obtain a mortgage loan. HUD Form No. 1 is a standard settlement form that itemizes all charges to be paid by borrower and seller as part of the final settlement. A good faith estimate must be provided by the lender within three working days of receiving a completed loan application. At the time of loan application, the lender must provide the borrower with a booklet entitled *Shopping for Your Home Loan HUD's Settlement Cost Booklet*

66. D

Siding, stucco, doors and trim, drywall and paint, HVAC, plumbing, electrical, and major structural defects generally have builder warranties for various statutory periods depending on the item warranted and state law. Household appliances are generally warranted by the manufacturer.

67. C

Components already covered under a manufacturer's warranty are not covered by the builder's new home warranty. Limited coverage on workmanship and materials, a definition of the repair procedure, and the duration of coverage are all included in a builder's new home warranty.

68. C

Consuela's activities are allowed under the Mortgage Debt Relief Act of 2007 that generally allows taxpayers to exclude income from the discharge of debt on their principal residence. Debt reduced through mortgage restructuring, as well as mortgage debt forgiven in connection with a foreclosure, qualifies under the Act. The Act applies to debt forgiven from 2007 through 2012. Up to $2 million of forgiven debt is eligible for this exclusion ($1 million if married, filing separately). The Real Estate Settlement Procedures Act applies to disclosure requirements by lenders in making and closing a mortgage loan. The Community Reinvestment Act has to do with lender activity in low-income neighborhoods. IRS Form 1040 is an income tax reporting form.

69. A

The Mortgage Debt Relief Act of 2007 generally allows taxpayers to exclude income from the discharge of debt on their principal residence. The Act covers debt reduced through mortgage restructuring, as well as mortgage debt forgiven in connection with a foreclosure. The Act applies only to qualified principal residences, not commercial property. The Act applies to debt forgiven from 2007 through 2012. Up to $2 million of forgiven debt is eligible for this exclusion ($1 million if married, filing separately).

70. D

With a short sale, both the borrower and lender must agree to the sale. Unless there is an agreement between the borrower and lender to the contrary, the borrower may still be liable for the deficiency or balance of the unpaid mortgage debt. In a short sale, the borrower *does* sell the property for less than the mortgage balance, but this type of sale is generally faster and less costly than a foreclosure proceeding.

71. C

Sometimes called a friendly foreclosure, but more formally a deed in lieu of foreclosure, a borrower in default conveys the title to the property to the lender, to avoid a record of foreclosure. If the proceeds of a foreclosure sale do not satisfy the balance due the lender, the lender can sue for a deficiency judgment on the note. A deficiency judgment is a court order stating that the borrower still owes the lender money. After default, and up to the time a foreclosure sale is held, the borrower has an equitable right to redeem his or her property by paying the principal amount of the debt, accrued interest, and lender costs in initiating the foreclosure. A short sale is a sale of real property in which the sale proceeds are less than the balance owed to the lender. It is used if a borrower is in economic difficulty and cannot pay back a mortgage loan on his or her property.

72. A

Involuntary alienation can occur if an individual is forced to give up title to his or her property if property taxes remain unpaid and the municipality proceeds with a tax foreclosure. Voluntary alienation occurs when there is a willing transfer of property such as by deed or will. *Caveat emptor* is Latin for "let the buyer beware." Escheat occurs when a decedent's property reverts to the state if there is no will and no heirs can be found.

73. C

According to federal statute, the long-term (12 or more months) capital gains tax is 15% for property owners in the 15% tax bracket and above.

74. B

Capital gain is the profit realized from the sale of any capital investment including real estate. Capital loss occurs when an investment or other types of property is sold at a loss. The capitalization rate is the percentage of the investment the investor will receive back each year from the net income from a property. The adjusted basis is the value of property used to determine the amount of gain or loss realized by an owner upon sale of the property. The adjusted basis equals the acquisition cost plus capital improvements minus depreciation taken.

75. D

Performing an IRS Code 1031 tax deferred exchange allows an individual to defer capital gains taxes on real estate bought and sold for investment purposes. The IRS Code provides that for a qualified exchange of property, some or all of the capital gain need not be recognized for tax purposes in that year. The property exchanged must be investment property or business property, must be "like-kind properties," cannot be an exchange of residence between two homeowners, and cannot involve foreign property.

76. C

According to the IRS, property taxes are federal tax deductions for property ownership. Homeowners cannot deduct maintenance and repairs, mortgage principal, or fuel and water bills for tax purposes.

77. D

A special exclusion to the IRS law gives home sellers a tax break on the capital gains when they are selling their home. Home sellers may be eligible to exclude up to $250,000 if single or up to $500,000 if married of the capital gain on the sale of the residence. To claim the exclusion, the home sellers must have owned and resided in his home for at least two of the last five years before the sale of the residence. Annie and Xavier do not have to pay a capital gains tax on the sale of their property. They have lived in their house for five years and the profit on the sale of $50,000 is less than their $500,000 married couple exclusion.

78. B

The IRS age 59½ rule allows first-time homebuyers to use IRA distributions to fund up to $10,000 of their new home cost without paying an early distribution penalty. A first-time homebuyer may be an individual, a spouse, a child, a grandchild or a parent of the individual or spouse. To qualify, a buyer must have had no present ownership interest in a principal residence during the two-year period ending on the date he or she acquires the new residence. Safe harbor laws apply to independent contractor status.

79. D

In a tax-deferred exchange, if an exchanger receives cash or some other type of nonqualifying property in addition to like-kind property, the transaction may still partially qualify as a tax-deferred exchange. The recipient of the cash in the exchange, called the boot, or other nonqualifying property incurs a tax liability on the boot or other "unlike-kind" property in the calendar year of the exchange. "Unlike-kind" property is property that is not similar in nature and character to the property exchanged.

80. B

If an exchanger receives cash or some other type of nonqualifying property in addition to like-kind property, the transaction may still partially qualify as a tax-deferred exchange. The recipient of the cash in the exchange, called the boot, or other nonqualifying property incurs a tax liability on the boot or other unlike-kind property in the calendar year of the exchange.

Topic 8: Leases, Rents, and Property Management

1. A

   Estate and tenancy can describe a temporary right of possession. Freehold would describe the interest of an owner, not a renter.

2. C

   Sam is a tenant at sufferance. At one time, Sam had rightful possession, but he no longer has the permission of the owner to continue to possess the property. An estate for years is a leasehold estate of definite duration. An estate at will is a leasehold estate that may be terminated at the desire of either party. A trespasser is one who inhabits a property but was never in lawful possession.

3. A

   Jenkins has an estate for years, for which no notice to terminate is required. An estate for years is a leasehold estate of definite duration. A periodic estate or tenancy is a lease that automatically renews for successive periods unless terminated by either party; also called an estate from year to year. An estate at will is a leasehold estate that may be terminated at the desire of either party. Notice is required to terminate a periodic estate and an estate at will. An estate at sufferance describes a tenant who is originally in lawful possession of another's property but refuses to leave when his right to possession terminates.

4. C

   With an estate at will, there is no formal agreement regarding the termination except the need to provide notice. An estate for years has a definite termination date. A periodic lease renews itself automatically. An estate at sufferance means occupying a property after lawful authorization to do so has expired.

5. A

   Tenants who do not have leases and pay rent on a monthly basis are called month-to-month tenants. Tenants at sufferance are those who were once in lawful possession of the leased premises but their lease has expired. Trespassers are those who occupy the lease premises but do not and did not have lawful possession.

6. D

   Continuing to occupy property after lawful authorization has expired is an estate at sufferance and a form of leasehold estate. One would not negotiate an estate at sufferance. It would exist only after one of the other estates in the question terminated without the tenant properly vacating. An estate for years is a leasehold estate of definite duration. A periodic estate or tenancy is a lease that automatically renews for successive periods unless terminated by either party; also called an estate from year to year. An estate at will is a leasehold estate that may be terminated at the desire of either party.

7. C

   A lease is a contract that temporarily transfers the right of possession to a property. A deed transfers title and ownership to real property. Tenancy describes the rights of possession, and is not a contract. An option to purchase is a contract in which the owner sells a right to purchase his or her property to a prospect.

8. B

   A lease is a contract that must have consideration. The consideration is generally the rent.

9. C

   A lease must have the terms and conditions of termination. A legal description would be required only if the lease were to be recorded, which is not always necessary. An option to renew is not required, but may be included in the lease.

10. C

    A lease may have any term; there is no minimum. Notice is not always required to terminate a lease (e.g., with an estate for years). However, a breach of the lease *would* shorten a lease.

11. B

The loss factor is the area that is part of the rented space that is not specifically usable to the tenant.

12. B

The owner (the party transferring the right to possession) is the *lessor*. The tenant is also referred to as the *lessee*. A vendor is a seller.

13. D

The warranty of habitability clause in a lease requires that tenants have a livable, safe, and sanitary living space. Failure to provide heat or hot water on a regular basis, or rid a premise of insect infestation violates this warranty. The warranty of habitability also generally covers public areas of the building.

14. D

A lease clause that states that future owners cannot terminate a lease if the tenant fulfills lease obligations is a nondisturbance clause. An escalation clause allows for increments in the lease payment. An estoppel clause confirms the lease terms. A subordination clause in a lease generally states that the tenant's lease is subordinate to all mortgages, past and future.

15. D

A lease is a form of a contract and generally can be among any number of interested parties.

16. A

A type of lease escalation clause is the Porter's wage formula that allows lease increments according to the porter's hourly wage. Estoppel, use, and subordination clauses are other types of lease clauses. An estoppel clause confirms the lease terms. A use clause describes the uses and limitations of use for the leased premises. A subordination clause in a lease generally states that the tenant's lease is subordinate to all mortgages, past and future.

17. D

A security deposit is intended to ensure the return of the property in good repair. The tenant's credit-worthiness is verified by credit reports or checking references. A security deposit is not used automatically for the final month of the lease or for maintenance during the term of the lease.

18. B

Subleasing is generally permitted under a lease unless prohibited by the lease agreement. Assignment is allowed unless prohibited by the lease agreement. Apartment sharing is subject to certain lease restrictions and possibly zoning requirements.

19. A

Property owners lease commercial space according to the rentable square footage. The rentable square footage of most commercial space is the square footage in the total area, some of which cannot be used, or sometimes seen, but the property owner charges the tenant rent for the space anyway. The rentable square footage equals the entire space including the usable square footage and the tenant's pro rata share of the building common areas, such as the lobby, hallways, and restrooms. The usable square footage does not include elevators and hallways, for example. The usable square footage is the area contained within the space that the tenant occupies. The carpetable area is the space that is covered by carpet or flooring and walked upon within the interior walls of the space.

20. B

Unlike many residential leases, a commercial lease is generally customized. This is because most commercial spaces are unique and there are different tenant needs for each.

21. C

Assignment is the transfer or sale of contract rights that the new owner acquired from the former owner. Novation is the substitution of a new contract for a prior contract or a new party for an old party resulting in a new contract. Specific performance is a court decision that the contract will be completed as agreed. Accord and satisfaction is a new agreement between parties to the contract termination.

22. A

A tax pass through escalation clause allows a property owner to increase the lease payment as the property taxes increase. The expense stop lease provides a way that expenses are shared between the tenant and the owner. The owner pays a predetermined amount for the property expenses. The tenant pays expenses above that amount. The estimated expenses determine the expense stop for the first operating year. A form of rent escalation for commercial tenants in certain cities, Porter's wage lease escalation clause ties rent escalation to the wage rate of cleaning and maintenance personnel (classified as "porters"). The formula provides that the rent will increase a specific amount per square foot for a specified increase in the porter's hourly wage. An index lease is a method of determining rent on long-term leases. The rent is tied to an index. An index is a value estimate and economic indicator used by banks to adjust interest rates.

23. B

A package can describe a type of mortgage in which personal property, in addition to real property, is pledged to secure payment of the mortgage loan. A ground lease is a lease on unimproved land. A percentage mortgage is a lease in which the lessor participates in the profits of the business by taking a percentage of the profits as payment on the lease. A net lease is a lease in which the lessee pays some or all of the expenses of the property.

24. B

A lease that has a base rent plus a percentage of the gross sales of a business is known as a percentage lease. A lessee who contracts for a triple net lease pays all the expenses associated with the property in addition to the rent except for the debt service. An index lease is a method of determining rent on long-term leases. The rent is tied to an index. An index is a value estimate and economic indicator used by banks to adjust interest rates. A ground lease is a long-term lease of unimproved land, usually for construction purposes. The ground lease normally contains a provision that the lessee will construct a building on the land.

25. D

A ground lease is a long-term lease of unimproved land, usually for construction purposes. A percentage lease includes a base rent plus a percentage of the lessee's gross sales. The rent in an index lease is tied to an index; an economic indicator used by banks to adjust interest rates. A graduated lease is one in which the rent changes from period to period over the term.

26. D

A triple net lease is one in which the lessee pays all expenses associated with the property in addition to rent. Expenses may include property taxes, landlord's insurance, liability insurance, and maintenance. A gross lease provides for the landlord to pay all expenses. A percentage lease has a base rent and an additional fee that is a percentage of the lessee's gross sales.

27. A

Sublet allows another party to live in a dwelling but does not transfer the lease contract. Assignment is the transfer of legal rights and obligations from one party to another. Constructive eviction occurs if the tenant is prevented from the quiet enjoyment of the premises. In a net lease, the tenant pays some or all of the expenses.

28. C

State law and possibly local laws, such as zoning ordinances, may affect the terms of the contract, but the individual lease contract itself is most relevant in determining owner–tenant rights. Common law is law by judicial precedent or tradition as contrasted with written statute. The lease contract would have much more relevance to the owner–tenant relationship.

29. B

A new owner cannot raise the rents until the lease renews. The owner cannot breach a contract to collect more rent.

30. C

An owner would have a duty to make sure the tenant is provided with heat. Failure to install window screens, replace air filters, or fix a broken window would not generally be considered an act of negligence. A leaky gas heater is the most severe of the problems in terms of the potential harm.

31. A

The Civil Rights Law of 1866 was the first law prohibiting discrimination based on race without exception and under all circumstances. Race as a protected class is also covered under the Federal Fair Housing Law of 1968 and other fair housing laws.

32. A

Assignment is the transfer of legal rights and obligations from one party to another. Sublet allows another party to live in a dwelling but does not transfer the lease contract. An option to renew is a provision in a lease setting forth the method and terms for renewal. Breach of lease is failing to perform any promise in the lease agreement.

33. D

Expiration of the lease, mutual cancellation by lessor and lessee, and eviction are methods of lease termination. Negligence does not constitute a termination of the lease.

34. A

The simplest way for a lease to terminate is to expire. The tenant vacates the premises, and possession reverts to the landlord. Constructive eviction occurs if the landlord does not provide habitable living conditions and this type of eviction may require court action. A breach of the lease terms can also result in a court action. A sublet does not terminate the lease. With a sublet, another party resides in the premises and pays the lessee.

35. B

If a building becomes unlivable, the tenant has been evicted for all practical purposes because enjoyment of the premises is not available. Tenants may vacate their lease obligations if the circumstances are unlivable. Tenants, not owners, can be evicted. Self-help occurs when an owner violates statutory law by physically removing a tenant from the premises or prevents the tenant access.

36. B

If the property manager or owner is careful in selecting tenants, legal actions for eviction and collection of rents are minimal. The owner/manager should attempt to resolve any disputes before they become a lawsuit. If there is a lawsuit, the owner's or property manager's records must show their compliance with all lease agreement terms.

37. A

Self-help is a term that describes a landlord who violates statutory law by physically removing the tenants and their belongings. Legal eviction occurs if the court takes action to remove the tenant and his belongings. Constructive eviction occurs if a tenant is prevented from the quiet enjoyment of the premises.

38. A

Should a landlord take matters into his or her own hands, without the aide or control of the court system, and remove a tenant from the premises, this is called actual eviction. Actual eviction is wrongful use of self-help. Self-help occurs if the landlord violates the law by physically removing the tenants and their belongings from the premises or prevents tenant-access to the premises. Constructive eviction occurs if the tenant is prevented from the quiet enjoyment of the premises.

39. A

If a tenant is forced to leave because of lack of basic services, it may be a constructive eviction. Actual eviction occurs if a landlord physically forces tenants to leave the premises. A *lis pendens* is a pending lawsuit regarding a property.

40. B

Actual eviction is the illegal removal of a tenant by the owner because the tenant breached a condition of a lease or other rental contract. Eviction refers to an owner's action that interferes with the tenant's use or possession of the property. Constructive eviction results from some action or inaction by the owner that renders the premises unsuitable for the use agreed to in a lease or other rental contract.

41. B

If a real estate broker enters into a property management agreement with an owner, an agency or fiduciary relationship is created.

42. A

The relationship between the property manager and the owner is most similar to the relationship of a seller and listing agent. The property manager will have a greater variety of tasks to perform than the listing agent who is hired to sell or rent the property only.

43. C

The terms property manager and resident manager are not the same because a resident manager generally lives on the premises and is a salaried employee of the owner. Property management is a specialized, growing field in the real estate industry, and a property manager through a management agreement is an agent and fiduciary of the owner.

44. D

A management agreement includes a complete description of the property, the duration of the agreement, and a document citing the management fee. Building codes are not in the management agreement but the manager should have some knowledge of local code requirements and should have the building checked by professionals who can ensure the building meets minimal code requirements.

45. C

Jamison is both a fiduciary and a general agent in his role as property manager. A fiduciary is one who is in a position of trust. A general agent is someone authorized to handle all affairs of the principal concerning a certain matter or property, usually with some limited power to enter into contracts. A special agent is someone who has narrow authorization to act on behalf of the principal. Real estate salespersons and brokers are special agents.

46. A

One of the first duties of a property manager is to submit a management proposal to the owner, setting forth the commitments of the manager if employed. The owner–manager relationship is formalized by a management agreement. This contract creates an agency relationship in which the owner is the principal and the property manager is the agent for the purposes specified in the agreement. The operating budget is an annual budget and includes income and expenses for week-to-week operation.

47. D

A property manager's function is to solicit tenants, hire, train, and supervise employees, and maintain adequate insurance for the owner. It would be a violation of federal and state fair housing laws for a property manager to maintain records on the racial composition of the neighborhood.

48. D

Aside from the other obligations created under the property management contract, a fiduciary relationship is created between the property manager and the principal through the property management agreement.

49. B

Certified Property Manager is a National Association of REALTORS® designation given through the Institute of Real Estate Management (IREM), an NAR affiliate.

50. C

   Real estate asset managers closely follow business trends. They periodically review their company's real estate holdings. Asset managers identify properties that are no longer financially profitable. They may negotiate the sale or termination of the lease on such properties. Asset managers focus on long-term financial planning. Real estate agents sell real estate. Property managers rent, sell, and lease property. Insurance brokers provide insurance coverage for the property.

51. D

   The property owner and the manager negotiate the fee, which commonly consists of a base fee and a percentage of rents collected, depending on the size and income of the property.

52. D

   Although the property manager's fee is typically a base fee and/or a percentage of the rents actually collected, it is negotiable between the owner and the manager.

53. C

   In many cases, a residential manager is not able to represent the owner in court cases such as evictions. Some courts require that an attorney represent the property manager. A property manager can dispatch repairmen, make decisions regarding delinquent tenants, and check the credit histories and other data for tenants.

54. B

   The property manager should provide a periodic (usually monthly) accounting of all funds received and disbursed called a property management report. It contains detailed information of all receipts and expenditures for the period covered (plus the year-to-date figures). The report relates each item to the operating budget for the period. The owner–manager relationship is formalized by a management agreement. This contract creates an agency relationship in which the owner is the principal and the property manager is the agent for the purposes specified in the agreement. The current rent roll is the number of rental units that are currently occupied in a building multiplied by the rental amount per unit. The stabilized budget is a forecast of income and expenses as may be reasonably projected over a short-term, typically five years.

55. A

   Property managers rent, sell, and lease property. Deeds are prepared by attorneys.

56. C

   The management agreement, and not the management proposal, formalizes the agency relationship between the property owner and the property manager. All of the other statements in the question are true.

57. A

   The term risk management describes the concern for controlling and limiting risk in property ownership. Controlling risk includes the purchase of appropriate insurance coverage for the property including obtaining public liability insurance.

58. D

   Alexa is breaching her fiduciary duty of accountability to the owner. A property manager must disclose to the owner, and receive consent to accept, any fees outside of the agency relationship.

59. B

   The type of insurance that covers a building owner in case of an injury is liability insurance. Liability insurance covers the risks an owner assumes when the public enters the premises. Homeowner's insurance protects individual residential properties.

60. B

   The insurable interest clause in an insurance policy maintains that the insured has a legitimate financial interest. The loss payee clause in an insurance policy provides that in case of payment being made under the policy in relation to the insured risk, payment will be made to a third party rather than to the insured beneficiary of the policy. Insurable risk is the concern for controlling and limiting risk in property ownership. The coinsurance clause in an insurance policy is a clause in which the underinsured owner is "coinsuring" with the insurance company or taking on a portion of the risk of any loss.

61. B

In the management of office space, property managers must deal with competing vacant office space and keep vacancies at a minimum in a competitive market.

62. B

An anchor tenant is a large department store that serves as a draw for a mall. A planned unit development (PUD) is a neighborhood of cluster housing or other design with supporting businesses. A PUD may also contain common areas such as swimming pools, tennis courts, nature paths, and meeting rooms.

63. D

Generally, retail customers do not come to an industrial property. The transportation system is important to transport materials and the finished products. Customized utility services are required for machinery and equipment. Adjacent infrastructure supports the industrial park, plant, or development.

64. A

A strip shopping center and neighborhood shopping center may have an anchor tenant but probably not several. A regional shopping mall usually has several anchors, around which the smaller retailers are located.

65. D

Apartments, condominiums, and mobile home parks all require a property manager.

66. B

Corrective maintenance cannot be a fixed expense because it is unplanned-for maintenance. The purpose of corrective maintenance is to fix a nonfunctioning item that a tenant has reported.

67. D

The property manager must consider supply and demand and present vacancy rates. The manager adjusts rental rates only after a neighborhood survey and analysis of the factors affecting rental. If a building is 98% occupied, the property manager may feel justified in raising the rents, since the laws of supply and demand are working in favor of the property.

68. C

Capital expenses are required to improve or maintain a building. The operating budget is an annual budget that includes income and expenses for week-to-week operations. A capital reserve budget is a projected budget over the economic life of the property. A variable expense is an expense that is not predictable but subject to the needs of the property at any time.

69. B

Income received on a property without deducting expenses is gross income. Once expenses are deducted, the remaining monies are net income. Debt service is the payment of principal and interest.

70. D

The principle of supply and demand states that the greater the supply of any commodity in comparison to the demand for that commodity, the lower its value. Conversely, the smaller the supply and the greater the demand, the higher the value. In setting rental prices, a property manager would lower or raise the rent dependent on this principle. The principle of anticipation is based on expectations or hopes of the future benefits of ownership. This is the underlying principle of the income approach to value. The principle of conformity states that general conformity among properties in a neighborhood produces maximum value for these properties. The principle of substitution states that all other things being equal, a buyer will purchase a property among other similar properties that is offered at the lowest price. This is the basis for the sales comparison approach.

71. D

Income from any source, including laundry and vending machines, increases the potential gross income. The vacancy rate, credit losses, and tenants leaving before expiration of the lease term all contribute to reducing the potential gross income of a property. The credit loss may include uncollected rent from defaulting tenants.

72. D

The natural breakeven point describes when a property will generate a positive return. Leverage is the use of other people's money. Expense stop is a type of lease payment arrangement.

73. A

The property operating budget includes expenses such as debt service, insurance, taxes, utilities, and maintenance. The effective gross rent is the income.

74. B

The capital reserve budget, also called a replacement reserve, is a projected budget over the economic life of the property. It includes variable expenses such as repairs, decorating, remodeling, and capital improvements.

75. C

Preventive maintenance requires a periodic check of mechanical equipment to minimize excessive wear and tear from improper operation. An example is changing the air filters in air conditioners and furnaces. The purpose of corrective maintenance is to fix a nonfunctioning item that a tenant has reported. An example is a leaky faucet.

76. B

Corrective maintenance, the correct answer, is performed only as needed and is not predictable. Preventative maintenance refers to routine, planned upkeep. Reserve for capital replacement is created in anticipation of repairs, remodeling, and capital improvements. Construction is not really a form of maintenance and is typically planned and budgeted for in advance.

77. A

Income:

$425 per month × 12 months per year = $5,100 per year income

Expenses:

$420 repairs + $2,192 interest + $621 taxes + $297 insurance + $240 pest control + $1,222 depreciation = $4,992 total deductible expenses

$5,100 income − $4,992 expenses = $108 annual net rental income

78. A

$124,000 value × 0.11 capitalization rate = $13,640 net income per year

$13,640 per year ÷ 12 months = $1,136.67 per month rounded to $1,137

79. D

2,400 × $1.20 per square foot = $2,880 per month

$2,880 per month × 48 months = $138,240 total rent

$138,240 × 0.065 commission rate = $8,985.60 commission

80. B

5 × $1,245 = $6,225

6 × $2,400 = $14,400

9 × $1,010 = $9,090

$6,225 + $14,400 + $9,090 = $29,715 = total monthly rent

$29,715 × 4 months = $118,860

$118,860 × 0.03 = $3,565.80 rounded to $3,566

Topic 9: Brokerage Operations and the Practice of Real Estate

1. B

The MLS fees from agents in the office must be forwarded to the MLS. Only funds that are to be held in escrow for a temporary time such as security deposits, earnest money deposits, and deposits on a binder (a form of real estate contract) can be placed in a trust account.

2. D

Brokers must keep the office operating account and the escrow (deposit account) separate. If the broker mixes the operating funds with the escrow or trust account, he or she is guilty of commingling. Conversion is the illegal use of another's money that a broker may have in escrow.

3. D

Deposits for real estate transactions may be held by real estate brokers, attorneys, or lenders. The seller does not generally hold the deposit if the transaction is negotiated by a broker.

4. B

The broker's action constituted an act of conversion and, as such, was improper and possibly illegal. The deposit money does not belong to the broker at this point in the transaction (although it may be used as part or all of the broker's commission at closing). The broker improperly converted the deposit money to another purpose.

5. C

Agents should not accept deposits from purchasers if they have some reason to believe the seller cannot perform on the contract.

6. D

Illegal commingling occurs when brokers mix their business escrow account with their personal account. Brokers must maintain two separate accounts: an office operating account to pay business expenses and an escrow account for deposit monies. A net listing is one in which a broker sets a sales price for a property and uses any amount that the property sells above that amount for his or her commission. A blind ad is an ad placed by a broker for a property that does not indicate that the ad is placed by a broker or brokerage firm.

7. D

Broker Carole may be vicariously liable for the activities of her salespeople who are in violation of license law, rules, and regulations. Carole is guilty of failure to supervise and possible conversion of funds. Even though a broker does not commit an unlawful act, a court may find him or her responsible for the acts of salespersons in his or her employ.

8. A

Generally, real estate brokers must maintain their financial records at the brokerage firm's main office or branch office.

9. C

Once a broker receives a deposit, he or she must immediately deposit it in an escrow account until the money is needed such as at closing. At closing, sometimes the deposit money comprises some or all of the broker's commission. In certain areas, brokers turn over deposit money to the seller's attorney who places it in his or her escrow account.

10. A

The listing agreement defines the relationship between the real estate broker and the seller. It specifies the point at which the broker is to have earned his commission. Although a broker is generally entitled to a commission when he produces a ready, willing and able buyer to purchase the subject property on terms *acceptable* to the seller, the broker's right to a commission may be varied by agreement. Accountability refers to financial accountability. Assignment is the transfer of a contract from one person or entity to another. Assumption may refer to a mortgage assumption in which a purchaser assumes the mortgage of a seller.

11. A

A real estate broker's advertisement for the sale of condominium units or rental apartments containing pictures that show owners or tenants of only one race on the property does not comply with fair housing law. According to HUD advertising guidelines, housing advertisements should depict diversity.

12. A

Regulation Z of the Truth in Lending Act defines disclosure requirements in advertising credit terms for consumer loans.

13. D

Owners of multi-family housing cannot discriminate because of race or against families with children. If 80% of the units in a development have persons aged 55 or older, and it is deemed a community for older adults, then target advertising to this older population is legal.

14. C

It is legal to discriminate against smokers, but it is not legal to discriminate based on race, familial status, or sex. Although certain exemptions apply, they never apply to race, and generally do not apply to advertising.

15. C

Guidelines for Internet advertising for real estate brokers are provided by the Association of Real Estate License Law Officials (ARELLO). ARELLO addresses various issues for real estate brokers using the Internet. Brokers should also check the real estate commission of their state for guidelines. The Appraisal Standards Board of the Appraisal Foundation provides Uniform Standards of Professional Appraisal Practice for the Appraisal Profession. The National Association of REALTORS® also publishes a Code of Ethics.

16. B

This ad is discriminatory according to the Federal Fair Housing Act because it discriminates against families with children (familial status). Age is a protected class in some states and municipalities but not under the Federal Fair Housing Act.

17. D

The employer does not have the right to control the details of the worker's performance such as hours worked in the independent contractor relationship. However, under special regulations in the IRS code, the broker may supervise the work of the sales agents in the brokerage firm. Employers who file a quarterly 941 with the IRS have salaried employees, not independent contractors.

18. B

In order to qualify under IRS rules for the independent contractor relationship between a real estate sales agent and broker, the agent must be licensed. He or she can be a broker, associate broker, or salesperson.

19. C

Since Reuben is an independent contractor, he may terminate his employment arrangement with his broker at any time.

20. B

A person who has a set salary would be classified under IRS rules as an employee rather than an independent contractor.

21. A

Compensation not based on hours worked, no specified workplace, and either party terminating at any time are components of the independent contractor relationship. Only workers who are classified as employees and *not* independent contractors have federal, state, and social security taxes withheld from their pay.

22. B

According to the IRS Code sections 3508 (a)(b), real estate licensees may be classified as statutory nonemployees and are therefore independent contractors. Common-law employees have generally been accepted as holding employee status. Statutory employees mean that the work, trade, or profession has employee status. The IRS Code does not categorize real estate licensees as to full- or part-time status.

23. A

Whether a salesperson is an independent contractor or employee is important for income tax purposes. If the salesperson is an independent contractor, the broker does not withhold federal, state, and social security taxes. The licensure process asks for broker sponsorship and not an employment statement. Listing agreements belong to the broker. Escrow accounts are kept by the broker and are not a part of any employment arrangement.

24. A

According to the IRS Code sections 3508 (a)(b), real estate licensees may be classified as statutory nonemployees and are therefore independent contractors. Statutory law, and not common law, governs the independent contractor relationship.

25. D

A salesperson is not compensated by hours worked in an independent contractor relationship but may engage in outside employment. However, commissions are paid without deduction for taxes.

26. B

For the independent contractor relationship, the broker must only file IRS tax Form 1099 misc. if the salesperson earns $600 or more. Form 1040 is used by individuals to file their yearly IRS income taxes. FICA filings are for monies withheld toward social security. Form 941 reports quarterly income.

27. C

In order to preserve independent contractor status, a licensee may not be compensated according to the number of hours worked. However, commissions are directly related to work performed, the licensee must hold a current real estate license, and enter into an independent contractor agreement.

28. B

Although salespeople are independent contractors, the broker *has* a duty to supervise the salespeople. The broker does not file quarterly employment forms, track work hours, or provide vacation and sick pay for the salesperson who is an independent contractor.

29. A

Agents may have their licenses suspended or revoked for engaging in fraudulent practices. Agents may not give legal advice and generally cannot draft real estate contracts from scratch. Real estate agents may not accept any compensation except from their sponsoring broker. Agents may only accept compensation from more than one party in a transaction with full disclosure to all the parties and informed consent.

30. C

Seaver committed an act of misrepresentation and may be liable for the resulting financial loss the seller incurred. Although Seaver had access to the correct comparable sales and listing information, he did not properly research this information, causing the seller to refuse several offers on his property. Eventually, the seller was forced to sell the property below the competitive market value.

31. C

An injunction is a court order that demands that parties stop a certain activity or action. Rescission is to annul a contract. Reformation allows the court to rewrite a contract that may, for example, have a clerical mistake. Assignment is the giving of contract rights to another.

32. B

Generally, a broker may not interfere with a lease or contract of sale that a principal has with another broker. A nonsolicitation order is a directive from an agency such as the real estate commission or a court prohibiting licensees from soliciting listings in certain areas. Failure to disclose information is another license law violation. Brokers may not commingle the funds of others with their business or personal accounts.

33. D

Reciprocity is a mutual agreement by certain states to extend licensing privileges to each other. A kickback is a payment by a broker of any part of compensation in a real estate transaction to anyone who is not licensed or who is not exempt from license law. A market allocation agreement is between competitors to divide or assign a certain area or territory for sales. A multiple listing service is a system that pools the listings of its member real estate firms.

34. D

Kickbacks are payments by a broker of any part of compensation from a real estate transaction to anyone who is not licensed or who is not exempt from license law. A net listing occurs if a seller specifies the amount of money he or she wants to receive from the sale of the property, and the sales agent retains any additional funds made from the sale. Breach of contract occurs if one or both parties to a contract do not perform according to its terms. Commingling occurs if a broker mixes the funds or property of others with his or her business or personal funds.

35. B

In many states, sales agents and brokers can fill in the blanks in real estate contracts but cannot draw a legal document from scratch. Noreen may have engaged in the illegal practice of law.

36. D

It is not necessary for brokers to hire sales agents. A broker may work for himself or herself without any other agents. It is generally necessary to clear the name of the firm with the real estate commission, find a location that is in compliance with zoning laws, and decide the type of business entity for the brokerage practice.

37. D

Listing, negotiating the exchange of real property, and negotiating the sale of a business in which a substantial amount of real estate is transferred are allowable with a real estate license. The drawing of a contract constitutes the unauthorized practice of law.

38. C

A broker should not adhere to any commission schedule proposed by a board of REALTORS® or any other individual or entity. The broker's commission is negotiable between the broker and the principal. The broker is responsible for the acts of sales agents, appropriate handling of funds, and representing clients and customers fairly and honestly.

39. D

A false statement regarding an important matter in a real estate transaction to induce someone to contract is called misrepresentation. Reciprocity refers to licensure arrangements between certain states. Buyer beware refers to prudent acts by buyers protect themselves from fraudulent activities.

40. A

Magda committed an act of misrepresentation and may be liable to the developer for any loss the developer may have as a consequence. A real estate broker cannot divulge information to a client if he or she is not certain that the information is correct. If a client relies on the erroneous information given to him or her by a real estate broker, the broker may be liable for misrepresentation.

41. B

A lease is a legal contract and the termination clause may be complicated. Sales agents and their brokers should not give out legal advice. George should advise his client to consult an attorney.

42. C

Brokers must keep records of income and disbursements for real estate transaction for tax purposes for a specified time according to IRS regulations. In addition, the state real estate commission may have a required time for record keeping. A broker is not required to file quarterly FICA payments, track hours worked for licensees, or record outside employment, as licensees are independent contractors.

43. C

Certain franchises offer a referral fee for clients that are relocating. This practice is not illegal. Referral fees must be disclosed to the party being referred and are generally distributed to the agent who originated the referral. Referral fees may involve services rendered by another party related to the transaction. This can occur if an agent receives a referral fee from a mortgage broker for referring buyers to that mortgage broker for financing assistance.

44. A

With a corporation, stockholders are liable to the extent of their investment. A Chapter 11 bankruptcy petition is a form of a business organization that allows the corporation to stay in business while the finances of the company are reorganized and plans to pay creditors are formulated.

45. C

A C corporation does not have to issue publicly traded shares of stock. A corporation may or may not be for profit, is subject to a double tax, and must have bylaws that govern the company. The double tax of a C corporation is a tax on both the corporate and the shareholder level therefore paying a double tax on corporate income.

46. A

Both sole proprietorships and general partnerships create unlimited liability for the owners. In a sole proprietorship, the business and the owner are the same. The owner's personal assets can be attached to pay for business debt. With a general partnership, the partners are jointly liable for the partnership's debts and creditors can attach the assets of any or all the partners to satisfy the debt. In a corporation, the owners are shielded by the business structure from the debts of the business. Members of a limited liability company or limited liability partnership are not personally liable for the obligations of the company.

47. D

A sole proprietorship is not taxed as a partnership. The individual owner of the business is taxed. According to IRS rules, S corporations, limited liability companies, and limited liability partnerships are taxed as a partnership.

48. A

Arbitration is a form of resolving a dispute between two or more opposing parties by a neutral third party. With arbitration, a final decision is made. Mediation involves the use of a neutral third party to discuss and attempt to resolve a dispute. Litigation is another name for a lawsuit. Torts are a body of substantive law that deals with civil lawsuits.

49. C

A disadvantage of a C corporation as a form of business organization is that it is taxed on both the corporate and the shareholder level therefore paying a double tax on corporate income.

50. D

Limited partners in a partnership organization are not liable for the debts of the partnership beyond the amount of money they have contributed. Limited partners are a legitimate form of business organization and can be a form of organization generally for real estate brokers.

51. D

A C corporation is not taxed as a partnership. A C corporation must pay corporate income tax to the IRS, and the shareholders are also taxed on their dividends that are profits of the corporation; therefore, a *double tax* is paid at the corporate level and the shareholder level. General partnerships, limited partnerships, and S corporations are taxed as a partnership and do not pay the double tax.

52. A

A prospectus is used in connection with a stock offering. In the formation of a condominium or cooperative, the developer or sponsor must include a prospectus in the offering plan.

53. D

A trade-name broker is a broker conducting business as a sole proprietorship, using a name other than his or her personal name.

54. D

A disadvantage of conducting business as a sole proprietorship instead of a corporation is that the broker is personally financially liable for any debts and/or lawsuits against the business. A corporate set-up offers some protection against these liabilities.

55. B

A form of business organization, which is an artificial being, that exists only pursuant to law, with tax rates that are separate from taxes on individuals, is known as a corporation. Sole proprietorships and trade-name companies are owned by one individual.

56. A

Bankruptcy cases are heard in federal district courts.

57. C

If a property is part of a Chapter 7 bankruptcy, the broker must contact the bankruptcy trustee before selling the property of the debtor. The bankruptcy trustee is appointed by the bankruptcy court to manage the bankruptcy.

58. D

According to the Association of Real Estate License Law Officials (ARELLO) guidelines, online listings posted on a real estate brokerage firm's website should be consistent with the property description, contain the actual status of the listing, and material changes to the listing status should be updated in a timely manner.

59. B

If Judy discloses the national origin of her buyers, then she has violated the Federal Fair Housing Act. Real estate agents should not take listings from clients who coerce them to violate fair housing laws.

60. C

Jennie cannot take the listing as discrimination against race is not allowed under the Civil Rights Act of 1866 as well as federal and state human rights laws. There are no exemptions to the law when discrimination involves race. A nonsolicitation area is a geographic area where a real estate commission or other entity may prohibit brokers from soliciting business.

61. B

Individuals posing as prospective home seekers, but who are actually volunteers who investigate equal treatment by brokerage firms, are known as testers. The findings of testers are admissible in court.

62. B

Familial status, under the Federal Fair Housing Act, is defined as an adult with children under 18.

63. B

Because Belinda is able to meet all of the lease terms, the Whitleys are in violation of the Federal Fair Housing Act. Because they are landlords of a multi-family dwelling and Belinda belongs to a protected class (familial status), the Whitleys cannot discriminate against her.

64. C

Steering is a violation of the Federal Fair Housing Act and occurs if real estate agents encourage culturally diverse people to or away from certain areas. Blockbusting is another discriminatory act by real estate agents that cause people to panic and sell their property because of the entry into the neighborhood of a culturally diverse family. Redlining is an illegal practice by lenders to exclude people from culturally diverse neighborhoods from receiving housing loans.

65. C

Choice Bank is guilty of redlining. Redlining is an illegal, discriminatory practice by lenders to exclude people from culturally diverse neighborhoods from receiving housing loans. Blockbusting is another violation by brokers that make people panic and sell their property because of the entry into the neighborhood of a culturally diverse family. Steering is a violation of the Federal Fair Housing Act and is practiced by real estate brokers that encourage culturally diverse people to or away from certain areas.

66. B

According to certain exemptions in the Federal Fair Housing Act, and in many state and local laws, because Royce lives in the other apartment of the duplex, she has certain choices in renting the duplex. However, she cannot discriminate based on race. The Civil Rights Act of 1866 states that there can be no discrimination based on race, no exemptions.

67. A

Rental applications that ask about race violate the Federal Fair Housing Act and the Civil Rights Act of 1866.

68. C

Requesting a certain type of housing is not housing discrimination.

69. B

Showing buyers properties based on affordability is not an example of steering.

70. C

Blockbusting is inducing present property owners to sell by telling them that a person from a particular race, color, or national origin is moving into the neighborhood. Steering is the practice of directing prospective purchasers toward or away from certain neighborhoods. Redlining is a lender refusal to make loans to purchase, construct, or repair a dwelling by discriminating against any of the protected classes. Discriminatory advertising is any ad that states a preference, limitation, or discrimination on the basis of protected traits.

71. B

Asking about an applicant's income is not discriminatory since it is directly related to whether or not credit would be granted. Questions about familial status, national origin, or racial background violate the Federal Fair Housing Act.

72. D

If a seller requests that a real estate salesperson not show the seller's property to minorities, the salesperson should withdraw from the listing. No other broker should assist in this illegal instruction. Reporting the seller to HUD might not result in an offense since, at this point, the seller has not yet discriminated.

73. D

In the scenario in the question, the applicants have an excellent credit rating. The lender is guilty of redlining and discriminatory practices. Redlining is refusing to make loans to purchase, construct, or repair a dwelling by discriminating against any of the protected classes. The lender may also be guilty of discrimination based on national origin and race.

74. B

At the end of the tenancy, the tenant must return the premises to its original condition at his or her own expense. If the owner agrees, some changes may remain as changed. The tenant typically bears all expenses.

75. A

Sexual orientation is a protected class under certain state laws but not under the Federal Fair Housing Act. National origin, race, and familial status are protected classes under federal law.

76. D

Familial status (families with children), race, and religion are all protected classes under the Federal Fair Housing Act. Marital status is not.

77. A

Under the Federal Fair Housing Act, exemptions exist for housing for older people if the housing has at least one person who is 55 or older in at least 80% of the occupied units, and the development adheres to a policy that demonstrates intent to house persons who are 55 or older.

78. A

A fine that may be imposed through HUD for a first offense for violation of the Federal Fair Housing Act is $10,000. A fine of $50,000 may be imposed for repeated violations.

79. A

Federal and state laws and regulations govern ads and communication for housing and rental property. The real estate agent should consider the intent of the message and the exclusion of any groups when creating ads or communicating in any way with customers or clients. Discrimination includes specific directions to a property that refer to well-known racial, ethnic, or religious landmarks, or other landmarks indicating a preference for a specific type of person or community.

80. D

Under Federal Fair Housing laws, a lender may not offer a different loan interest rate based on minority status. Unemployment may be a reason to refuse a loan applicant. Most lenders do require a credit report and an appraisal of the property that is the subject of the mortgage.

81. D

Familial status (families with children), race, and religion are all protected classes under the Federal Fair Housing Act. Lawful occupation is not a protected class under federal law.

82. C

All citizens do have the right to inherit, buy, sell, and lease real and personal property. The Civil Rights Act of 1866 prohibits discrimination because of race and is in full force today and not declared null and void after the Civil War.

83. D

The civil penalty for multiple discriminatory acts in violation of the Federal Fair Housing Act is $50,000.

84. A

Testers are volunteers who visit real estate firms and other business to assess equal treatment for all. Discriminatory advertising, steering, and discrimination against families with children are all prohibited under the Federal Fair Housing Act.

85. D

Dewey, Cheatum, and Howe Savings and Loan would violate the Federal Fair Housing Act by denying a loan to Seymour because of his religion. Discrimination by lending institutions on the basis of religion is a violation of the Federal Fair Housing Act.

86. C

The Civil Rights Act of 1866 prohibits discrimination based on race, no exceptions. This means that even if the federal, state, or local laws have exemptions to the fair housing law, no one can discriminate based on a person's race, no matter what the reason.

87. B

In Plessy v. Ferguson (1866), the Supreme Court ruled that separate but equal is legally acceptable. Therefore, as long as separate housing accommodations or facilities for African Americans and whites were deemed equal, they were legal. In Brown v. Board of Education (1954), the Supreme Court reversed this decision. This Supreme Court decision stated that separate but equal facilities were unconstitutional. In Buchanan v. Warley (1917), the Supreme Court decided that city ordinances that denied minorities the right to occupy housing in blocks where whites lived was unconstitutional.

88. A

The Federal Fair Housing Act does not cover discrimination in the sale or rental of commercial property, only residential housing. State and local laws may cover commercial property as well as residential property.

89. C

Familial status and persons with disabilities were added as protected classes to the 1988 amendments to the Federal Fair Housing Act of 1968. Religion was included as a protected class in the 1968 Federal Fair Housing Act. Sex was added as a protected class in the Housing and Community Development Act of 1974. Race, color, and national origin were included as a protected class in the 1968 Federal Fair Housing Act. Pets are not a protected class at this time.

90. B

Sex or gender as a protected class was added to fair housing law by the Housing and Community Development Act of 1974. The Federal Fair Housing Act of 1968 included national origin as a protected class. The Fair Housing Amendments Act of 1988 added familial status as a protected class. The Civil Rights Act of 1866 first included race as a protected class.

91. C

The only choice in the question that is not exempt under the Federal Fair Housing Act is real estate brokers acting as brokers. Real estate brokers cannot participate in any of the exemptions in the Act. Note that state and municipal laws may be more restrictive than the federal law as to exemptions in the federal law.

92. B

Financial penalty, action by the U.S. Attorney General, and civil suit in federal court are possible HUD sanctions. Enforcement of the Federal Fair Housing Act through HUD does *not* include the revocation of a real estate license.

93. B

Fair housing complaints may be referred to the U.S. Department of Housing and Urban Development (HUD). States and municipalities may also have human rights commissions where complaints may be filed.

94. A

Individuals with AIDS are protected under the Federal Fair Housing Act and the Americans with Disabilities Act as persons with disabilities.

95. A

Disability, religion, and national origin are all protected classes under the Federal Fair Housing Act. Although age is not a protected class under the federal law, it is a protected class under some state and municipal laws.

96. A

The federal regulatory agency that oversees human rights complaints and legislation is HUD or Department of Housing and Urban Development. The FHA or Federal Housing Authority is a private agency that insures mortgage loans. Fannie Mae is short for Federal National Mortgage Association and is an agency of the federal government that buys mortgage loans on the secondary market. The USDA stands for the U.S. Department of Agriculture.

97. C

The Civil Rights Act of 1866 has the blanket statement that citizens have the same rights to inherit, buy, sell, or lease real and personal property, prohibiting racial discrimination. The Federal Fair Housing Act of 1968 also prohibits discrimination based on race. The Bill of Rights is part of the U.S. Constitution. The Civil Rights Act of 1964 prohibits discrimination in any program receiving federal funds.

98. B

Megan's Law mandated the disclosure of sex offenders in a neighborhood. The states have regulations and case law as to the responsibility of the real estate agent in this disclosure. The Federal Fair Housing Act addresses discrimination in housing. Filtering down describes the economic decline in a neighborhood. Testers are individuals who visit real estate firms posing as home seekers to assess if the firm is in compliance with fair housing laws.

99. A

Free competition is not illegal under antitrust law; however, tie-in arrangements, group boycotts, and price fixing are. A tie-in arrangement is between a party selling a service to a buyer, that as a condition of sale, the buyer will buy another product from the seller. A group boycott is a conspiracy in which a person or group is coerced into not doing business with another person or group. Price fixing occurs when competitors in a certain group conspire to charge the same or similar price.

100. C

The Americans with Disabilities Act covers commercial and public facilities, not single-family homes.

101. D

A business activity where there is a monopoly or conspiracy that negatively impacts another individual's or company's ability to do business is called an illegal restraint of trade and violates antitrust laws. Injunction is a court order to stop a certain act. A kickback occurs if a broker improperly pays a fee to another such as an unlicensed individual.

102. A

The supreme law of our country is the U.S. Constitution.

103. A

Violation of the Sherman Antitrust Act will not result in capital punishment, but a felony charge, imprisonment, or monetary damages could be penalties.

104. B

The governmental commission that has the power to declare trade practices unfair is the Federal Trade Commission, also known as the FTC. The FTC oversees antitrust violations. The other examples in the question are fictitious.

105. B

A major purpose of the license law is to protect the public from dishonest dealings by brokers and salespersons.

106. A

A tie-in arrangement is an agreement between a party selling a product or service with a buyer that, as a condition of the sale, the buyer will buy another product from the seller or the buyer will not buy a product or use a service of another. An agreement between competitors to divide or assign a certain area of territory for sales is also a violation of antitrust laws and is called market allocation. Illegal price fixing occurs when competitors conspire to charge the same amount for services. A group boycott is a conspiracy in which a person or group is persuaded or coerced into not doing business with another person or group.

107. A

The example in the question illustrates an illegal market allocation agreement in which competitors divide or allocate a market area for sales and agree not to compete in those areas. A tie-in arrangement is between a party selling a service to a buyer, that as a condition of sale, the buyer will buy another product from the seller or not do business with another. Price fixing occurs when competitors in a certain group conspire to charge the same or similar price. A group boycott is a conspiracy in which a person or group is coerced into not doing business with another person or group.

108. A

It is illegal for two or more brokers to agree to charge certain commission rates to listing sellers. This is "price fixing" and is a restraint of trade that violates antitrust laws.

109. D

Real estate boards may not publish prescribed commission rates or amounts. This is a violation of antitrust laws including the Sherman Antitrust Act.

110. B

The dollar amount of the federal annual exclusion per person to the federal gift tax is $13,000. This means that a taxpayer does not have to report or pay taxes on a gift of $13,000 or less to another.

111. C

Illegal price fixing is a violation of antitrust laws. An illegal group boycott occurs when one group or person is persuaded or coerced to not do business with another group or person. An illegal market allocation agreement occurs when competing companies agree to split a territory among them.

112. B

The Federal Trade Commission settled a lawsuit with several multiple listing services (MLS) and made an agreement that said the MLS must carry exclusive agency listings and other lawful listings without restrictions. The agreement was made because some multiple listing services refused discount brokers access. The MLS should not make brokers charge the same fee and there is generally a fee for sales agents to belong to MLS.

113. B

The Clayton Antitrust Act was enacted to preserve a system of free economic enterprise, similar to the Sherman Antitrust Act, and also covers interstate trade or commerce. The Federal Trade Commission is a U.S. government agency that has the power to declare trade practices unfair.

114. D

Zoning laws may not be used to establish neighborhoods restricted to people of a certain race. This would be a violation of fair housing laws. Zoning laws can prevent the demolition of historic buildings, regulate the architectural style of buildings, and control growth and development.

115. B

Tie-in arrangements are agreements between a party selling a product or service with a buyer that, as a condition of the sale, the buyer will buy another product from the seller or the buyer will not buy a product or use a service of another. This example in the question is an illegal restraint of trade and violates antitrust laws.

116. B

Police power is the power of government to protect the health, safety, and welfare of its citizens. Civil procedure refers to the body of law that defines the exact steps that must be followed in the development of a lawsuit.

117. A

A fine of $50,000 for a first offense, $100,000 for subsequent offenses, and injunctions against operation of a business are actions to enforce the Americans with Disabilities Act. The Act is not, however, enforceable by a jail sentence.

118. D

All of the choices in the question are subject to the Americans with Disabilities Act (ADA), passed in 1992. This law prohibits discrimination by any public or commercial facility or public transportation against persons with a mental or physical impairment that substantially limits one or more of the major life activities.

119. D

The Community Reinvestment Act (CRA) (1977, last revised 2010), also known as the Fair Lending Law, was enacted to encourage lenders to help meet the credit needs of communities where the bank is located. The Act requires that each lender's record in helping meet the credit needs of its entire community be periodically evaluated.

120. B

One of the main purposes of the Sherman Antitrust Act is to allow small businesses to compete effectively with larger companies. The Act applies to many industries including the real estate industry.

Topic 10: Real Estate Math

1. B

   sales price × rate of commission = total commission

   $6,000 ÷ $100,000 = 0.06 = 6% commission rate

2. A

   sales price × rate of commission = total commission

   $7,215 commission ÷ $111,000 sales price = 0.065 or 6.5% commission rate

3. D

   3,500 square feet × $1.85 per square foot = $6,475 per month

   $6,475 per month × 24 months = $155,400 total rent

   $155,400 × 0.03 = $4,662 commission

4. B

   sales prices × rate of commission = total commission

   $124,500 price × 0.06 = $7,470 total commission

   $7,470 × 0.70 = $5,229 commission

5. B

   $72,000 total cost − $36,000 A's share − $12,000 B's share = $24,000 C's share

   $24,000 ÷ $72,000 = 0.33333 or 33.3% is C's ownership share

6. C

   sales prices × rate of commission = total commission

   $116,500 price × 0.065 commission rate = $7,572.50 total commission

   All other information is irrelevant

7. C

   sales price × rate = commission

   $85,000 × 0.08 = $6,800

   $6,800 × 0.80 = $5,440 commission

8. B

   $45,000 × 1.20 (120%) = $54,000 asking price

   $54,000 × 0.90 = $48,600 selling price

9. D

   sales prices × rate of commission = total commission

   $7,000 + $48,000 = $55,000

   100% − 7% commission = 93%

   $55,000 ÷ 0.93 = $59,140 price at which property must be sold (rounded)

10. B

    sales prices × rate of commission = total commission

    $64,000 price × 0.08 = $5,120

    $5,120 × 0.65 = $3,328 Simpson's commission split

11. B

    43,560 square feet per acre × 0.84 acres = 36,590 square feet (rounded)

12. B

    9 inches thick on each of two ends = 1.5 feet

    35 feet − 1.5 feet = 33.5 feet

    26.5 feet − 1.5 feet = 25 feet

    33.5 feet × 25 feet = 837.5 square feet

13. A

    490 feet × 356 feet = 174,440 square feet

    174,440 ÷ 43,560 square feet per acre = 4 acres

14. C
    area = length × width
    43,560 ÷ 450 = 96.8 feet = 97 feet (rounded)

15. D
    .264 feet × 660 feet = 174,240 square feet 174,240 × $8.50 per square foot = $1,481,040 total cost

16. C
    $128,000 price × 0.90 loan-to-value ratio = $115,200 loan
    $115,200 loan × 0.0225 points = $2,592 in points

17. C
    $12,500 loan × 0.095 interest rate = $1,187.50 interest per year
    $1,187.50 ÷ 12 months = $98.9583 per month
    $98.9583 monthly × 6 months = $593.75 total interest paid

18. B
    loan ÷ value = ratio
    $375,000 ÷ $450,000 = 0.83333 = 80% loan-to-value ratio (rounded)

19. C
    $962.50 interest per month × 12 months = $11,550 per year
    $11,550 ÷ 0.105 interest rate = $110,000 loan balance

20. C
    $86,300 price × 0.85 loan-to-value ratio = $73,355 loan
    $73,355 loan × 0.01 loan origination fee = $734 (rounded)

    For the buyer's required cash:
    $86,300 price + $734 loan origination fee + $2,625 additional closing costs = $89,659 total charges
    $89,659 − $73,355 loan = $16,304
    $16,304 − $3,000 earnest money deposit = $13,304 total due at closing

21. B
    loan balance × rate = annual interest
    $500 × 12 months = $6,000 annual interest
    $6,000 ÷ 0.065 = $92,307.69 loan balance

22. A
    points: loan × number of points as percentage = dollars in points
    $155,000 × 0.055 = $8,525 dollars in points
    commission: sales price × rate of commission = total commission
    $165,000 × 0.06 = $9,900 total commission
    $9,900 + $8,525 = $18,425 total expenses
    $165,000 − $18,425 = $146,575 net to seller

23. B
    To avoid PMI, the borrower must put a 20% down payment for a maximum loan amount of 80%
    $128,000 price × 0.20 down payment = $25,600 down payment

24. D
    Debt service equals principal and interest payments on a given loan for an entire year.
    $225 interest + $70 principal = $295 per month
    $295 × 12 months = $3,540 annual debt service

25. B
    $1,200 ÷ 30 = $40 rent per day
    $40 × 20 days not used
    $800 rent credit to buyer

26. A

$28,000 × 0.0775 = $2,170 yearly

$2,170 ÷ 12 months = $180.83/month

$180.83 ÷ 30 days = $6.03/day

$6.03 × 12 days = $72.36 used portion

(as payments are made in arrears, this amount is a credit to buyer and a debit to seller)

27. A

$5,000 ÷ 12 = $416.66666 taxes per month

$416.66666 ÷ 31 = 13.44086 taxes per day

13.44086 × 15 = $201.6129 taxes through January 15

$5,000 − $201.6129 = $4,798.387 = $4,798 taxes credited to the seller (rounded)

28. B

The time for which the seller has already paid but will not own the property includes 8 days remaining in September and 90 days for the three months of October, November, and December for a total of 98 days

98 days ÷ 360 days per year = 0.27222

$920 per year × 0.27222 = $250.44 taxes credited to seller

29. D

10 × $780 = $7,800 per month

$7,800 ÷ 31 = $251.6129 per day

$251.6129 × 13 = $3,270.9677 = $3,271 debit to K (rounded)

30. B

$240 ÷ 6 = $40 per month × 1 month (July 1–July 31) = $40 credit to buyer

31. A

$105,000 × 0.35 assessment ratio = $36,750 assessed value

$36,750 × 0.066 tax rate = $2,425.50 tax per year

$2,425.50 ÷ 4 quarters = $606.375 per quarter rounded to $606.38

32. B

$72,000 × 0.70 assessment ratio = $50,400 assessed value

$50,400 × 0.0575 tax rate = $2,898 annual tax bill

33. C

rate = tax dollars required ÷ taxable assessed value

rate = $5 million ÷ 100 million = 0.05

0.05 × $1,000 = $50 per $1,000 tax rate

34. C

$750 increase ÷ $3.75 = $200 ($100 units)

$200 ($100 units) × $100/unit = $20,000 tax value

$20,000 ÷ 0.60 = $33,333.33 increase in value

35. C

assessed value × tax rate = annual tax

$540 ÷ 0.0150 = $36,000 selling price

36. B

assessed value × tax rate = annual taxes

$4,250 ÷ $340,000 = 0.0125

per $100 = $1.25 tax rate

37. C

income ÷ rate of return = investment

$390,000 × 0.13 = $50,700 income

38. D
    original value × percentage of appreciated value = new value
    $200,000 × 0.02 = $4,000
    one year $4,000 + $200,000 = $204,000
    $204,000 × 0.02 = $4,080
    two years $4,080 + $204,000 = $208,080 appreciated value

39. A
    $1,200 (cost of improvements) × 0.0225 = $27 allowed rental increase
    $415 − $380 = $35 actual rental increase
    $35 − $27 = $8 exceeded lease terms

40. D
    Investment × rate of return = annual net income
    $12,000 ÷ 0.085 = $141,176 selling price (rounded)

Salesperson 100-Question Practice Exam

Property Ownership

1. A
   The words "estate" or "tenancy" generally imply the right to possession. There are several types of estates in real property including leasehold or rental estates and freehold, which are ownership estates.

2. A
   An important economic characteristic of real property is its *scarcity*, or availability. Scarcity follows the principle of supply and demand that states the greater the supply of any commodity in comparison to demand, the lower the value. Uniqueness means that no two parcels of land are identical.

3. C
   A plat is a *map* of land that may contain many references including legal descriptions of many parcels. A deed transfers or clears title. Land descriptions by metes and bounds do not use a plat.

4. C
   Residential tenants may enter into an agreement with the property owner to remove all fixtures, even if attached, when the lease ends. Preexisting fixtures do not belong to the current tenant. Fixtures may be attached by tenants usually by agreement with the property owner.

5. D
   A *freehold estate* is ownership for an undetermined length of time. An example of a freehold estate is home ownership. A *nonfreehold*, or *leasehold*, *estate* is possession with a determinable end. An example of a leasehold estate is an apartment rental. A bill of sale is a document for the sale of personal property.

6. D
   A timeshare is ownership that shares the use of the unit with many different owners based upon prescribed time intervals. It works by allowing several different individuals to purchase the condominium unit in fee and then divide the use by weeks or months. A Real Estate Investment Trust (REIT) is a business trust owned by shareholders making mortgage loans. A fee simple absolute ownership is an inheritable estate in land providing the greatest interest of any title. A planned unit development (PUD) is a cluster zoning providing for both residential and commercial land uses within a zoned area.

7. A
   Title to the common areas within and without the condominium is held as tenants in common, which is a form of co-ownership that does not include the right of survivorship. A partnership is a business organization owned by two or more people. Joint tenancy is a form of co-ownership that includes the right of survivorship. Ownership in severalty occurs when title to real property is held in the name of one party.

8. B

A lien is a claim or charge against another. Mortgages are a type of lien. The deed is the document to convey title legally to real property. A judgment is a court decree resulting from a lawsuit. A writ of attachment is an involuntary lien.

9. D

An encroachment is created by the intrusion of some structure or object across a boundary line. Appurtenances in real property are the ownership rights that are a natural consequence of owning property. An easement by necessity exists when a property has no access to roads except across another property. A negative easement appurtenant occurs if the dominant tenement does not have the right to enter the land of the servient tenement, but has the right to restrict some activity or use of the servient tenement.

10. A

Aviva's lien was filed first so it has priority to be paid over the other liens.

Property Valuation, Market Analysis, and the Appraisal Process

11. C

Nonhomogeneity, which is not an economic characteristic, means that no two parcels of land are identical. Economics characteristics include permanence of investment, which refers to the fact that land is indestructible and immobile. Location also greatly affects a property's value. Modification by improvements to the land impacts value as well. As a parcel of real estate changes from a plot of vacant land to a completed dwelling, the land's appeal increases resulting in increased value.

12. C

Obtaining financing, and therefore mortgage value, is an important consideration when marketing property. Assessed value, hazard insurance value, and condemnation value are not always important to real estate sales.

13. C

The principle of substitution states that, all other things being equal, a buyer will purchase a property that is offered at the lowest price. An appraiser uses this principle in comparing properties to one another to arrive at a value for the subject property. The principle of conformity states that general conformity among properties in a neighborhood produces maximum value for these properties. The principle of anticipation is based on expectations or hopes of the future benefits of ownership. The principle of contribution states the each portion of a property contributes to the property's ability to produce income.

14. D

The income, sales comparison, and cost approaches are all appraisal approaches to value. The comparative market analysis is generally employed by real estate sales agents to derive a market value.

15. B

In many areas, there are not a plentiful number of properties for comparison. An example might be a rural area where properties are few and far between. In this instance, it is difficult for the appraiser to find suitable comparable properties. This may also happen to the real estate agent who is creating a comparative market analysis.

16. A

The depreciation or loss in value of the property, the value of the site, and the cost to replace the property are all considerations in the cost approach. Financing terms are generally not evaluated in the cost approach.

17. C

A real estate agent must be able to adjust the listing price according to the market. Pricing the property at the lowest possible price for a quick sale should only be done with the permission of the seller.

18. A

Generally, the more dollars the investor risks or puts up for an investment, the greater his return. There is a saying that sometimes works: "Risk equals reward."

19. A

Once expenses are deducted, the remaining monies are net income. Income received on a property without deducting expenses is gross income. The net operating income (NOI) is the operating income minus operating expenses and debt service or the cash flow. Debt service is the annual amount needed to pay off or reduce a loan.

20. C

The first level of licensure to become a licensed real estate property appraiser is to begin at the first level, which is an appraisal trainee. After a certain amount of experience, the trainee can move up to higher levels of appraisal licensure. This level requires certain prescribed appraisal education. No other type of real estate licensure is necessary.

Land Use Controls and Regulations

21. D

Deed restrictions may be terminated in certain circumstances. For example, if property owners do not act to enforce restrictive covenants on a timely basis, the court will not apply the restriction against the violator and the restriction may be terminated. Termination of a covenant in this manner is an application of the doctrine of laches that states if landowners are lax in protecting their rights, they may lose them. All of the other choices are true. Covenants and conditions run with the land, and must benefit all property owners.

22. D

Many buyers do not realize the power of a homeowners' association to make and enforce rules governing every property in a given subdivision. Homeowners' associations can enforce rules through fines and even court action to force compliance.

23. D

Condemnation occurs when a property is taken by government under its right of eminent domain. Escheat occurs when the government takes property of the deceased if no heirs are found. Estoppel is generally a court order to stop an act. *In rem* is a type of legal proceeding.

24. C

Setbacks are specific distances from the front property line to the building line that must be maintained. The doctrine of laches states that property owners may lose their rights if they do not exercise them. Incentive zoning offers incentives to property owners and developers to make certain modifications or improvements to property. Taking is the government acting on its power of eminent domain.

25. B

A moratorium imposed by a municipality is a delay in allowing development of property, which is imposed only for public welfare. A census is a recordation of each individual and property in a municipality. A referendum is a community-wide vote on an issue of importance. An injunction is usually ordered by a court to stop an act.

26. A

Linda should suggest that Claudia attach a radon inspection contingency along with the contract for purchase and sale. This contingency provides for a qualified inspector to test for and measure the radon level of the property. If radon is present and the level is above four picocuries, the seller must take action to remediate the problem. If the seller refuses to remediate the problem, Claudia can terminate the contract.

27. B

Most state and/or local governments require a full environmental assessment before a developer initiates or changes a land use that may have an adverse effect on the environment. The report of this assessment is called an environmental impact statement. A property report is a disclosure required under the Interstate Land Sales Full Disclosure Act that gives specific information about the land offered for purchase. An appraisal is an estimate of value of a property. A feasibility study is a detailed economic analysis that considers the cost of site development, construction, financing, tax considerations, rates of return on similar investments, and the benefit to the community.

28. A

The assessment roll that describes all properties and their assessed value is published each year. Taxpayers have the right to look at the assessment of their property and compare it with other properties on the assessment roll, and if a property owner believes the assessment is wrong, the owner may file a written complaint, called a grievance, with the local board of assessment review. The other choices in the question are fictitious.

29. B

If a property owner believes the assessment is wrong, the owner may file a written complaint, called a grievance, with the local board of assessment review. A judicial review of a tax case in court is called a tax certiorari proceeding. This is an appeal following the grievance procedure. A subpoena is a court order for a witness to appear in court.

30. C

The tax rate is set by the municipality to meet the needs of the annual budget. The assessor determines assessments, and not the tax rate.

Contracts and Relationships with Buyers and Sellers

31. B

An earnest money deposit is not legally necessary for an offer to purchase. The deposit shows the sincerity of the buyer, demonstrates financial capability of the buyer, and could serve as liquidated damages to the seller if the purchaser defaults on the contract.

32. D

The precocious 16-year-old is a minor (not having legal capacity) who may hold an adult to a contract, but the adult cannot hold the minor responsible. Consideration, the giving of something of value, makes a contract valid. Reality of consent requires the parties to voluntarily enter into a contract. Offer and acceptance is a meeting of the minds.

33. B

Belinda must pay Diamond Real Estate a full commission on the sale. Under an exclusive-right-to-sell listing contract, if anyone else sells the property during the term of the listing contract, including the owner, the broker is still legally entitled to the commission.

34. D

100% = gross sales price
100% − 7% = 93% net to owner
sales price × rate of commission = total commission
$160,000 ÷ 0.93 = $172,043

35. B

The lead-based paint disclosure form can be completed upon signing a contract of sale, but only applies to properties built before 1978. Riders are part of a contract of sale. The mortgage contingency is a clause in the real estate contract. An agency disclosure form is signed at the first significant meeting between an agent and the principal or customer.

36. **D**

Installment sales contracts create a transaction in which the seller receives the sales price over a specified period of time and title is transferred upon full payment of the purchase price. An option to buy is a contract in which a property owner sells a right to purchase his property to a prospective buyer. A binder is a written document for the purchase or sale of real property. A lease is a contract between an owner and a tenant.

37. **B**

When a party purchases an option, the optionee is purchasing an agreed-upon time to exercise or not exercise the option contract.

38. **C**

In this example, there was a meeting of the minds or agreement between the two parties. Julius is the *offeree* and Constance ended up as the *offeror*. A unilateral contract is a contract where only one party makes a promise.

39. **C**

Assignment transfers only the rights of the contract, but does not eliminate the contract obligations, and is not a means of discharging a contract. The Statute of Limitations is a law establishing the time within which certain lawsuits may be brought. If the time to sue on the contract runs out, then the contract may terminate. A bankruptcy petition filing may terminate a contract, and alteration of a contract may result in the cancellation or discharge of a contract.

40. **A**

Real estate agents have a duty to communicate all information affecting the listing to the sellers. All offers should be communicated to the sellers whether they are in writing or not.

Financing

41. **D**

The *mortgagor* is the borrower and the one who signs the note and gives the mortgage. The *mortgagee* or lender lends the funds, holds the mortgage liens, and receives the payments.

42. **C**

loan balance × rate = annual interest
$570 × 12 = $6,840 annual interest
$6,840 ÷ 0.06 = $114,000 mortgage balance

43. **B**

The alienation clause allows the lender to declare the balance due if the mortgagor sells the property during the mortgage term. The prepayment penalty clause is a fine imposed by the lender if the mortgage is paid off before it is due. The granting clause is part of a deed. The defeasance clause in a mortgage or deed of trust gives the borrower the right to redeem the title and have the mortgage lien released at any time before default by paying the debt in full.

44. **D**

A purchase money mortgage is a type of seller financing in which the seller holds the mortgage on the property. A second mortgage is one that is subordinate to another mortgage. With an installment land contract, title is not transferred to the buyer until the mortgage is paid. A deed of trust conveys title to a trustee.

45. **C**

As of March, 2011 a VA (Department of Veterans Affairs) mortgage limits the maximum loan amount with no down payment to $417,000. This loan program applies to qualified buyers. Therefore, the VA loan provides the maximum amount of leverage (use of other people's money) than other loan programs mentioned in the answer choices. FHA (Federal Housing Authority) loans generally require a down payment as do conventional loans (those that are not insured or given by a government agency).

46. D

Loan underwriting is the process in which the financial data and credit history of a prospective borrower are analyzed by the lender. The alienation clause in a mortgage allows the lender to declare the balance due if the mortgagor sells the property during the mortgage term. Preapproval requires that a lender validate a borrower's credit and employment history. This evaluation precedes the underwriting process and is not detailed.

47. B

Regulation Z of the Truth in Lending Act addresses the accurate advertising of credit terms. The Real Estate Settlement Procedures Act addresses a lender's disclosure of borrower costs in obtaining a mortgage loan. The Community Reinvestment Act encourages lenders to meet the credit needs of communities. The Equal Credit Opportunity Act addresses discrimination in the lending process.

48. A

Subprime lenders are companies that provide loans to homebuyers who do not have good credit histories, or, because of their income, are riskier candidates for loans. A nonconforming loan is one that does not follow the guidelines as set forth by the Federal Reserve Bank. An example of low equity would be a mortgagor having paid a small down payment and a relatively small amount of cash towards payment of the mortgage.

Law of Agency

49. D

An individual who is hired to work on another's behalf and for his or her best interests is called an agent. Upon creation of the relationship, the agent is in a position of trust and loyalty to the principal. A customer is the party whom an agent brings to the principal to purchase or lease a property. The client or principal is the party or parties who hire the agent.

50. B

The agent should not be liable if the principal withholds information causing the agent to make incorrect representations to third parties. If the agent is found liable to third parties for the principal's misrepresentation, the agent is entitled to repayment from the principal. The repayment is indemnification to the agent and makes the agent financially whole.

51. D

An agency relationship can be created unintentionally such as by the conduct of the parties. This is known as an implied agency. It can also be created by a written agreement generally called a listing contract, an express agreement between the broker and seller.

52. C

An agency disclosure form is presented at important events in the real estate transaction such as the signing of the listing agreement or when a buyer is first shown a property. The form explains and describes whom the agent represents in the real estate transaction. The form is mandatory in many states. A property condition disclosure statement is generally completed by sellers and describes details about their property. HUD Form No. 1 is mandated by the Real Estate Settlement Procedures Act and is used by lenders to describe settlement costs at closing. A contract contingency contains provisions for inspection or remediation before the parties become obligated under a contract.

53. D

In an exclusive agency agreement, if the owner sells the property, the broker is not entitled to the commission. In a net listing, a seller specifies a net amount of money he or she wants to receive upon sale of a property. This listing is illegal in many states. In an open listing agreement, the property is shown by more than one broker and the one with the sale is entitled to the commission. An exclusive-right-to-sell agreement means that only one broker lists the property, and the broker is entitled to the commission no matter who sells it.

54. A

An agent's fiduciary duty is to the principal or client. Unless the agent is a buyer agent, he owes no fiduciary duty to the buyer. A customer or buyer is a third party whom the agent brings to the seller. The other agents in the firm do not have a fiduciary relationship with each other.

55. B

A positive misrepresentation by a seller broker occurs when the broker conceals a defect in the property from the buyer or misrepresents to the buyer the existence of a defect. A positive misrepresentation can occur by omission of facts about the property even if the buyer does not ask such as the case in this question.

56. C

The brokerage firm is the primary agent, who the individual agent works for, and represents the seller only. In this case, the buyer is a customer, even though brought to the seller from a branch office. So far, no one represents the buyer, although the buyer could elect to be represented by the agent, and then a dual agency would arise.

57. D

The disadvantage of a transaction agent, who may also be called a facilitator or intermediary, is that a seller or buyer does not receive any of the fiduciary duties and advantages of an agency relationship. The client is not offered the personalized services of an agency relationship in which an agent may only work in the best interests of one or the other party. Transaction agents offer many of the same services as an agent, will negotiate with all of the parties to the transaction, and are licensed agents.

58. D

An agency agreement can be terminated like any other contract. If the purpose of the agency is satisfied, the listing agreement has expired, or if the parties mutually agree to terminate the contract, the agreement may be terminated.

Property Conditions, Disclosures, and Transfer of Title

59. B

Fraudulent practices are acts meant to deceive or misrepresent. Shanice, in not disclosing property defects, would be committing fraudulent misrepresentation. Real estate agents may be held responsible for what they know, or should have known, regarding defects in a property.

60. B

The real estate agent will arrange and generally take a prospective purchaser for a "walk through" of the property immediately before closing. The purchaser can look around one last time and determine that the property is in the same condition as when last viewed.

61. B

All target properties covered under the Residential Lead-Based Hazard Reduction Act, those built before 1978, must have specific disclosure and acknowledgement language regarding the presence of lead-based paint. The law does not apply to commercial properties. Target properties include most residential housing for sale or lease including cooperative apartments. Certain types of residential housing are exempt, such as senior citizen housing.

62. C

For a deed to be eligible for recording, it must have an acknowledgment or oath of subscribing witness. A grantor must appear before a public officer, such as a notary public. A deed is valid between the grantor and grantee without an acknowledgment but the grantee cannot record the deed. Then the grantee has no protection to title against purchasers of the same property from the same grantor who records his deed. A metes and bounds description, *habendum* clause (have and to hold clause), and covenant of warranty (title) are not in all deeds.

63. A

HUD Form No. 1, mandated by the Real Estate Settlement Procedures Act (RESPA), is used by lenders to itemize closing costs for a mortgage loan. The form must be available for the borrower's inspection at or before final settlement. One business day before the settlement, borrowers have the right to inspect the form. HUD Form No. 1 is *not* required for assumptions and nonresidential loans. A certificate of title sets forth the title examiner's opinion of the title. A satisfaction of mortgage is a document from the lender stating that the loan is paid in full. A bill of sale is a document transferring ownership of personal property.

64. D

New home warranties are generally provided by the builder, independent companies from whom the builder purchases coverage, or other third-party companies contracted by the homeowner that supplement the builder's coverage.

65. C

An unbroken transfer of successive titles to real property is called a chain of title. The chain must be unbroken for the title to be good and therefore marketable. It involves tracing the successive conveyances of title, starting with the current deed and going back an appropriate time (typically 40 to 60 years). An abstract of title is a condensed history of the title and an abstract continuation is an update of an abstract of title. A title search finds evidence of marketable title.

66. C

Within three working days of receiving a completed loan application, the lender must provide the borrower with a good faith estimate of the likely mortgage costs and associated costs at settlement.

67. B

A short sale is a sale of real property in which the sale proceeds are less than the balance owed to the lender. If a borrower is in economic difficulty and cannot pay back a mortgage loan on his or her property, the borrower may consider a short sale. The lender and the borrower must both consent to sell the property at less than the amount that would satisfy the loan. The short sale allows the borrower to avoid a foreclosure on the property.

68. C

Performing an IRS Code 1031 tax-deferred exchange allows an individual to defer capital gains taxes on real estate bought and sold for investment purposes. Investment property would include any industrial property, commercial property, and hotel or motel. According to regulations for a 1031 exchange, a personal residence is not eligible for a tax-deferred exchange.

Leases, Rents, and Property Management

69. B

The question describes a periodic estate, which continues for an additional period if no notice is given. A periodic tenancy terminates only with notice. An estate for years does not automatically renew itself when the termination date is reached. An estate at will does not have a set termination date and may be terminated by either party at will. An estate at sufferance occurs if a tenant occupies a property after lawful authorization to do so has expired.

70. D

The possessor, tenant, or lessee (one and the same) do not have a reversionary interest in the property. Possession of the property will revert to the lessor (the owner).

71. C

In a net lease, the tenant (lessee) pays some or all of the expenses. Sometimes, net leases are called net, double net, or triple net. It depends upon how many property expenses the tenant pays. A lessee who contracts for a triple net lease pays all expenses associated with the property in addition to the rent, except for the debt service. Expenses may include property taxes, landlord's insurance, liability insurance, and maintenance. A gross lease provides for the landlord (lessor) to pay all expenses. A ground lease is a lease for unimproved land.

72. C

The right of quiet enjoyment means that the owner is allowed to enter the premises only in emergencies and not at will. The right of quiet enjoyment does not pertain to noise made by other tenants. A livable condition for the apartment must be provided at the outset of the lease, but this right does not pertain to the upkeep of the general premises.

73. A

Eviction is the proper legal process to remove a tenant from the premises. An actual eviction, that is, to remove a tenant without the aid or control of the court system, is illegal. To mitigate damages means to minimize damages. A holdover tenant is one who refuses to vacate the property.

74. B

Generally, a lease does not terminate upon the death of the tenant. Rather, it becomes the property of the tenant's estate. The estate is entitled to possession of the apartment for the remainder of the time left on the lease provided all the rent is paid.

75. B

The management agreement automatically creates a general agency relationship between the owner and the manager. The property manager becomes a fiduciary, a position of trust, in the owner–manager relationship. In his position of a general agent, the manager can perform a variety of tasks for the owner as designated in the property management agreement. Joint tenancy is ownership by two or more parties with the right of survivorship.

76. C

Public relations serve a twofold role in the property management office. First, a management company uses public relations to market itself. Second, public relations market client properties. Some property management companies use a professional firm. A property manager will make effective use of the media, promote community involvement when necessary and promote good relations between an owner and tenant. Feasibility studies are used in the valuation of property, which is not a public relations task of the property manager.

77. A

Although not always involved with leasing or renting, a manager for a condominium, cooperative, or PUD homeowners' association is very involved in the physical management of the property. The responsibility begins with budgeting expenses and collecting assessments. It progresses to coordinating common facility maintenance, landscaping, security, and enforcement of the association's or board of directors' regulations. Drafting and developing the proprietary lease, offering plan, and communicating with the state attorney general are accomplished by the sponsors of the development and their attorneys.

78. D

The operating budget is an annual budget and includes income and expenses for week-to-week operation. The capital reserve budget, also called a replacement reserve, is a projected budget over the economic life of the property. It includes variable expenses such as repairs, decorating, remodeling, and capital improvements. A variable expense is one that is not predictable but subject to the needs of the property at any time. The stabilized budget is a forecast of income and expenses as may be reasonably projected over a short term, typically five years.

79. D

With regard to maintenance, a property manager must supervise physical property maintenance and routinely inspect the building. Efficient maintenance requires analysis of the building's needs, together with consideration of repair costs. To save payroll and other employee costs, the property manager may subcontract individuals and companies.

80. A

$750 \times 6 = \$4,500$ per month $\times 12 = \$54,000$ per year
$1,050 \times 7 = \$7,350$ per month $\times 12 = \$88,200$ per year
$54,000 + \$88,200 = \$142,200$ total rental income
$0.05 \times \$142,200 = \$7,110$
$142,200 - \$7,110 = \$135,090$

Brokerage Operations and the Practice of Real Estate

81. C

An escrow account is a separate trust account for any deposits received that do not belong to the broker. The earnest money deposit is the deposit on a contract for a property. Commingling is the illegal mixing of deposits and personal/business funds by the broker. Conversion is the apportionment of other people's money from one use to another.

82. B

This ad is a blind ad because it does not indicate that the ad is placed by a real estate broker, or gives his or her name. The ad, as described in the question, does not violate any fair housing laws although blind ads placed by real estate brokers are illegal in many states. A net listing is a type of listing in which a broker sets a sales price for a property and keeps any amount he or she procures above the sales price as his or her commission. This type of listing is illegal in many states.

83. C

Under the IRS code, real estate licensees are independent contractors. As such, work hours for an independent contractor cannot be mandated by a broker. Independent contractors must set their own hours and are paid for work product, not for hours worked.

84. B

Aliyah must include the commission arrangement with the sales agent in the employment agreement. Under an independent contractor agreement, Aliyah would not be required to share employee information with them, such as minimum wage, health care, unemployment, or required work hours.

85. D

A broker may not violate license law to comply with other laws. Conversely, a broker may not violate zoning laws to comply with license laws. The broker can find another location or apply for a variance so that the firm can have a sign that is in compliance with the zoning at the desired location.

86. C

Agent Richard is guilty of illegal self-dealing and a breach of his fiduciary duty to the principal, Kathleen. He did not disclose his own interest in the property nor did he tell his client about the developer who would pay more than the listed price.

87. A

The commission fees for a real estate transaction are strictly negotiable between the principal and the real estate agent. Should a multiple listing service or real estate board establish commission fees, this would be a violation of antitrust laws.

88. C

An individual can conduct business under his or her own name as a sole proprietor and may choose to give the business a name such as Jason Wake doing business as (d/b/a) Roundout Realty. Roundout Realty would be a trade name.

89. A

A type of organization that avoids a double tax on trust income is a REIT or real estate investment trust. This is because the trust is not taxed at the corporate level if income is distributed to the beneficiaries. An S corporation's major significance is that it usually avoids corporate income tax. Corporate losses can be claimed by the shareholders. A trust fund is an amount of capital that a person (the trustor) places in the custody of a trustee to be administered for the benefit of another (the beneficiary). An LLC is a limited liability company or, more rarely, a company with limited liability (WLL), and is a business organization that blends elements of partnership and corporate structures.

90. A

When a real estate brokerage firm establishes active online communication with a consumer about real estate services with the intent to form a brokerage relationship through e-mail, instant message, web-cam, or VON (voice on net), this is known as active solicitation.

91. C

Steering is a violation of the Federal Fair Housing Act and is practiced by real estate brokers who encourage culturally diverse people to move to or away from certain areas. Blockbusting is another violation by brokers that make people panic and sell their property because of the entry into the neighborhood of a culturally diverse family. Redlining is an illegal practice by lenders to exclude people from culturally diverse neighborhoods from receiving housing loans.

92. B

Blockbusting occurs when real estate firms sell a home in a neighborhood to a person from a protected class with the intent to cause property owners to panic and place their property for sale at reduced prices.

93. A

Under the Fair Housing Act, the Fair Housing Poster must be displayed in the broker's office. State real estate commissions have different laws as to the display of the salesperson and broker licenses. The NAR Code of Ethics promulgated by the National Association of REALTORS® is not a law but a credo that its members must follow if they are members of NAR.

94. C

The Americans with Disabilities Act applies mainly to commercial and public facilities and multi-family housing.

95. A

Illegal price fixing occurs when competitors in a group or an industry conspire to charge the same or similar prices for services rendered. Any discussion of commission rates between or among brokers could be a violation of antitrust laws.

96. C

Megan's Law requires a public registry of known sex offenders.

Real Estate Math

97. C

sales price × rate of commission = total commission
$100,000 × 0.07 = $7,000
$10,000 − $7,000 = $3,000
$3000 ÷ 0.06 = $50,000
$100,000 + $50,000 = $150,000

98. D

128.5 feet × 236.2 feet = 30,351.7 square feet
30,351.7 ÷ 43,560 square feet per acre = 0.69678 or 70% of an acre

99. C

$849.43 interest per month × 12 months = $10,193.16 interest per year
$10,193.16 ÷ 0.1175 interest rate = $86,750 loan balance

100. A

assessed value × tax rate = annual tax

$89,990 × 0.5 = $44,995

4.10 ÷ 100 = 0.041

$44,995 × 0.041 = $1,844.80 annual tax (rounded)

Broker 100-Question Practice Exam

Property Ownership

1. D

   The mineral rights to real property and the right to profit from or to mortgage real property are included in the bundle of rights. Chattel is another name for personal property.

2. C

   Of all the characteristics of land, location has the greatest effect on property value. Uniqueness means that no two pieces of land are identical. Scarcity is the availability of land.

3. B

   Description by monument is used by surveyors when describing multiple-acre tracts of land that might be quite expensive to survey. The description uses permanent objects such as a stone wall, large trees, or boulders. In the metes and bounds description, metes are the distances from point to point and bounds are the directions from one point to another. Property may be described by reference to section, block, and lot on a tax map or other document. A description by reference to a plat may refer to a plat (map) and lot number as part of a recorded subdivision.

4. A

   Adaptation refers to how an object fits the real estate. Custom draperies or cabinets that are sized for a certain area, even if not attached, are examples. *Agreement* refers to those items specified by an owner that include part of real estate and those that are not. *Attachment* refers to the physical connection of objects to the real estate.

5. B

   Tenancy in common, the correct answer, is an estate characterized by two or more people who hold title to a property at the same time with no rights of survivorship. Another indicator of tenancy in common is differing percentages of ownership as is between Fiona and Osborn. Joint tenancy and joint tenancy as husband and wife (which has different names in different states) provide for survivorship to co-owners. Fiona and Osborn do not have an estate for years, which is the relationship between owners and tenants.

6. A

   The term "right of survivorship" refers to the right of surviving co-owners to automatically receive the interest of the deceased co-owner upon his or her death. The right of heirs to receive the co-owner's share of real estate as provided in his or her last will and testament is known as the right of inheritance. Tenancy in common is characterized by two or more people holding title to a property at the same time. The bank does not automatically inherit the mortgaged property of the deceased.

7. A

   The co-owners, having equal percentages of ownership and having received their title at the same time from the same source, define a joint tenancy. In a tenancy in common, two or more people hold title to a property at the same time but with no rights of survivorship. A leasehold is a rental estate. Fabian and Frannie do not have an estate for years, which is the relationship between owners and tenants.

8. B

An easement is a nonpossessory use of land by another.

9. C

A lien is a claim that one person has against the property of another for a debt.

10. C

A license is a temporary privilege and is given to a licensee for a prescribed time.

Property Valuation, Market Analysis, and the Appraisal Process

11. D

The law of supply and demand states that the greater the supply of any commodity in comparison to the demand for that commodity, the lower its value. Conversely, the smaller the supply and greater the demand, the higher the value. The principle of immobility states that land cannot be moved. This is why location is so important in real estate value. The principle of scarcity refers to the availability of land or property. Situs refers to the location of a property.

12. B

Cost is the dollar expenditure for labor, materials, legal services, and financing. Price is the amount a purchaser agrees to pay and a seller accepts. Investment value is the highest price an investor will pay. Mortgage value is what a property will bring at foreclosure.

13. C

The gross rent multiplier is used to value properties that rely on rental income and is therefore not used for valuing single-family residential properties.

14. B

Because there are few, if any, comparables and the properties are not income producing, the cost approach is generally used to appraise schools, hospitals, and office buildings.

15. B

In making an adjustment using the sales comparison approach, if the comparable is inferior to the subject, then a plus adjustment is made to the comparable.

16. A

An appraisal is an estimate or opinion of value only. There is no such thing as the legal value of a property nor does an appraisal address the amount a seller will accept. Book value is the accounting cost of an item.

17. C

The aim of an accurate comparative market analysis is to find properties in as close proximity as possible to the subject property.

18. B

For income tax purposes, buildings, equipment, and machinery are depreciable assets. Personal property does not qualify for this depreciation allowance.

19. B

A process that calculates the value of an asset in the past, present, and future is called the time value of money. Leverage is the use of other people's money. Debt service is the payment of principal and interest. Net operating income is property expenses deducted from gross income.

20. C

The first step in becoming a State Licensed Real Property Appraiser is to begin at the first level, which is an appraisal trainee. After a certain amount of experience, the trainee can move up to higher levels of appraisal licensure. The first level requires certain prescribed appraisal education. No other type of real estate or real estate related licensure licensure is necessary and does not count toward appraisal licensure.

Land Use Controls and Regulations

21. A

Subdivision regulations maintain the standards of the subdivision therefore protecting the purchaser's investment.

22. D

Homeowners' associations (HOAs) throughout the country have tried and succeeded with various actions to force compliance by homeowners. HOA actions have included lawsuits, eviction proceedings, and steep fines to homeowners. Real estate agents should familiarize prospective purchasers with HOA rules and regulations before they sell a property.

23. B

Eminent domain is the government's right to take property with just compensation in the name of the public good. Escheat occurs when the state acquires the property of a deceased because no heirs are found. Voluntary alienation and a grant imply that the owner willingly gives up the property, which is not the case in this example.

24. A

Both police power and eminent domain actions are taken by a governmental agency. In both circumstances, the owner's use is affected. Compensation is the difference between police power and eminent domain. In a police power action, such as the creation of zoning ordinances, no compensation is paid if affected property owners suffer a loss. Under eminent domain, the owner is compensated for any loss in value.

25. D

Nonconforming use occurs when a preexisting use of a property in a zoned area is different from that specified by the zoning. Xavier can continue to operate his grocery store. He cannot attempt to change zoning except through a variance or court action if the variance is not allowed.

26. C

The municipality sets the special assessment, not a state taxing agency, and decides as to the special assessment. The special assessment is a specific lien against the property, and not against the owner, until paid. If the lien is not paid, the taxing unit may execute on the lien, forcing a sale of the property for payment of the assessment.

27. D

The purpose of the Toxic Substances Control Act is to allow the Environmental Protection Agency to regulate new commercial chemicals before they enter the market, and to regulate existing chemicals when they pose an unreasonable risk to health or environment. The Superfund Amendment and the Comprehensive Environmental Response, Compensation, and Liability Act regulate the transfer, penalties, and cleanup of a property containing hazardous substances. The Interstate Land Sales Full Disclosure Act regulates developers who sell subdivisions of 25 or more lots offered across state lines.

28. B

In the sale of large tracts of land or other types of commercial property, due-diligence reviews of the property are conducted in order that these issues are not passed on to the next owner. Feasibility studies and highest and best use studies are types of property valuation studies.

29. C

Ad valorem is Latin meaning "according to the value." Real property is taxed on an *ad valorem* basis. An *in rem* legal proceeding is an action that is brought against the real property. A tax certiorari proceeding is a judicial review of a proceeding in court. "As is" are words in a contract of sale indicating that a property is sold without warranty as to condition.

30. D

    Both liens must be paid before transfer, most probably by Rafe. The purchasers can also satisfy the liens if Rafe cannot. If not paid, then the indebtedness would transfer to the new owners. Also, depending on the time frame of the property tax lien, the taxing jurisdiction may have a claim on the property if the back taxes are not paid.

Contracts and Relationships with Buyers and Sellers

31. C

    An arm's-length transaction is between a buyer and seller, from equal bargaining positions and not related by business interest, friendship, or familial relationships. An agency relationship occurs when a principal hires an agent to represent him. A fiduciary relationship is based on the trust and confidence of one party to serve another. Parol evidence allows oral explanations to support the written words of a contract.

32. B

    The term "meeting of the minds" is synonymous with offer and acceptance. Consideration refers to the item of value given in the contract, such as money. Competence is the legal capacity of a party to contract with another. Legality of object has to do with the legal purpose of the contract.

33. B

    The court probably ruled that Lionel's contract is unenforceable since oral real estate contracts should be in writing to be enforceable. An executory contract is one that is not fully performed. A unilateral contract is when one party makes a promise to a second party.

34. C

    The developer's contract to purchase the land is terminated because of impossibility to perform the contract. The state is making the land unavailable for private development because of the eminent domain condemnation. There is no evidence in the question of incompetent parties or lack of consideration.

35. C

    If tracts of unimproved land or lots are sold, a tax map, plat, or survey is generally attached to a contract of sale for identification and verification purposes.

36. C

    Legal title through an installment land contract is transferred to the purchaser upon full payment of the purchase price and transfer of the deed.

37. A

    With an option contract, only one party, the optionor, makes a promise. The *optionor* promises to allow the *optionee* the sole right to purchase the property by a specific date, and the *optionee* pays for the right to purchase by a specific date but does not promise to purchase. Because only one promise is made, the option contract is unilateral.

38. D

    In this example, the seller has rejected the buyer's offer and made a counteroffer to the buyer. It is now up to the buyer to accept or reject the counteroffer or to make *his* or *her* new (counter) offer to the seller.

39. A

    Liquidated damages are an amount of money to be paid upon certain breaches of the contract. Rescission means to take back, remove, or annul. Rescission may occur when a contract is not performed by either party or when a party breaches it. Assignment is the giving over of the contract to another. Novation is the substitution of a new contract for a prior contract.

40. A

    Brokers must present all offers to the seller even if there is a pending contract.

Financing

41. **D**

   Amortization is a method of payment of a mortgage debt in which uniform installment payments include payment of principal and interest. The payment toward principal increases over the life of the payback while the amount of interest owed decreases. Underwriting is a lender investigation into a loan application. PITI stands for principal, interest, taxes, and insurance. Loan to value compares the loan amount to the property value.

42. **B**

   $250 × 12 months = $3,000
   $3,000 ÷ $50,000 = 6% interest rate

43. **B**

   A defeasance gives the borrower the right to remove the lien by paying the mortgage debt in full. The alienation clause makes the mortgage debt due on the sale of the property. The *habendum* clause, meaning "to have and to hold," is part of a deed. The acceleration clause permits the lender to declare the entire principal balance of the debt immediately due and payable if the borrower is in default.

44. **D**

   A sale leaseback would assist Paul in freeing up his equity in the property. Sale leaseback is a transaction in which a property owner sells a property to an investor who immediately leases back the property to the seller as agreed in the sales contract. A gross lease is a lease in which the lessor pays all costs of operating and maintaining the property including the real property taxes. A net lease is a type of lease in which the lessee pays a fixed amount of rent plus the costs of operation of the property. A percentage lease is one in which the rental amount is a combination of a fixed amount plus a percentage of the lessee's gross sales.

45. **A**

   Conventional loans involve no participation by an agency of the federal government. Conventional loan programs *are* available throughout the country, and for first-time buyers. Government loan programs include other options besides single-family home purchases.

46. **B**

   FHA (Federal Housing Authority) insured loans protect lenders against financial loss. The buyer pays for this insurance protection by paying an up-front mortgage insurance premium (MIP) at closing and an annual MIP prorated monthly and paid with the monthly mortgage payment. Life insurance is not required for an FHA mortgage. An appraisal and/or survey would have been completed before closing and does not protect the lender against default.

47. **A**

   Regulation Z does *not* regulate interest rates. However, Regulation Z *does* provide specific consumer protections concerning mortgage loans and loans for personal, family, household, or agricultural purposes, and does not apply to commercial transactions.

48. **C**

   Although subprime borrowers may have poor credit ratings, have an income that is insufficient to carry the mortgage debt, and pay higher than normal interest rates, they may obtain and "qualify" for a mortgage that they cannot afford.

Law of Agency

49. **A**

   A real estate agent is a special agent who has narrow authorization to act on behalf of the principal. A general agent has more authority to act on behalf of a principal, for example, a property manager. An attorney-in-fact is someone who has the complete power of attorney over another's affairs, which does not describe a real estate agent. The agent works on behalf of the principal in a fiduciary relationship.

50. D

Agents who work together to bring about the real estate transaction are cooperating agents. A dual agent is an agent who represents the buyer and the seller in the same transaction. A single agent may represent the buyer or the seller. There is no requirement that all agents belong to a multiple listing service.

51. B

Agency by estoppel is a type of implied agency and occurs if an individual claims incorrectly that someone is his or her agent, and a third party relies on this information. Since Armand made this representation to a third party, he cannot now retract that representation; thus, a valid agency relationship may exist.

52. A

Real estate agents may accept referral fees and other compensation from parties not represented by them as long as they give disclosure and receive consent from the parties to the transaction. Generally, real estate agents may not receive compensation directly, but through their sponsoring broker.

53. D

In an option to purchase, the property owner sells the right to purchase his or her property to a prospective buyer. The buyer can decide by a specified date indicated in the contract whether to move forward with the purchase or lose the right to purchase. An exclusive-right-to-sell agreement means that only one broker lists the property, and the broker is entitled to the commission no matter who sells it. In an exclusive agency agreement, if the owner sells the property, the broker is not entitled to the commission. In an open listing agreement, the property is shown by more than one broker and the one with the sale is entitled to the commission.

54. D

The brokerage contract, which most often is the listing contract, details the obligations of the parties (seller and broker) in the agency relationship. A contract of sale is a contract between the buyer and seller outlining the duties of each party and including contingencies that must be met before sale. A property disclosure statement, generally completed by the seller, discloses the history and conditions affecting the property. The agency disclosure form assists consumers in choosing agent representation and understanding agency relationships.

55. A

Mick is guilty of positive misrepresentation, which is a form of illegal self-dealing. A positive misrepresentation occurs by omission of facts about the property even if the buyer does not ask. Positive misrepresentation may take place when an agent engages in self-dealing and can occur when a broker has an undisclosed interest in a property. The broker must disclose his or her interest in a property to the principal and all other parties to the transaction. An unintentional misrepresentation occurs when the seller broker makes a false statement to the buyer about the property, and the broker does not know whether the statement is true or false. The words or actions of the principal and agent indicating that they have an agreement may create an implied agency.

56. A

In this scenario, broker Blue is acting as a dual agent. He is representing himself as a buyer of the property and representing the sellers as the listing agent. He can only have this arrangement with the disclosure and informed consent of the sellers.

57. B

A real estate broker who represents neither the seller nor the buyer in an agency relationship in a real estate transaction is a transaction broker. The transaction broker is a facilitator who manages the transaction and attempts to bring about an agreement to purchase real property. A dual agent is an agent who represents both buyer and seller in the same transaction. A subagent is an agent of the seller.

58. A

Once an agency contract terminates, the agent no longer has any authority to act on behalf of the principal. Generally, listing agreements, once expired, cannot be renewed without express agreement between the agent and the principal. They do not renew automatically. The principal is generally free to contract with another brokerage firm once the agency contract terminates. However, there may be wording in the terminated contract that allows an agent to collect a commission if a customer brought by the agent under the terminated contract purchases the property. This contract provision generally has a limited duration such as three months from the termination of the contract.

Property Conditions, Disclosures and Transfer of Title

59. A

The Residential Lead-Based Paint Hazard Reduction Act applies to both the sale and rental of residential property built before 1978. However, real estate agents who act on behalf of a buyer or lessee and receive payment exclusively by the buyer or lessee are not required to comply with disclosure requirements.

60. D

Under federal law, various parties may be liable for environmental contamination on a property once the property is transferred. Because of this liability, in the sale of large tracts of land or other types of commercial property, lenders, purchasers, and tenants often conduct due-diligence reviews of the property. The parties to the transfer of property evaluate these reviews.

61. B

The Comprehensive Environmental Response, Compensation, and Liability Act defines persons liable for hazardous waste cleanup costs. The Real Estate Settlement Procedures Act has to do with lender disclosure in making mortgage loans for housing. The Interstate Land Sales Full Disclosure Act covers disclosure requirements for certain properties sold across state lines. The Residential Lead-Based Paint Hazard Reduction Act provides disclosure requirements for the presence of lead-based paint.

62. C

Jackson's recording of the deed provides constructive or public notice of the transfer of title. Actual transfer of a deed indicates delivery and acceptance only. Recording of a deed will not protect against those with prior claims to the property. The property may or may not have free and clear title.

63. C

Outstanding liens would generally delay a closing because the title would not be clear. Discount points, which are lender fees, the hiring of an attorney by the purchaser, and a purchase money mortgage are all common closing events.

64. A

A title insurance policy is required by the lender and is not issued without an acceptable abstract of title. An abstract of title is a history of the title showing the transfers of property over the years. State insurance departments have nothing to do with this process.

65. D

The type of policy in the question is not for a new home. Generally, home warranty programs do not cover items such as a sprinkler system, swimming pool, or items that are in violation of local codes. A sprinkler system or pool may be covered by the manufacturer. A furnace would generally be covered by a home warranty policy depending on its age and condition.

66. A

The Real Estate Settlement Procedures Act (RESPA) regulates activities of lending institutions in making mortgage loans for housing. The Act applies only to residential federally financed or refinanced properties, not all properties. The Act does not apply to commercial properties, cash deals, or owner-financed loans. Condominiums and cooperatives are included under the Act as long as the properties are not for business purposes. The Act originally took effect in 1974 (last revised 2010).

67. C

A lender will take a deficiency judgment against a borrower if the foreclosure does not bring in enough proceeds to cover the debt and expenses of foreclosure. Equity of redemption occurs when the borrower redeems his or her property before foreclosure. A construction lien is for unpaid labor performed or materials furnished to a property. A *lis pendens* is a notice that a lawsuit has been filed affecting a property's title.

68. D

A special exclusion to the IRS law gives home sellers a tax break on the capital gains when they are selling their home. Home sellers may be eligible to exclude up to $250,000 if single or up to $500,000 if married of the capital gain on the sale of the residence. To claim the exclusion, the home sellers must have owned and resided in his home for at least two of the last five years before the sale of the residence. Marcus is in the 10% tax bracket so his capital gains are taxed at 5%. Marcus has exceeded his exclusion by $100,000, so he must pay capital gains tax on that amount.
$100,000 \times 0.05 = $5,000$

Leases, Rents, and Property Management

69. A

An estate for years is for a fixed time period. An estate at will has a duration that is unknown when the estate is created. A freehold estate is an ownership estate. A periodic estate is renewable at the end of the period and can be for any duration.

70. C

A *habendum* clause may be part of a deed, not a lease. In addition to the granting clause, the deed sometimes contains a *habendum* clause, which describes the estate granted and always must agree with the granting clause. This clause begins with the words "to have and to hold." A demising clause addresses when the lessor (landlord) leases the premises and the lessee (tenant) takes possession of the property leased—"the demised premises." To record a lease, it must be signed by the lessor and lessee. Generally, a formal legal description of the property is not required. A street address or other informal reference that is identifiable to both parties is acceptable.

71. D

An option to renew and right of first refusal is not only used for office buildings but for other types of commercial establishments. Most residential leases do not contain options to renew and rights of first refusal. A proprietary lease is used in the ownership of cooperative apartments.

72. B

The owner cannot deny the person with disabilities the right to make reasonable modifications to the premises to fit his or her needs, but at the tenant's expense. The tenant is responsible for returning the premises to its original status upon lease termination.

73. B

Upon the death of the owner, the lease agreement is still binding on the heirs. A lease agreement does not terminate because of the death of the owner or the tenant, nor does it revert to another form, or is it considered void.

74. B

A constructive eviction occurs if the tenant is prevented from the quiet enjoyment of the premises such as if a tenant moves out because the landlord has failed to maintain the premises in a habitable condition. To claim constructive eviction, the tenant must actually vacate the premises while the conditions that make the premises uninhabitable still exist, which Patsy did not do. She may be in breach of her lease. An actual eviction occurs if a landlord removes the tenant's belongings and locks the doors of the premises so that the tenant does not have access. This is an illegal use of self-help.

75. D

A marketing plan is a manager's plan for acquiring tenants. In a management proposal, the manager sets forth the commitment he or she will fulfill for the property. The management agreement creates an agency relationship between the owner and the property manager. A property management report is a periodic accounting of all funds received and disbursed.

76. D

Providing the greatest net return possible for the owner is the primary function of the property manager. Most other functions serve to produce this net maximum return. Collecting rents, residing on the property, and screening and locating tenants are possible functions of a property manager, but not required.

77. A

With cooperative property, the cooperative corporation owns the cooperative and the property managers are generally employees of the cooperative corporation.

78. D

A stabilized budget is a forecast of income and expenses as may be reasonably projected over a certain term, typically five years. A capital expense budget is needed to plan for improvements or maintenance to a building. The operating budget is an annual budget that includes income and expenses for week-to-week operations. A variable expense budget is a budget that is not predictable but subject to the needs of the property at any time.

79. A

One of the most important functions of a property manager is to supervise physical property maintenance. The property manager must routinely inspect the building. To save payroll and other employee costs, the property manager may subcontract individuals and companies. Preventive maintenance requires a periodic check of mechanical equipment to minimize excessive wear and tear from improper operation. Corrective maintenance is to fix a nonfunctioning item that a tenant has reported.

80. A

$83,500 gross income − $44,000 expenses = $39,500 net income
$39,500 ÷ $625,000 investment = 0.0632 or 6.32% return

Brokerage Operations and the Practice of Real Estate

81. A

Any licensee who deposits an earnest money check in his or her personal checking account instead of in the broker's escrow account and uses the money for his or her personal use is guilty of conversion. Conversion occurs when an individual spends or uses another's money that is entrusted to him or her.

82. D

Generally, in most states, brokers must reveal in their ads that they are a real estate broker. If they do not, this is known as a blind ad. Antitrust laws have to do with fair competition practices in the marketplace.

83. D

According to the IRS code, although sales agents are independent contractors, a broker still has the duty to supervise the agents in his or her employ. The use of W-2s, the enforcement of strict work hours, and the payment of a base salary would indicate that the worker is an employee and not an independent contractor.

84. A

Broker Lately should not allow these salespeople to transact real estate. Brokers have a duty to supervise sales agents and also to make sure the brokerage firm is in full compliance with license laws at all times. Sales agents cannot transact real estate for others without a license.

85. D

A broker is responsible for what he or she knows or should have known. The seller's miscalculation and the broker's omission in verifying the measurements of the property make the broker guilty of misrepresentation. The broker may be able to prevail in a lawsuit against seller. Whether the broker prevails or not is for a court to decide.

86. C

Generally, Andy is entitled to the full commission as originally agreed upon. Courts have concluded that a broker earns the commission upon procuring a purchaser who had reached agreement with a seller on essential terms and is ready, willing, and able to perform. It is not based upon an actual sale or transfer of title to the property.

87. B

The company dollar is the portion of revenue that ends up belonging to the brokerage firm. It does not include deductions for the cost of business. However, to arrive at the company dollar, the firm deducts all commissions and fees paid to its own salespeople and other firms. These fees include cooperating sales and listings. The company dollar is important because it indicates the amount of business a firm does. Because the operating costs are not yet deducted, it does not indicate the firm's profit.

88. D

In a general partnership, the correct answer, the partners are personally liable for partnership debts exceeding partnership assets. Partners are jointly (together) and severally (separately) liable for these debts. Limited partners are not liable for the debts of the partnership beyond the amount of money they have contributed.

89. C

A corporation is a taxable legal entity recognized by law, with tax rates separate from individual income tax rates. It is recognized by the abbreviation "Inc." after the name of the company. A sole proprietorship is a business owned by one person. A trade name is sole proprietorship doing business as a name other than that of the proprietor or owner.

90. B

When advertising on the Internet, brokers should obtain legal advice so they are in compliance with local, state, and federal guidelines. Many real estate commissions also publish guidelines for Internet advertising and website publishing. Brokers should adhere to these guidelines.

91. C

Blockbusting, a violation of federal, state, and local fair housing laws, is a practice by real estate agents to induce people to panic and sell their properties with the goal of obtaining new listings (and ultimately sales). Eminent domain is the right of government to take private property for public use.

92. A

Redlining is an illegal discriminatory practice by lenders to exclude people from culturally diverse neighborhoods from receiving housing loans. Steering is a violation of the Federal Fair Housing Act and is practiced by real estate brokers who encourage culturally diverse people to move to or away from certain areas. Blockbusting is another violation by brokers who make people panic and sell their property because of the entry into the neighborhood of a culturally diverse family.

93. C

Testers look for unlawful racial steering practices. The U.S. Supreme Court and most, if not all, real estate commissions regard testers as a legitimate method of gathering evidence of housing violations. Steering is a violation of the Federal Fair Housing Act and is practice by real estate brokers who encourage culturally diverse people to move to or away from certain areas. Redlining is an illegal discriminatory practice by lenders to exclude people from culturally diverse neighborhoods from receiving housing loans. Blockbusting is violation by brokers who make people panic and sell their property because of the entry into the neighborhood of a culturally diverse family. Price fixing is an antitrust violation in which competitors conspire to charge the same or similar price of services.

94. A

The board is illegally promoting a group boycott against Commercial Properties because it does not belong to the local board of REALTORS® or multiple listing service. The board's activity is an illegal restraint of trade according to the Sherman Antitrust Act.

95. D

To comply with the Americans with Disabilities Act (ADA), alterations must be made to existing public accommodations and commercial facilities if readily achievable.

96. D

A multiple listing service (MLS) cannot refuse listings because of a certain fee percentage, or dictate commission agreements between the broker and client. This conduct is a violation of antitrust laws. The MLS may circulate information regarding the commission that a broker has agreed upon with his or her client. Only licensed brokers and salespersons may participate in the MLS.

Real Estate Math

97. D

$95,000 loan × 0.11 interest rate = $10,450 interest per year
$10,450 ÷ 12 months = $870.83 interest for the first month
$898.93 principal and interest payment − $870.83 interest = $28.10 principal
$95,000 old balance − $28.10 principal repaid = $94,971.90 new balance

98. B

$142,000 × 1.18 = $167,560 increased valuation
$167,560 × 0.80 = $134,048 new tax basis
assessed value × tax rate = annual taxes
2.12 ÷ 100 = 0.0212
$134,048 × 0.0212 = $2,841.82 annual taxes

99. D

$4,600 × 12 = $55,200 yearly income
income ÷ rate = value
$55,200 ÷ 0.06 = $920,000 value of building

100. C

12 months × $1,200 = $14,400 minimum annual rent
$16,600 − 14,400 = $2,200 above minimum
$2,200 ÷ 0.03 = $73,333.33 over $260,000
$260,000 + $73,333.33 = $333,333.33 total sales